FRONTLINE
COOKBOOK

FRONTLINE COOKBOOK

BATTLEFIELD RECIPES FROM THE SECOND WORLD WAR

ANDREW ROBERTSHAW

First published 2012
by Spellmount, an imprint of

The History Press
The Mill, Brimscombe Port
Stroud, Gloucestershire, GL5 2QG
www.thehistorypress.co.uk

British Library Cataloguing in Publication Data.
A catalogue record for this book is available from the British Library.

ISBN 978 0 7524 7665 0

Typesetting and origination by The History Press

Manufacturing Managed by Jellyfish Print Solutions Ltd

Printed in Malta by Gutenberg Press.

Contents

Foreword by Valentine Warner   7

Part One: An Army Marches on its Stomach   9
Frontline Food before the Second World War   11
The Making of an Army Cook: Training, Equipment and Logistics   25
    The Formation of the Army Catering Corps   26
    Training   31
    Equipment   38
    Logistics   59
'Waste Not, Want Not': The Army Ration   63
    Hospital Food   86
    The 'Mess-Tin Cook'   86
Food Wherever You Are   91
    India   95
    The Jungle   98
    Africa   100
    Middle East   101

North Africa   113

East Africa   113

Iceland   113

'If it's burnt, it's cooked': Conclusion   115

Part Two: Battlefield Recipes   119

Index   223

Foreword

MILITARY HISTORY IS littered with defeats caused by a broken food supply chain or troops made to march too far on an empty stomach.

Andrew Robertshaw's *Frontline Cookbook* is a fascinating insight into the logistics of feeding an army, an account of how innovation and imagination produced essential solutions to combat starvation – as no matter how many weapons an armed force may carry, without food neither can be used to best effect.

As a chef I have found feeding just a few strenuous at times, so just imagine how to approach feeding hundreds of thousands of troops spread across the globe in thick jungle, bone-cracking cold or the searing desert heat.

Covering such subjects as equipment, rationing, training and location, Andrew's knowledge is second to none and the well-illustrated, recipe-plump writing makes *Frontline Cookbook* informative reading for not only those with an interest in military history, but anyone interested in food and human endeavour.

Valentine Warner, 2012

Part One

An Army Marches on its Stomach

Frontline Food before the Second World War

THE QUOTATION THAT 'an army marches on its stomach' has been attributed to both Napoleon Bonaparte and Frederick the Great. What matters is not who made the original statement but that it demonstrates that two of the world's great military commanders clearly understood the connection between feeding an army and its ability to fight. Although it is commonly appreciated that soldiers need ammunition, and more recently fuel for their vehicles, they have always needed something to eat and drink, whether on the march or in camp. Soldiers can survive without ammunition but not without food and water. The Chief Minister to Louis XIV noted that neglect of supply and organisation could frustrate military operations. He states that 'history knows more armies ruined by want and disorder than by the efforts of their enemies'.[1] It is coincidental that Napoleon, who is supposed to have stressed the importance of food to armies, neglected to supply his troops in Spain and Portugal during the campaign in the Peninsula. To reduce the burden of supply he used a system by which his troops foraged (i.e., stole) from the Spanish and French civilians as they marched. Foraging parties were sent ahead and on the flanks of the army to strip the countryside of food to keep the army supplied. This situation was made worse by repeated campaigning in the same areas, and by

---

1   Cardinal de Richelieu, *Le Testament Politique*

the requirement of armies to remain stationary for weeks or months at a time. Despite acts of terror intended to force the unarmed farmers and labourers to provide the French troops with food, resistance increased as the armies drove the population to the verge of starvation. Rather than comply with the invaders, civilians hid their stocks of food and animals, and then began to systematically hunt down and kill the French soldiers and their wives who had been sent in search of provisions. This created the first 'Guerrilla' war and was largely responsibly for allowing Wellington's numerically inferior army to tie down Napoleon's forces in what became known as the 'Spanish Ulcer'. Wellington did not suffer from the same problems as Napoleon because he was both regarded as an ally by the local populace and his quartermasters paid for supplies they required.

Supplying armies with food has provided a number of terms which are still familiar today. Although rationing is associated with restricted supply to civilians on the Home Front in the Second World War, a 'ration' was originally a quota of food and drink provided for soldiers and sailors as part of their service. Originally, rations consisted of the provision of a few basic, staple items, normally meat, fresh or preserved (salted); bread or biscuit and a liquid that was safe to drink, unlike the water, such as beer or wine. The actual amount of these staples varied over time and was normally supplemented with privately purchased food items such as vegetables, preservatives and flavourings. Because individual cooking is time consuming and wasteful of fuel, larger medieval households used a form of mass catering in which a group of people were provided with a set amount of prepared food which they shared amongst themselves. These groups were known as 'a Mess' and the term was then adopted by both sailors and soldiers. This gives us expressions such as 'messmate', 'messdeck' and 'Officers' and Sergeants' Mess'. It is worth noting that these messes were formed of groups of around ten or twelve people and this continues to be reflected in military organisations as the 'file', 'squad' or 'section'. These reflect both the communal nature of eating and the need to organise armies into regular-sized military sub-units.

It was recognised that although some soldiers were accompanied by their wives on campaign, the so-called 'camp-followers', many were not and their cooking skills could range from poor to diabolical. In consequence, the role of 'Sutler' was created to manage the procurement of rations and their cooking, making a profit on both transactions as they provided less cooked food than raw materials. As the Sutler was often a relative or agent to commanding officers, the system was open to abuse and the soldiers' diet and health could suffer in consequence. However, in 1680 the English garrison of Tangier in North Africa was recorded as being 'better than any other part of the world, for [the soldiers] have fresh and wholesome quarters with small gardens; coal for dressing the provision they have out of the store at the King's charges. Every Monday morning each man receives a piece of beef; one of pork, seven pounds of bread; a quart of oatmeal, besides butter and cheese for his week's allowance.'[2]

During Marlborough's campaigns (1704–10), it was ordered that men should mess regularly and that they should have bacon or other fresh meat twice a week, the cost of which was to be met by stoppages from the soldiers' pay. Parties of troops were sent out to gather root vegetables, although the Sutlers could always provide something better. Regulations required commanding officers to encourage butchers to follow their regiments with good stocks of butchered meat, and cattle on the hoof. It was these arrangements which the Duke of Marlborough had in mind when he stated that 'No soldier can fight unless he is properly fed on beef and beer'.[3] It's worth adding that at one point the English garrison of Elizabethan Dublin threatened to mutiny because they were being supplied with too much salmon and too many oysters, when what they really wanted was beef and beer!

As has already been noted, Wellington's preparation for the campaign in the Peninsula included the development of a working Commissariat, responsible for the supply of provisions for the forces, but this does not mean that this was easy or that the Treasury in Whitehall were happy with the additional expense. One problem was that on the outset of the operations the Commissaries were mostly inexperienced and they had a skeleton staff to superintend the supplies to all units. At this time rations were issued by the Commissariat in the evening, usually for three days at a time. One day's ration was issued to the men, the others were held at a regimental headquarters. In Spain in 1813, every soldier was entitled to a daily ration of a pound of meat, a pound of biscuit (or 1½ pound of bread), and a quart of beer (or a pint of wine or ⅓ pint of spirits). When the army halted, ovens were built so that bread could be baked and meat obtained from butchered cattle which had been driven along behind the marching columns. The meat was usually boiled by small messes of soldiers in a

---

2   Howard N. Cole, *The Story of the Army Catering Corps and its Predecessors* (Army Catering Corps Association: 1984), p. 9

3   Howard N. Cole, *The Story of the Army Catering Corps and its Predecessors* (Army Catering Corps Association: 1984), p. 9

communal pot to which was added pulses and vegetables. This provided a soup for the evening and a joint of cooked meat which could be eaten cold the next day. It was during the Peninsula War that British soldiers first received a standard issue individual cooking vessel called, not surprisingly, the 'mess-tin'. This was a two-part tin-plated steel item, roughly D-shaped, to fit against the body or pack, and provided with a handle so it could be held over a fire or used as an eating vessel. It was far from ideal as too much heat would cause the tin plate to melt and soldiers cooking for themselves used vastly more fuel than communal cookery. However, the ability to make tea, and in some cases coffee, was recognised as a valuable contribution to the soldier's diet.

In the period after the Battle of Waterloo in 1815, greater importance had been attached to feeding the army and the construction of barracks throughout the country meant that it was easy to superintend the feeding of troops. Previously they had been quartered on willing civilians or in public houses where they were supplied by the residents at the government's expense. At the beginning of the nineteenth century the soldiers' ration at home comprised 1lb of bread and ¾ pound of meat daily – for this food, 6d per day was stopped from his pay – cooking facilities were available in the new barracks, but they were of a very basic character. The cooking utensils available to each company were two coppers (cooking pots), one for potatoes and the other for meat, which was always boiled as no ovens were available for roasting or baking, and so the solider had to put up with the eternal boiled beef and beef broth served hot, or cold meat at his two meals per day – 7.30am breakfast and 12.30pm dinner – after which he was without food unless he was able to purchase something to sustain him for the next nineteen hours.[4] Although this might seem surprising to modern diners, it was clearly perfectly acceptable at the time and an order for the army issued by the Adjutant General's Office dated 1 January 1882 makes it clear that the system was carefully regulated:

> In Camp or Barracks the Captain or Subaltern of the Day must visit and inspect the kettles at the hour appointed for Cooking, and no kettle is to be taken from the Kitchens till this inspection is made, and the Signal is given for the Men to dine, which should be at the same hour throughout the Garrison or Camp. Independent of this Regimental Arrangement, the Officers must daily

4   Howard N. Cole, *The Story of the Army Catering Corps and its Predecessors* (Army Catering Corps Association: 1984), p. 13

and hourly attend to the Messing, and to every circumstance connected with the Economy of their Troops and Companies.[5]

In the period of peace that followed the end of the Napoleonic Wars there were few occasions when the Home Army had the opportunity for collective training, and in 1853 a 'camp of exercise' was established on Chobham Common under the direction of the Prince Consort and the Duke of Cambridge. This two-month exercise was designed to give every regiment of cavalry and infantry, together with the artillery, engineers and all supporting services, the opportunity to cooperate as a force under active service conditions. Wells had already been sunk to supply fresh water, and the kitchens were specially built from mud over trenches. The results of the experiment were not conclusive, however they were a useful preparation for the force that would be sent to the Crimea just two years later. Although the invasion of the Crimea was successful and the Battle of the Alma also a success, the Siege of Sebastopol – which began in the autumn of 1854 – was to be a disaster. The principle reason for the high death rate at Sebastopol was not enemy action, but the inability of the army to supply the soldiers in the trenches overlooking the city with food, fuel or safe water. This situation has commonly been ascribed to the army's neglect of supply in the preceding period of peace. It was in fact the result of Treasury penny pinching, particularly with the abolition of the Royal Wagon Train in 1833 which had been established in the Peninsula War to assist the Commissariat. The intention was that, in peacetime, the Wagon Train had no function and could be axed. It was planned, at least by the Treasury, that local wagons and horses would be hired in any future campaign. These were not forthcoming when the 'Army of the East' landed on Russian soil and supply handicapped the first year of the war until the innovative solution of a specially constructed military railway provided a 'modern' form of transport.

Another innovation of the campaign came with the arrival of Alexis Soyer, who was born in France but by 1837 had become head chef at the Reform Club and an expert on economical charity cookery.[6] Soyer took with him the first prototypes of his famous field cooking stove. This was cylindrical and it stood on

5   Howard N. Cole, *The Story of the Army Catering Corps and its Predecessors* (Army Catering Corps Association: 1984), p. 13

6   Ruth Cowen, *Relish: The Extraordinary Life of Alexis Soyer, Victorian Celebrity Chef* (Phoenix: 2006)

three short legs. Under the lid was a copper and below was the fire, fed through a small hatch in the front centre, the cowled chimney rising up from the back. The inventor had refused to patent it in case anyone would think that his offer of the 'Soyer Stove' to the army had been made for his personal profit.[7] The stove took his name and would continue to be used by the British Army on campaigns as varied as the Zulu War, the First and Second World Wars, the Falklands and finally the First Gulf War of 1991. The great advantages of the Soyer Stove was the economical way in which it used fuel, and that it was light and portable and could be used without the flame being seen. As the stove could be used for stews, roasting, baking and steaming, plus making tea, coffee and hot chocolate, its adaptability was a great asset and an enormous advantage over previous systems of open fire cookery. Soyer started work in the hospitals at Scutari, where he revised the diets and introduced new catering procedures, so that instead of the so-called cooking of the basic rations of a pound of meat, bread and potatoes, he drew up numerous menus of soups, stews and seasoned meat, supplemented the diet by local purchases and introduced beef tea, jellies, and rice for the invalid diet. In late August 1855 he officially opened his first camp and bivouac kitchen before Sebastopol and, using seven large Soyer Stoves, a banquet was prepared entirely from army rations. His rations were distributed and a succession of Army Cooks were introduced to the new system. This was a necessary development as the Commission of Enquiry held in 1857 into the Sanitary State of the Army stated that 'the first step must be to instruct our soldiers in the rudiments of the art of cooking, of which they are now lamentably deficient'.[8]

---

7   Howard N. Cole, *The Story of the Army Catering Corps and its Predecessors* (Army Catering Corps Association: 1984), p. 21

8   Howard N. Cole, *The Story of the Army Catering Corps and its Predecessors* (Army Catering Corps Association: 1984), p. 27

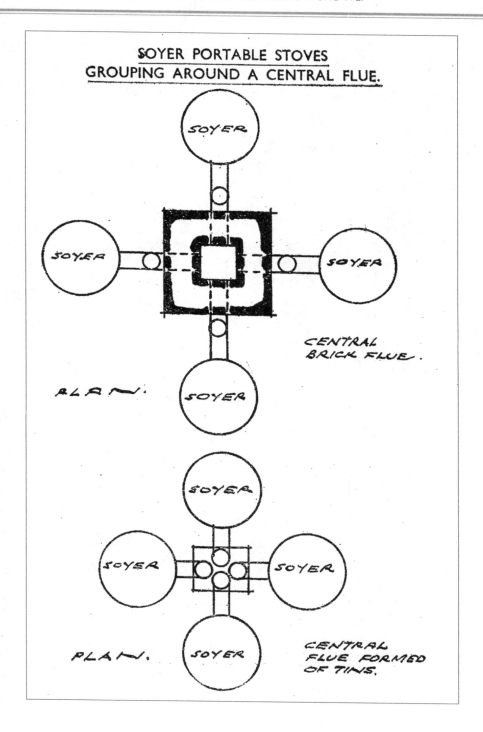

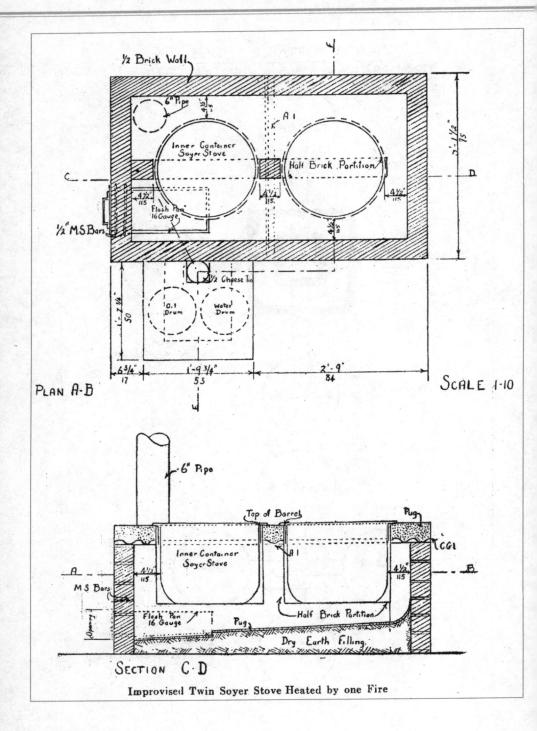

Improvised Twin Soyer Stove Heated by one Fire

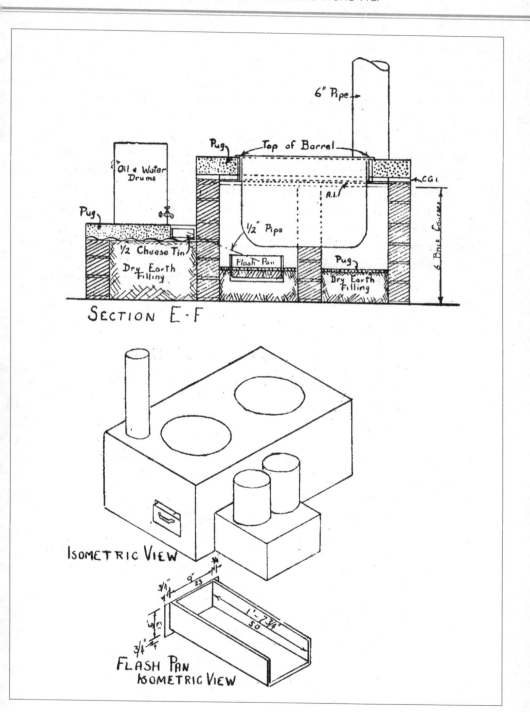

6" Pipe

Pug
Top of Barrel

Oil & Water Drums

Pug

C.G.I.

R.L.

1/2" Pipe

1/2 Cheese Tin

Dry Earth Filling

Flash Pan

Pug

Dry Earth Filling

6 Brick Courses

SECTION E-F

ISOMETRIC VIEW

3/4"

9" / 23

1

1'-7 3/4" / 50

6 / 12

3/4"

FLASH PAN
ISOMETRIC VIEW

It was not, however, until 1870 that 'one sergeant cook is to be appointed to every regiment of cavalry, battalion of infantry... brigade of artillery or command of engineers or military train ...'[9] The Queen's Regulations and Orders for 1889 stated that non-commissioned officers (NCOs) could not hold the appointment without undergoing a course of training at the 'Instructional Kitchen at Aldershot'. The Adjutant-General stated that the candidate should fulfil conditions which included being 'steady and trustworthy' to 'write with accuracy and quickness', and that they should have 'five years to serve'. His duties, as laid out in Queen's Regulations, include 'personally superintending all cooking done in Regimental Cookhouses', 'to instruct those under him in all operations connected with cookery' and 'he will enforce order, punctuality and cleanliness'.[10] The result was great improvement in the standard of rations and by 1896 the first Army Cookery Competition was held at Aldershot.

Horace Wyndham, who enlisted in 1890, made this observation concerning the period:

> ...during the last six years especially barrack feeding has made brilliant strides. Dishes of meat are supplied for breakfast; roast, stews, curries, puddings and pies for dinner; and even the despised tea meal is generally supplemented by some appetising repasts that have been replaced not only by an abundance, but by such variety of savoury food that the soldier who still complains of hunger must be either a fool or a glutton.[11]

By contrast he singles out some of the men taken into regimental cookhouses who were without the slightest aptitude for the work; 'they were taken haphazardly taken from the ranks, and pitch-forked in a kitchen'.[12] Wyndham also remained unconvinced that catering was well organised and commented on

---

9 Howard N. Cole, *The Story of the Army Catering Corps and Its Predecessors* (Army Catering Corps Association: 1984), p. 32

10 Howard N. Cole, *The Story of the Army Catering Corps and its Predecessors* (Army Catering Corps Association: 1984), pp. 32–33

11 Horace Wyndham, *The Queen's Service* (1899) in Howard N. Cole, *The Story of the Army Catering Corps and its Predecessors* (Army Catering Corps Association: 1984), p. 39

12 Howard N. Cole, *The Story of the Army Catering Corps and its Predecessors* (Army Catering Corps Association: 1984), p. 40

overcrowded cookhouses, badly cooked meat and the delay between food being prepared for inspection and service.

If food in barracks was often poor, preparing hot meals for troops in the field was dealt with by a combination of Soyer Stoves, improvised ovens using trenches and constructions of clay, turf or even hollowed-out anthills in the tropics, and the more conventional 'Aldershot Oven' – made of curved and straight steel sheets, these could be transported easily on wagons, roofed over earth or clay and used for baking and roasting. During the campaign in South Africa (1899–1902), mention is frequently made of corned beef (bully beef) and a new innovation 'Machonochie' ration of meat and vegetables. These could be eaten from the tin or added to the camp kettles or 'dixies' to produce an all-in-one stew. These tinned rations would form a staple for the war that followed.

On 3 August 1914 Britain was at war with Imperial Germany, and the British Expeditionary Force (BEF) mobilised in support of France and to honour her treaty to preserve Belgium's neutrality. On the outbreak of war the scale of field-ration was divided into bread and meat, and the grocery ration:

Commodity	Weight (ozs)
Bread	12
Biscuits	2⅔
Meat	
Frozen	8
Preserved	3
Bacon	3
Vegetables (fresh)	8
Sugar	2½
Butter or Margarine	1
Jam	3
Cheese	2
Condensed milk	1
Rice	1
Oatmeal	1
Pork and Beans ration	2⅔
Meat and Vegetable ration	1½
Sugar	2

This ration for a frontline soldier produced a theoretical 4,129 calories, which compared well to the soldier behind the lines who received a reduced ration of 3,259 calories. Frontline soldiers also carried their 'Iron Ration', which consisted of 'a pound of preserved meat; 12ozs of biscuit, ⅝oz of tea; 2ozs of sugar; ½oz of salt; 3ozs of cheese and two cubes of meat extract.'[13] This was for emergency use only and could only be used on the orders of an officer.

As in previous campaigns, food could either be cooked in individual mess-tins or in the camp kettle or 'dixies'. The methods of cooking were based on experience of the past sixty years and cooks were trained in building improvised ovens and using Aldershot Ovens when the force was stationary. One innovation was, however, the provision of a 'Travelling Field Kitchen' for every company of infantry. This horse-drawn vehicle fitted with a chimney could be used as a stationary cooker and to keep the food warm even when on the march. Units such as the Royal Army Medical Corps (RAMC), who had to make do with the traditional Soyer Stove, regretted bitterly that they did not get the advantage of these field kitchens, as it took time to set up the stoves and prepare a hot meal or drink. Only the simplest meal could be produced from the travelling kitchen, the type of cooking being limited to boiling and frying.

Under the conditions of trench warfare, men in the frontline would not have the opportunity to use field kitchens or ovens and, although where possible food was sent up to the line from kitchens in the rear, most infantrymen had to make do with their mess-tins and a good deal of improvisation. One example of this is the use of strips of sandbags soaked in candle fat or tiny chips of wood that burnt quickly and were, in theory, smokeless. Another is using a galvanised bucket or latrine container with punctured sides as an improvised cooker. Perhaps more successful was the development of 'pan-packs' or 'hayboxes' and other insulated containers in which food could be taken to the trenches while it was still cooking. Soldiers often received a privately purchased device called the 'Tommy Cooker' from home, a tin containing a gel which could be used to heat a cup of tea or tin of stew. All of this took time to develop and in the autumn of 1914 Private Frank Richards records 'there was no such thing as cooked food or hot tea at this stage of the war, and the rations were very scarce, we were lucky if we got our four biscuits a man daily, a pound tin of 'bully' between two, a tin of jam between

13 Howard N. Cole, *The Story of the Army Catering Corps and its Predecessors* (Army Catering Corps Association: 1984), p. 59

six and the rum ration which was about a tablespoon and a half.'[14] It is interesting to note that although both 'bully beef' and Machonochie's stew are often mentioned in soldiers' memoirs, archaeological research carried out recently has demonstrated that, in addition to empty tins, a very large amount of full tins were abandoned by soldiers fed up with the weight and the monotonous nature of frontline rations. By the end of the Great War more than 6 million men and women were in uniform, nearly 2 million of them on the Western Front; despite the appalling conditions of trench warfare, transport problems, mud and the weather, these men and women were fed every day, meals which, if not always delicious, were filling and sustaining.

This logistical feat performed during the First World War was to pave the way for feeding the armies of the next world conflict.

A Note on Sources

Frontline Cookbook is illustrated throughout and in the Battlefield Recipes section with material from the following original war diaries, log books and manuals from the Royal Logistic Corps Museum archive:

Manual of Military Cooking and Dietary Part I – General 1940
Army Catering Corps Guide to Messing in the Middle East (Revised Edition)
Gnr Bell's Log book, Army School of Cookery, Poona, 25/5/43–3/6/43
Recipe Pamphlet No.1: Brighter 'Bully' Beef, Eastern Command, 1944
Catering and Cooking for Field Forces, Allied Land Forces, South East Asia, 1945
Operational Ration Packs and their Development, The War Office, 1958
Operational Feeding: Use of Special Ration Packs, The War Office, 1943
Pamphlet No.38: Combined Operations RASC, 1943
Operational Feeding: Use of Special Ration Packs, The War Office, 1945
Desert Recipes, 1942
Manual of Army Catering Services Part III – Cooking in the Field, including Improvised and Mess Tin Cookery, 1945

14 Howard N. Cole, The Story of the Army Catering Corps and its Predecessors (Army Catering Corps Association: 1984), p. 59

Pamphlet of Recipes for Cooking F.S. Rations, compiled 1942 (repr. 1943)
Sec/Leader E. Young Log book, Instructress Course, Aldershot School of Cookery,
22 April–May 1941
A Soldier's Log book, 1949
ACC Pamphlet: Christmas, 1946
ACC Scrap book, Messing Officers Training Centre, Scarborough, 1944–45

The Making of an Army Cook:
Training, Equipment and Logistics

the field truly contributes his full quota to keeping the men of his unit contented, in good health and fit to stand the rigours and hardships of modern war.

4.   The RATIONS may be the same along the length of the line; but the DINNERS will vary accordingly to the trouble that has been taken over them; and the wise officer will know that in war a hot meal before going into action represents a reinforcement out of all proportion to the trouble and the ingenuity its preparation demands.

The Formation of the Army Catering Corps

ONE DEVELOPMENT WITHIN the Royal Army Service Corps (RASC) of the Great War was a new appointment for officers. Their responsibility was catering and by January 1916 there were fourteen Catering Instructors who were distributed throughout the UK. By 1918 the number of instructors had expanded to forty and although the main Army School of Cookery was at Aldershot there were schools of instruction in all the theatres of war. These included Egypt, Palestine, Mesopotamia, Salonika and, from 1918, Russia. After the Armistice, the Catering Section was gradually disbanded and by June 1923 there was a single Inspector of Catering at the War Office.

In training, the soldier lived on a standard haversack ration – two thick cut, margarine-spread sandwiches of cheese or 'corned beef' and a portion of slab cake, or if on appeal or on manoeuvres he lived on stews – the produce of the field cookers, horse-drawn, which followed the columns of marching troops as they wended their way from Aldershot to Bordon, across Salisbury Plain or over Bellerby Moor at Catterick. With the last provided meal of the day being tea at 4pm or 4.30pm; after that the soldier had recourse to the services of the NAAFI (Navy, Army and Air Force Institutes) to meet his needs in the evening and these came in a friendly and efficient manner by providing a restaurant service in barracks, or in camp marquees where supper menus of soup, sausages and chips; 'chunky' (meat) pies; egg and chips; and tea and coffee were made available by cheerful NAAFI girls. This was the situation in the mid-1930s, at which time instruction in catering for the army was entirely back in the hands of the Army

School of Cookery at Aldershot and, at the War Office, one RASC Captain. The Army School of Cookery had been re-established at Chiseldon, near Swindon, in 1920. To send their regimental cooks on courses at the school, the fees were paid for out of Regimental Funds. In June of that year a new revised and enlarged edition of the 1917 booklet 'Managements of Soldiers' Messing – Notes for Guidance' was issued by the Inspector of Army Catering, and this became the handbook for Messing Officers and cooks between the wars. At this time, cooks were not recognised as tradesmen and, therefore, received no extra pay other than from Regimental Funds.[15]

In 1937 a committee was established by the War Office under the Chairmanship of Major General E.A. Beck to examine catering for the army and to make recommendations for improvements. Having visited permanent barracks and units on field training and during manoeuvres, the committee were soon convinced there was considerable room for improvement. The Beck Committee report included in its recommendations six main points, stressing the need for:

> More skilled supervision and more comprehensive training at the Army School of Cookery and with re-organisation of the courses; a better type of man and more continuity and with better pay and promotion prospects for men employed as cook; finally the report concluded with the recommendation that an early modernisation programme of all Army Kitchens and dining halls should be undertaken and that the provision of modern cooking utensils should be speeded up.[16]

This report came to the notice of the Secretary of State for War, Leslie Hore-Belisha. At the time, the regular army was 20,000 men short of its establishment and one of his most important tasks was recruitment. Hore-Belisha saw catering as a vital element in encouraging men to join the forces and having inspected army kitchens he invited Sir Isidore Salmon MP, the Chairman of J. Lyons and Co. Ltd, to be Honorary Catering Advisor in March 1938. Sir Isidore Salmon set to work with a newly recruited staff and by 3 June 1938 they had completed the Salmon Report on Catering and Cooking in the Army.

15 Howard N. Cole, *The Story of the Army Catering Corps and its Predecessors* (Army Catering Corps Association: 1984), p. 66

16 Howard N. Cole, *The Story of the Army Catering Corps and its Predecessors* (Army Catering Corps Association: 1984), p. 67

This comprehensive document covered all aspects of cooking and the service of food in the army, the recruitment and training of staff and the use of modern methods to improve the standard of food across the army, both at home and overseas. The implementation of its recommendations had far-reaching effects and can be seen as leading, two years and nine months later, to the formation of the Army Catering Corps (ACC). This was of course after the outbreak of the Second World War in September 1939. One significant change can be seen in the effect of Army Order No.60 of 1939:

George RI

Whereas We deem it expedient to revise the conditions of service of cooks and to improve the cooking and messing arrangements of Our Army.

Our Will and Pleasure is that soldiers trained in future as cooks shall be graded for pay as Army tradesmen; that soldiers at present employed as cook within the establishment laid down for this appointment for their units shall be granted a higher rate of additional pay pending their re-qualification under the new standards of trade skill to be introduced for Army cooks; and that non-commissioned officers holding the appointment of sergeant-cook shall, on attending the higher standards not prescribed for their appointment, be granted additional pay or tradesmen's rates of pay according to the standard attained by them.

Our Further Will and Pleasure is that amendments contained in the Schedule attached to this our Warrant shall be made to the Warrant of His Late Majesty King George V for the Pay, Appointment, Promotion and Non-Effective Pay of Our Army, date 12 February 1931.

Given at Our court at St James's, this
13 day of April 1939, in the 3rd
year of Our Reign.

By His Majesty's Command,
LESLIE HORE-BELISHA[17]

---

17 Howard N. Cole, *The Story of the Army Catering Corps and its Predecessors* (Army Catering Corps Association: 1984), p. 83

The result of this order was that, in future, Army Cooks were graded as 'trades-men' and would receive additional pay ranging between 3d and 9d per day. This does not appear much by modern standards but was considerably more than an unskilled soldier would receive at that time. Basic pay was obviously one incentive, but so was the possibility of promotion. There was a large increase in the number of non-commissioned ranks reserved for cooks, and a limited number of posts of the rank of Staff-Sergeant and Warrant Officer. Being an Army Cook was no longer a dead end for a career soldier.

The background to this reform was the opening campaigns of the Second World War. Although Britain and France had gone to war in defence of Poland, they were unable to prevent its defeat and occupation by combined German and Soviet invasion forces. As in 1914, the British Army was mobilised and dispatched to the Continent in support of France and other nations which were then neutral. Conditions during the first year of the war on the Western Front replicated those of trench warfare a generation before; a static campaign with all the advantages this offered. However, fear of enemy air attack on the Channel ports meant that the BEF of 1940 had an extended supply route running from ports in western France around St Nazaire, Cherbourg and St Malo. In consequence, when the German Panzer divisions heading the Blitzkrieg carved through the Allied armies to the coast near Amiens, these 'Lines of Communication' (L of C) were cut. At a stroke the BEF was deprived

RATES OF PAY FOR COOKS, MESS, INDIAN.

				Rs.	a.	p.	
Cook Learner Mess (under tuition at Schools of Cookery)							
Pay of Rank ...	...	...	...	17	0	0	per mensem
Trade Pay ...	...	...	...	0	2	0	per day
	Total p.m. (30 days)	...		20	12	0	
Cooks Mess grade III							
Pay of Rank ...	...	...	...	17	0	0	per mensem
Trade Pay ...	...	...	...	0	9	0	per day
	Total p.m. (30 days)	...		33	14	0	
Cooks Mess grade II							
Pay of Rank ...	...	...	...	17	0	0	per mensem
Trade Pay ...	...	...	...	1	0	0	per day
	Total p.m. (30 days)	...		47	0	0	
Cooks (Special) grade							
Pay of Rank ...	...	...	...	17	0	0	per mensem
Trade Pay ...	...	...	...	1	8	0	per day
	Total p.m. (30 days)	...		62	0	0	

of food, fuel and ammunition, and there was no choice other than to withdraw to the Channel ports. This led to the Dunkirk evacuation, Operation Dynamo, which began on 28 May 1940. Despite the enormous task of the arrival of 224,585 British and 112,546 French and Belgian troops, they were fed on arrival at the UK in a round-the-clock operation conducted by troops, assisted by the Women's Voluntary Service (WVS).

In the aftermath of this 'retreat to victory', the advantages of forming a Catering Corps separate from the Army Service Corps were hotly debated. One contributing factor was the very large number of complaints received from new conscripts who were not prepared for the poor quality of rations they received, especially in their early period of training. This was frequently due to lack of training by the cooks rather than poor quality of ingredients. Although Army catering and cooking sectors were recognised as 'a science and the business of experts', it was felt by some that this could be carried out by those expert in supply, transport and catering. This debate was eventually resolved by the Quartermaster-General, General Sir Walter Venning, who came to the pragmatic conclusion that as he saw no objection to an Army Education Corps he could not object to an Army Catering Corps, 'the one ... is no more military sounding than the other.'[18] General Venning was to become the first Colonel Commandant of the Corps and held his appointment until 1945.

Thus, the Army Catering Corps (ACC) came into existence on 22 March 1941 and on the 26th of the month this was announced in a Special Army Order (No.35 of 1941):

Royal Warrant
Formation of the Army Catering Corps

George RI
Whereas We deem it expedient to authorise the formation of a Corps to be entitled the Army Catering Corps;
Our Will and Pleasure is that the Army Catering Corps shall be deemed to be a Corps for the purposes of the Army Act, the Reserve Forces Act, 1882, and the Territorial and Reserve Forces Act, 1907.

....

18 Howard N. Cole, *The Story of the Army Catering Corps and its Predecessors* (Army Catering Corps Association: 1984), p. 107

Our Further Will and Pleasure is that the Schedule attached to the Warrant of His late Majesty King George V date 27 February 1926, shall be amended as shown in Part I of the Schedule attached to this Our Warrant.

Lastly, Our Will and Pleasure is that the rates of pay of personnel of Our Army Catering Corps shall be as prescribed in Part II of the Schedule attached to this Our Warrant.

Given at Our Court at St James's, this
22nd day of March, 1941, in the 5th
Year of Our Reign
By His Majesty's Command[19]

By the end of May 1945 there were 120 ACC officers and 24,000 other ranks serving with the British forces in France, Belgium, Holland and Germany.[20] At their highest capacity they produced over 2 million meals a day over four continents. During the war and in operations up until 31 March 1946, the Army Catering Corps suffered 1,316 casualties. One officer and 206 other ranks had been killed in actions, one officer and eighty-six other ranks had died of wounds, and five officers and 1,002 other ranks had been wounded. During the same period three officers and 256 other ranks had died of disease and four officers and 100 other ranks had died of injuries. One officer and twelve other ranks had become prisoners of war.[21]

Training

INITIALLY CANDIDATES FOR training as Army Cooks were to be selected from trained soldiers throughout all the regiments and corps of the army, of not less than nine months of service and with a minimum of four years still to

19 Howard N. Cole, *The Story of the Army Catering Corps and its Predecessors* (Army Catering Corps Association: 1984), p. 107

20 Howard N. Cole, *The Story of the Army Catering Corps and its Predecessors* (Army Catering Corps Association: 1984), p. 139

21 Howard N. Cole, *The Story of the Army Catering Corps and its Predecessors* (Army Catering Corps Association: 1984), p. 148

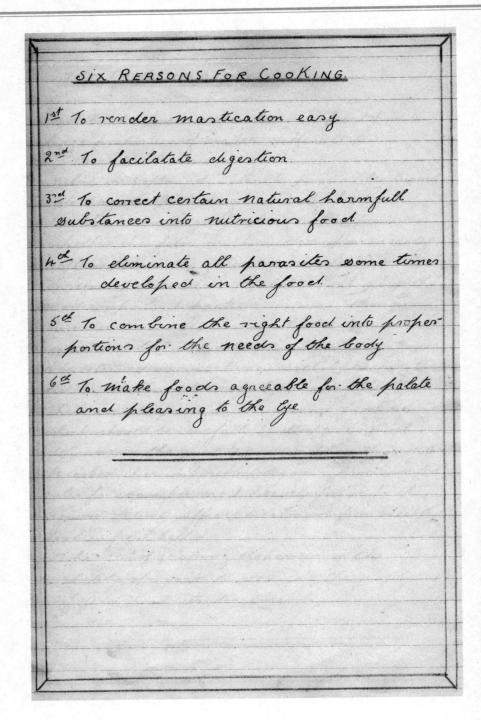

SIX REASONS FOR COOKING.

1st To render mastication easy

2nd To facilatate digestion

3rd To correct certain natural harmfull substances into nutricious food

4th To eliminate all parasites some times developed in the food

5th To combine the right food into proper portions for the needs of the body

6th To make foods agreeable for the palate and pleasing to the eye

serve, and who had already been employed in a Regimental Cookhouse. Others came from recruits who had enlisted as Army Cooks and from boy soldiers. The course consisted of nine months of training in the theory and practice of cookery at the Army School of Cookery in Aldershot. On the completion of the course they would be sent to rejoin a unit of their arm of service where there was a requirement for a cook.[22] On the establishment of the Army Catering Corps the number of officers, NCOs and other ranks required for the new organisation called for a rapid expansion in numbers. In April 1941, four grades of serving soldiers were transferred from the RASC to the new corps, all retaining their original rank. All were qualified Master or Sergeant Cooks together with rank and file who were qualified as Army Cooks and cooks who had passed the course of instruction as Unit Cooks.[23] Soldiers who were 'Called Up' could also become cooks if they passed a trade test at the Army School of Cookery and had not less than three years of civilian or military cooking experience.

The original officers for the new corps were all transferred from the RASC and were all catering specialists who had been employed in the hotel or catering industry and had been commissioned between the outbreak of war, in September 1939, and the formation of the Army Catering Corps.[24] Subsequently, all ACC officers were commissioned from the ranks and trained in specialist Officer Cadet Training Units (OCTU). These officers had, of course, to be suitably qualified and they served as Messing Officers before becoming Catering Advisers.[25]

The new Army School of Cookery, at St Omer Barracks, was opened on 9 March 1941, just fourteen days before the ACC was formed. From the outset there were insufficient qualified cooks to meet the needs of the army, but transfers and recruitment gradually eased this situation. By the time Queen Elizabeth, later the Queen Mother, and the Princess Royal, now the Queen, visited St Omer

22 Howard N. Cole, The Story of the Army Catering Corps and its Predecessors (Army Catering Corps Association: 1984), p. 85

23 Howard N. Cole, The Story of the Army Catering Corps and its Predecessors (Army Catering Corps Association: 1984), p. 108

24 Howard N. Cole, The Story of the Army Catering Corps and its Predecessors (Army Catering Corps Association: 1984), p. 108

25 Howard N. Cole, The Story of the Army Catering Corps and its Predecessors (Army Catering Corps Association: 1984), p. 108

MESSING.

The attainment of a satisfactory system of messing depends mainly on the following conditions

1. A good quality of supplies

2. The Purchase of provisions at reasonable rates

3. Close and constance suppervision of the preperation cooking and the serving of foods.

Commanding Officers will as far as possible carry out a system of messing discribed in the Manual. its object is to improve the food and reduce the waste to the fullest possible extent, The Battalion in central system of catering is preferable to that of a company central system. The Central system how ever does not releive the companie commanders of responsability for seeing that their men are properly fed

For large units in India central catering with cooks and dinning hall arrangements controled by Company commanders is usually most successfull.

Barracks in July 1944 over 1,000 students were in training.[26] Many of those students at the time were members of the Auxiliary Territorial Service (ATS), female conscripts who would be joined by others as the war progressed. One reason for the visit by the Princess Royal is that she was probably the most famous member of this unit. Later in the war there was a concerted effort to recruit female cooks to supplement the services of their male comrades. As Britain was waging a global war it was necessary to establish schools of cookery in all the principle theatres of war. One was opened in Egypt for the Eighth Army of Middle East Command, others for both British and Indian troops in India for the Fourth Army; at the Army School of Cookery in Arungabad members were given instruction in Hindustani. Other schools of cookery were set up in Accra in Ghana.[27]

Wherever in the world a member of the Army Catering Corps found himself, or later herself, the training syllabus had common basic content, although they varied according to the rank of the participant and his or her specialism. The 'Syllabus of Training for Hospital Cooks', which was run for eight students at the Army School of Catering, consisted of 174 training periods of forty-five minutes each. This was spread over four weeks and the largest amount of time was spent on practical work in the kitchen.[28] Among the archives of the Royal Logistic Corps Museum there is a remarkable record book in which the details of hospital courses run at the ACC Training Centre from January 1942 to May 1960 is recorded. This provides detail of the participants, their test results and the comments of the instructors. On the very first course the best student was a corporal from the RAMC who scored 85 per cent and was described by his instructor as a 'Good all round student with previous teaching experience. Recommended for Senior Hospital cook'. Not so successful was a sergeant from a Field Ambulance, who scored 67 per cent and was described as being 'Unsuitable as a Hospital Cook'.[29]

26 Howard N. Cole, *The Story of the Army Catering Corps and its Predecessors* (Army Catering Corps Association: 1984), p. 110

27 Howard N. Cole, *The Story of the Army Catering Corps and its Predecessors* (Army Catering Corps Association: 1984), pp. 128–129

28 Army School of Catering, *Course Hospital Cooks*

29 *Al Courses ACC Training Centre*, RLCA8255.

TESTS GIVEN TO E.C.T.C. DROITWICH ON 4.8.41.

1. Brown Stew, Boiled Potatoes, Cabbage,
              Steamed Chocolate Pudding.

2. Roast Beef and Gravy,
    Roast Potatoes and Greens,
    Figs and Custard.

3. Hot Pot,   Potatoes, Beans,
              Jam Tart.

4. Meat Croquettes and Gravy,
    Peas and Potatoes.
    Baked Rice Pudding.

Droitwich   4.8.41.

The basic course of Army Cookery included aspects of storage, hygiene and sanitation, the layout of kitchens at home and in the field, food preparation including bakery and butchery, ration scales, use of tools and equipment, recipes and improvised cookery. The training was a combination of theory and practical work using a range of cookers, including the 'build your own' variety of improvised cookery.[30] Well before the trainees were let loose on food preparation they would have spent long periods in taught lessons in which illustrations were copied from blackboards or the official manuals.[31] These notes and drawings were kept in notebooks which would be assessed and marked by the instructors. Some of the books are minor works of art and it is clear that some of the students used everything they had been taught in school art classes to enhance their work. What is striking about the training carried out is the scope of the instruction and the mix of theory and practice. Examples of the syllabus used in schools outside the United Kingdom indicate that local

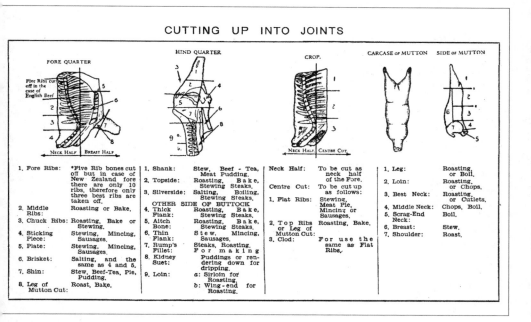

CUTTING UP INTO JOINTS

1. Fore Ribs:	*Five Rib bones cut off but in case of New Zealand fore there are only 10 ribs, therefore only three best ribs are taken off.	1. Shank:	Stew, Beef - Tea, Meat Pudding.	Neck Half:	To be cut as neck half of the Fore.	1. Leg:	Roasting, or Boil.
		2. Topside:	Roasting, Bake, Stewing Steaks.	Centre Cut:	To be cut up as follows:	2. Loin:	Roasting, or Chops.
		3. Silverside:	Salting, Boiling, Stewing Steaks.	1. Flat Ribs:	Stewing, Meat Pie, Mincing or Sausages.	3. Best Neck:	Roasting, or Cutlets.
			OTHER SIDE OF BUTTOCK			4. Middle Neck:	Chops, Boil.
2. Middle Ribs:	Roasting or Bake.	4. Thick Flank:	Roasting, Bake, Stewing Steaks.			5. Scrag-End Neck:	Boil.
3. Chuck Ribs:	Roasting, Bake or Stewing.	5. Aitch Bone:	Roasting, Bake, Stewing Steaks.	2. Top Ribs or Leg of Mutton Cut:	Roasting, Bake.	6. Breast:	Stew.
4. Sticking Piece:	Stewing, Mincing, Sausages.	6. Thin Flank:	Stew, Mincing, Sausages.	3. Clod:	For use the same as Flat Ribs.	7. Shoulder:	Roast.
5. Plate:	Stewing, Mincing, Sausages.	7. Rump's Fillet:	Steaks, Roasting, For making				
6. Brisket:	Salting, and the same as 4 and 5.	8. Kidney Suet:	Puddings or rendering down for dripping.				
7. Shin:	Stew, Beef-Tea, Pie, Pudding.	9. Loin:	a: Sirloin for Roasting.				
8. Leg of Mutton Cut:	Roast, Bake.		b: Wing - end for Roasting.				

30 This aspect of cookery is still taught to army chefs by the Royal Logistic Corps at Worthy Down in Hampshire.

31 The wartime manuals culminated in the multi-volume *Manual of Catering Service 1945*, one copy of each volume being issued to every cookhouse.

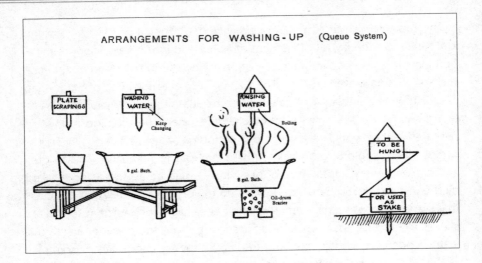

conditions, ingredients and the nature of the fighting were all taken into consideration. The result was that the students finished their course able to meet the considerable challenges they would face when they went into the field, in addition to behind the lines and in training camps. The importance placed on hot rations for soldiers in all theatres of war is borne out by this observation from the *Manual of Army Catering Services*:

> The Rations may be the same along the length of the line; but the Dinners will vary according to the trouble that has been taken over them; and the wise officer will know that in war a hot meal before going into action represents a reinforcement out of all proportion to the trouble and the ingenuity its preparation demands.[32]

Equipment

WITH THE MECHANISATION of the army, the proven and reliable horse-drawn travelling field kitchens were regarded as obsolete and a variety of cookers were now carried on trucks and lorries. These cookers were classified

---

32 *Manual of Army Catering Services, Part III – Cooking in the Field, including Improvised and Mess Tin Cookery* (1945), p. 1

as Portable No.1, 2, 3 and were introduced before the outbreak of war. The Cooker Portable No.1, or 'Hydro burner', which was introduced in 1938, was designed to cook for twenty-five men and consisted of a burner unit and a number of 6 gallon containers and insulators. The fuel used was petrol, sensible for a mechanised army, although there was always the danger of accidents. In operation pressurised petrol was projected along a trench covered by metal plates. The plates were pierced to take five 6 gallon cooking containers or frying pans and it was possible to fit a portable oven to the outfit. The noise was alarming and there was an ever-present risk of accident with the fuel. It was, however, easy to operate, efficient and remained in use for over forty years.

The Cooker Portable No.2 was a single burner designed to cook for approximately six to eight men. It consisted of a shallow metal box, which formed the stand, and an internal petrol tank and pump. Strapped to the cooker was a stainless steel cooking vessel which had a removable lid and could be used as a frying pan. Because of the weight of the unit it was usually issued to the crews of armoured vehicles. The Cooker Portable No.3 was a larger version of the No.2 with two burners and could cater for approximately fifteen men. It too used petrol as fuel and even when folded away was the size of a small suitcase. A compensation for its size was that it could be fitted with an oven. The Cooker Triplex No.4 was a portable oven with a cast iron range. This could use either solid fuel or a petrol burner unit and was a smaller version of the Bluff Range. These last two were adapted versions of commercial cookers. The Bluff Range was large and could prepare food for up to 250 men and could be put together in twenty minutes or so. In addition to this range of 'field' cookers which could be used on campaign, the army employed a vast array of 'static' fish fryers, vegetable cleaners, steamers, ovens, pressure cookers and ranges which were used in locations such as depots and training camps. Many of these were variations of civilian cookers and were often brought into military use by officers who had been recruited from hotel and restaurant catering for the duration of the war. The types used are well illustrated in the *Manual of Army Catering Services, 1945*.[33]

Despite the sophistication of these cookers, instruction continued to be given in using the venerable Soyer Stove, camp kettles, the Aldershot Oven, improvised cookery and various forms of insulated or 'haybox' cooking. The Soyer Stove

---

33 *Manual of Army Catering Services, Part IV – Static Cooking Apparatus and Cooking Equipment in the Field* (1945), pp. 1–55.

The "Hydra"

This consists of a 2-gallon petrol tank fitted with burner unit and pressure gauge. The principle is briefly to pass petrol through a jet and vapourising ring when it emerges as a gas.

(a) To operate:—

  (i) Close the burner stop cock.

  (ii) Disconnect the foot pump and open air release valve, to ensure that the tank is not under pressure.

  (iii) Close the air release valve.

  (iv) Fill the tank to within 3" of the top with petrol. Replace the filler cap and tighten up.

  (v) Connect up the pump.

  (vi) Open air release valve and pump up pressure until gauge registers 20 lbs per square inch.

(b) To light burner:—

  (i) Open the burner stop cock, as soon as the petrol issues from the jet, close the cock, and ignite the petrol.

  (ii) Keep the petrol alight by opening and closing the cock but avoid excessive flaring.

  (iii) When the burner is hot, open the cock slowly to the full position.

  (iv) Increase the air pressure in tank until the required flame is obtained. Do not exceed a pressure of 50 lbs per sq inch.

(c) To close down:—

  (i) Close the burner stop cock.

  (ii) When the flame is burnt out and *not* before, open the air release valve.

  (iii) When pressure is exhausted, close the air release valve.

(d) Care and Maintenance:—

  (i) Use clean petrol only.

  (ii) Ensure that no water is allowed to enter the petrol.

  (iii) Close the air release valve immediately after pumping to avoid loss of pressure.

  (iv) Decarbonise the burner once a week, using the special reamers provided, this is important and should be a routine job. To do this properly the burner must be disconnected from the tank, and the reamers worked down the vertical, horizontal, and inclined tubes until these are clear of carbon. Blow out all loose particles and prick out jet.

Components for Cooker, Portable, No. 1

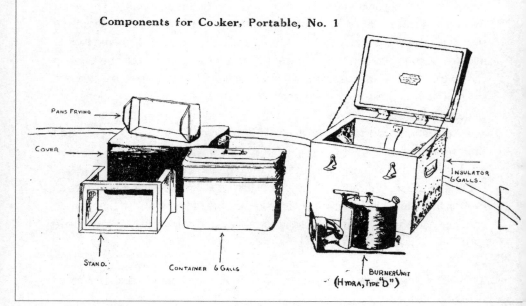

PANS FRYING

COVER

STAND.

CONTAINER 6 GALLS

INSULATOR 6 GALLS.

BURNER UNIT (HYDRA, TYPE "D")

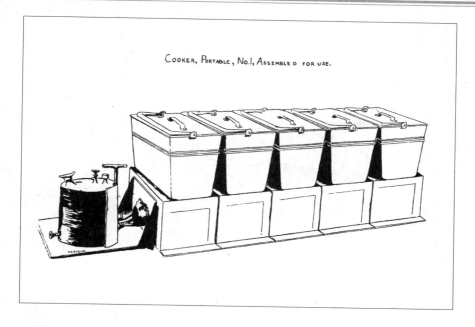

COOKER, PORTABLE, No.I, ASSEMBLED FOR USE.

remained a valuable addition to army catering because of its simplicity. The stove was capable of boiling 12 gallons of liquid and crucially could be carried by a mule into areas where motor vehicles could not reach. Depending upon where the troops were operating, Soyer Stoves could be fired with coal, coke or charcoal, wood, or in a desert area, dried dung. This meant that it was not dependant on petrol or fuel oil, although some were run on petrol burners.

Camp kettles were still used because they allowed quantities of food to be prepared over a limited number of heat sources. They could exploit the same range of fuels as the Soyer Stove, and could be employed either stacked up to create means to direct airflow, or the manual suggests that eight kettles are ideal to form a 'kitchen' and that meals can be cooked in about one and a half hours using this technique.[34] The kettles could also be used on a variety of improvised cookers. These could be as simple as a trench dug in the ground with the kettles rested on top, to upright ovens built from brick, clay blocks or tins filled with earth. Using these materials it was possible to form a firebox and flue to direct the heat above, while sheets of steel could be made into a hot plate and, with the

34 *Manual of Army Catering Services, Part III — Cooking in the Field, including Improvised and Mess Tin Cookery* (1945), p. 2

"BLUFF" PORTABLE STOVE

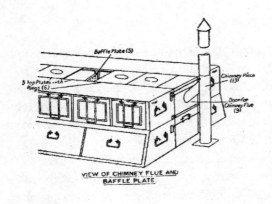

Door (10)
Top Section (4)
Door for Chimney Flue (9)
Plain Plate (7)
5 Top Plates with Rings (6)
Top Section (4)
Screw Bolts with Wing Nuts (11)
Plain Plate (7)
Bottom Section (1)
Hook Bolts (12)
Door (8)

COMPLETE STOVE.

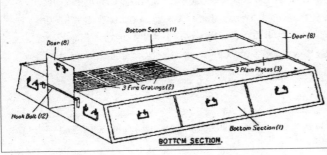

Baffle Plate (5)
Chimney Piece (13)
5 Top Plates with Rings (6)
Door for Chimney Flue (9)

VIEW OF CHIMNEY FLUE AND BAFFLE PLATE.

Bottom Section (1)
Door (8)
Door (8)
3 Plain Plates (3)
3 Fire Gratings (2)
Hook Bolt (12)
Bottom Section (1)

BOTTOM SECTION.

INSTRUCTION FOR ERECTION OF "BLUFF" PATTERN PORTABLE SERVICE STOVE.

(a) Choose a level site, if this is not possible, a short time spent in levelling will be well repaid by the ease of erection and efficient working. A level site is most essential.

(b) Place the two bottom sections (1) in position. Then place three fire gratings (2) and three plain plates (3) between the two bottom sections.

(c) Drop two top sections (4) into bottom section.

(d) Slide baffle plate (5) between runners in centre of fire space.

(e) Slide five top plates with rings (6) and two plain plates (7) between the top section as shown. The two plain plates (7) at either end.

(f) Drop doors (8) into grooves each end of bottom section.

(g) Drop door (9) into grooves at end of top section where chimney is required, and door (10) into corresponding grooves at other ends.

(h) Put screw bolts (11) in position at bolt ends, and tighten up wing nuts as much as possible. Put hook bolts (12) on bottom sections in position both ends.

(i) Place chimney piece (13) in position over nozzle on door (9) and secure in position by two hooks provided.

(j) Place plain chimney pipes on chimney (13) to required height.

NOTE:— There are two doors supplied to doors (8) one shorter than the other. This is for the purpose of decreasing or increasing draught required. There is also a regulating damper in the chimney piece (13) for this purpose.
It is imperative that the screw bolts (11) and hook bolts (12) are not interfered with once adjusted in position.

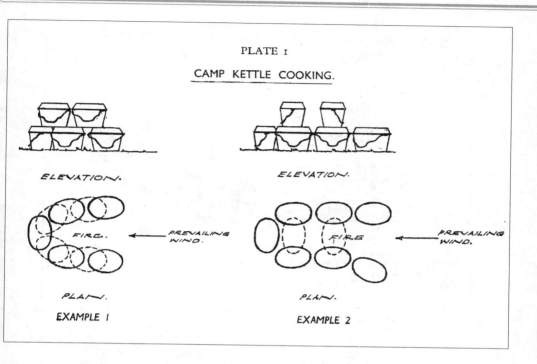

PLATE 1

CAMP KETTLE COOKING.

ELEVATION.

ELEVATION.

FIRE.

PREVAILING WIND.

FIRE

PREVAILING WIND.

PLAN.

PLAN.

EXAMPLE 1

EXAMPLE 2

addition of a chimney, the heat could be drawn through the system. In its most simple form the improvised cooker could be used as a means of heating camp kettles, but this could be enhanced by the addition of an oven, a tank for heating hot water, or a frying plate. The great advantage of all of these 'improvised' cookers was that they could use local materials and the ovens, chimneys and water tanks could be extemporised from empty petrol tins, fuel containers and food cans, especially for chimneys. Depending upon the circumstances, 'combination' cookers could be built which could be used for roasting, heating water, as a hot plate or any combination that took the cook's fancy. One technique to provide hot water for sanitary purposes called for an oil drum for water to be set above a heat source with an inlet in the very top. To get water out from the outlet, set just below the top of the barrel it was necessary to add cold water to raise the level to above that of the outlet so that a flow of water could be run off.[35]

35 *Manual of Army Catering Services, Part III – Cooking in the Field, including Improvised and Mess Tin Cookery* (1945), pp. 4–9, further illustrations pp. 10–11

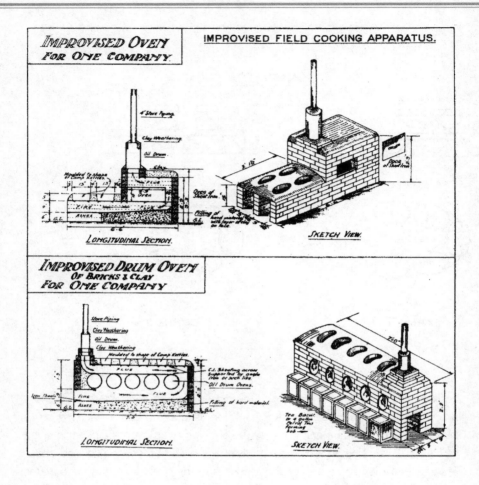

BOILING AND/OR FRYING.

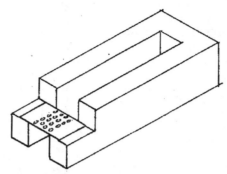

FIG. I. WALLS ALMOST COMPLETE.
'FIREBARS' IN POSITION.

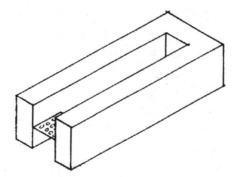

FIG II. WALLS COMPLETE.

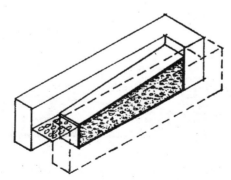

FIG III. FLUE BED FORMED.

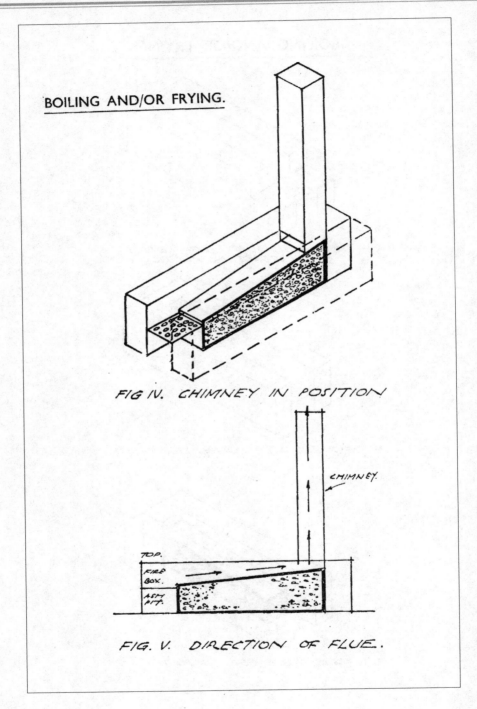

BOILING AND/OR FRYING.

FIG IV. CHIMNEY IN POSITION

FIG. V. DIRECTION OF FLUE.

BOILING AND/OR FRYING.

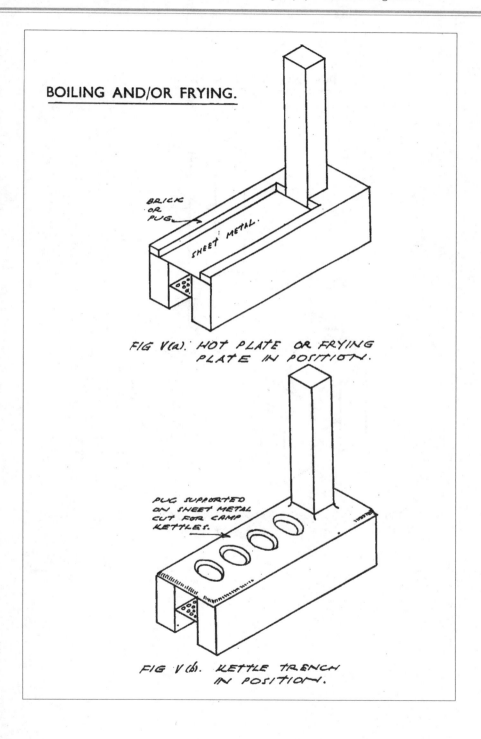

BRICK OR PUG

SHEET METAL.

FIG V(a). HOT PLATE OR FRYING PLATE IN POSITION.

PUG SUPPORTED ON SHEET METAL CUT FOR CAMP KETTLES.

FIG V (b). KETTLE TRENCH IN POSITION.

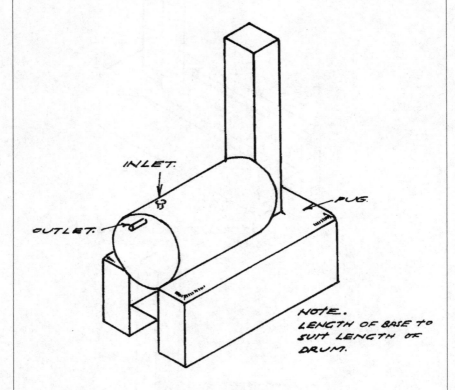

BOILING AND/OR FRYING.

INLET.

OUTLET.

PUG.

NOTE.
LENGTH OF BASE TO
SUIT LENGTH OF
DRUM.

FIG. V. (c). HOTWATER BOILER
IN POSITION.

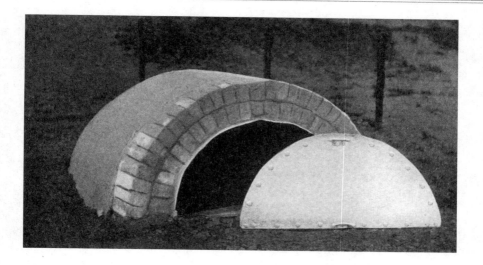

The elements that made up the Aldershot Oven (as pictured above) were a series of arches, plates and ends all made of sheet steel. These were heavy, at over 370lbs (168kg), but it provided for great variations in style of cooking. The metal components could not be used on their own and a casing of up to 100 bricks plus clay mixed with hay or straw to form 'pug' was required. In its simplest form it was operated very much like a pizza oven in which a wood fire was lit in the interior of the oven and allowed to burn for some time. This heated the metal plates forming the roof and walls, and the heat was retained by the covering of brick, clay, or turf. The heat created by the burning of fuel was reflected back and the oven could be used to prepare bread, roast meats, pies, milk or Yorkshire puddings. One feature of the oven was that, as the covering dried out, subsequent heatings used less fuel; also as the temperature dropped the style of food cooked could be varied. As it was not possible to tell the temperature of the oven, a simple test was developed using a hand held in front of the open oven door, if it became impossible to hold the hand in position for more than five seconds the oven was ready for meat and potatoes, ten seconds brown stew, and ten to fourteen seconds fruit pies. As with other cooking techniques, an improvised version of the Aldershot Oven was taught using barrels covered with clay which would burn out but still provide a roof, tin boxes filled with earth or even a hollowed out anthill.[36]

36 *Manual of Army Catering Services, Part III – Cooking in the Field, including Improvised and Mess Tin Cookery* (1945), pp. 56–63

Based on the experience of the Great War, insulated cookery was used to provide troops, with no means of cooking, with a hot meal. Using this system, food could be cooked behind the lines and be sent forward in either issue insulated containers or those which had been improvised. An additional advantage of this was that it actually conserved fuel as the cooking continued once the food was placed into the insulated container. In very bad weather conditions the advantages of being able to get hot drinks to soldiers in exposed conditions can be easily understood. It was possible to use the same technique to get food such as bacon and beans, porridge, soup, puddings, stews or deserts to those on the frontline. It was claimed in the manual that food could be kept hot for up to twenty hours if placed in a 'haybox' or insulator.[37] Although purpose-made insulated containers were provided, improvised 'hayboxes' were manufactured from timber in workshops or converted from tea chests. The *Manual of Military Cooking* also provides details of using a standard pack, lined with hay, in which hot soup or tea could be carried to the frontline.[38] To solve the problem of getting hot drinks to men in the frontline, a variety of insulated containers were developed. Some were not much bigger than a modern thermos flask whilst others could contain up to 1½ gallons of liquid.[39]

If the army was concerned about wasting fuel oil, it was also aware that there was a constant supply of waste oil available from vehicle sumps and cooling systems. The *Manual of Army Catering Services* makes it clear that most kinds of cooking apparatus can be adapted to burn oil and water which was mixed in proportion. This highly hazardous operation required the use of tanks to feed the cooker by gravity and a preheated oil pipe into which fuel was dripped from above. In one style of cooker the oil was dripped onto a U-shaped channel of metal which formed a flash pan. The flash pan was filled with fuel and ignited so that when additional oil and water were dripped onto the flash pan this would ignite. Problems encountered could include heavy smoke and a build up of soot, and the ever-present danger of a badly run system catching fire.[40]

....

37 *Manual of Army Catering Services, Part III – Cooking in the Field, including Improvised and Mess Tin Cookery* (1945), pp. 19–33

38 *Manual of Military Cooking and Dietary* (1933), pp. 117–119

39 *Manual of Army Catering Services, Part IV – Static cooking Apparatus and Cooking Equipment in the Field* (1945), p. 62.

40 *Manual of Army Catering Services, Part III – Cooking in the Field, including Improvised and Mess Tin Cooker* (1945), p. 12

Dishes.	Amount of wood required.	Time for heating oven.	Time for cooking	If pugged up.	No. of seconds for hand test.	Remarks.
Meat and potatoes.	Lbs. 112	Hrs. 2	2 to 2½ hrs.	Yes	5	Stock to cover bottom of dish. Full load nine dishes.
Meat pies ...	112	2	2 hrs.	Yes	10 to 12	No egg wash. Camp kettle of boiling water to be placed in oven. Full load eight pies.
Brown stew ...	112	2	2 hrs.	Yes	10	Stew must be complete and covered with other trays.
Bacon fried ...	50 to 60	1	5 mins.	No	Flash heat.	If glowing embers are left in back of oven, less time will be required.
Eggs, fried ...	50 to 60.	1	5 mins.	No	do.	do.
Liver	90 to 100.	1½	10 to 15 mins.	No	do.	do.
Sausages ...	do.	do.	do.	No	do.	Care must be taken to leave space in dishes to allow sausages to swell in cooking.
Chops and steaks.	do.	do.	15 mins.	No	do.	*See* remarks on bacon. Turn over after 7 or 8 minutes.
Milk puddings	100	1¾	1¼ hrs.	Yes	12 to 14	
Fruit pies ...	100	1¾	1¼ hrs.	Yes	10 to 12	*See* remarks on meat pies.
Jam tart ...	100	1¾	30 mins.	No	Flash heat.	
Yorkshire pudding.	100	1¾	45 mins.	No	do.	

NOTE.—The times quoted above are approximate as the different types of wood available, as fuel, vary. Fir and other resinous kinds burn away quickly, but give off great heat; while ash, beech, box, elm and oak burn very slowly, with little smoke, and give a maximum of heat. Quantities of wood, as well as heating times must, of necessity, be somewhat elastic.

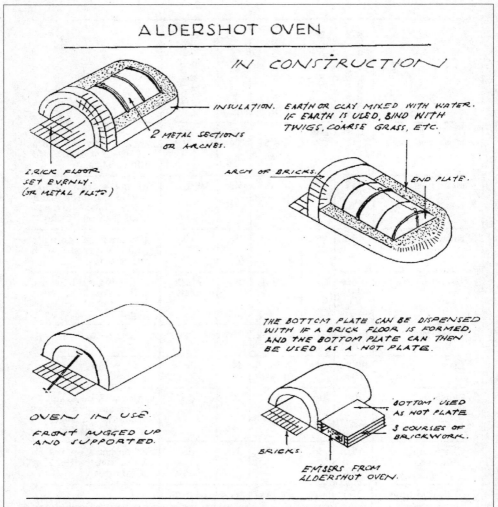

ALDERSHOT OVEN

IN CONSTRUCTION

INSULATION. EARTH OR CLAY MIXED WITH WATER. IF EARTH IS USED, BIND WITH TWIGS, COARSE GRASS, ETC.

2 METAL SECTIONS OR ARCHES.

BRICK FLOOR SET EVENLY. (OR METAL PLATE)

ARCH OF BRICKS.

END PLATE.

THE BOTTOM PLATE CAN BE DISPENSED WITH IF A BRICK FLOOR IS FORMED, AND THE BOTTOM PLATE CAN THEN BE USED AS A HOT PLATE.

OVEN IN USE.
FRONT PLUGGED UP AND SUPPORTED.

'BOTTOM' USED AS HOT PLATE

3 COURSES OF BRICKWORK.

BRICKS.

EMBERS FROM ALDERSHOT OVEN.

How to erect the Oven (*cont.*)

2 feet wide, and 6 feet long, leaving a space of 12 inches between the trench and the oven. The clay, or soil from the trench, being mixed with water and grass, rushes, etc., to assist in binding it, is then thrown on the oven and well beaten down. The depth of clay or earth should be at least 6 inches. The roof should slope backwards slightly, to carry off the rain. A wood fire is then lit in the oven. As the earth or clay bakes it naturally cracks and leaves crevices, which should be filled in with liquid pug or clay.

The oven is then ready for use.

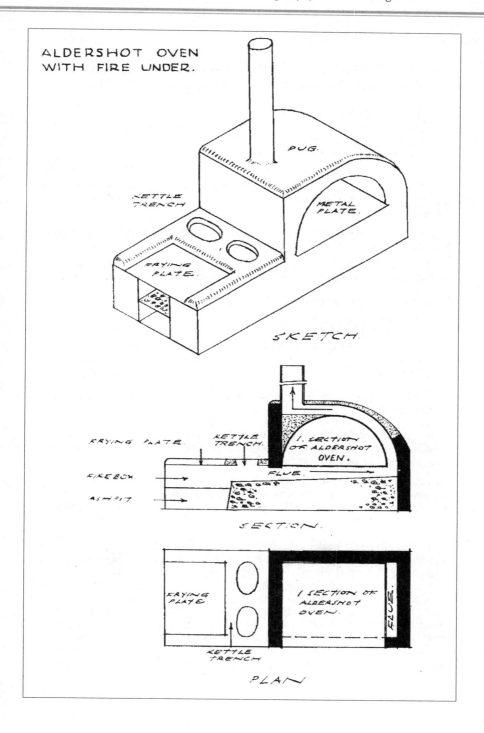

ALDERSHOT OVEN
WITH FIRE UNDER.

PUG.

KETTLE TRENCH

METAL PLATE.

FRYING PLATE.

SKETCH.

FRYING PLATE.

KETTLE TRENCH.

1. SECTION OF ALDERSHOT OVEN.

FIREBOX.

FLUE.

ASH PIT

SECTION.

FRYING PLATE.

1 SECTION OF ALDERSHOT OVEN.

FLUE.

KETTLE TRENCH

PLAN

DIRECTIONS FOR WORKING OVENS OF THE ALDERSHOT MUD- OR CLAY-COVERED TYPE

5. Fuel required for each oven

1st heating 1st day	300 lb. wood.
1st heating 2nd day	150 lb. wood.
2nd and subsequent heating	75 lb. (baking).
2nd and subsequent heating	Up to 150 lb. (cooking).

When not in use the oven should be loaded with wood ready for quick lighting as the preparation of wood for the Aldershot takes some little time.

An old tip worth remembering is that the Aldershot oven should always be full of food, fuel or fire.

When the oven is heated the embers are drawn out with a rake, and a small quantity of ashes left and raked evenly over the floor.

6. Time for heating, baking, cooking, etc.

1st heating 1st day	4 hours.
1st heating 2nd day	2 hours.
2nd and subsequent heating	$1\frac{1}{2}$ hours.
Baking	1 to $1\frac{1}{4}$ hours.
Cooking	Up to $2\frac{1}{2}$ hours.

7. When meat is to be cooked, it can be put in immediately the fire is drawn.

8. Immediately the oven is filled the door should be put up and wedged tightly with a piece of wood, the end of which should rest on the outer edge of the trench in front.

The crevices round the end should then be filled in with wet clay to prevent any steam escaping. If this is done properly the steam providing the necessary moisture is retained, and the bread or dinners will not be burnt.

9. Beer barrels make excellent ovens ; one end is knocked out, the ground slightly sloped, so that it may rest firmly, the sides, back and top being covered with clay, well wedged downwards, to become quite hard ; the fire is then lit and allowed to burn until the whole of the barrel is consumed ; the hoops will then support the clay, and the oven may be safely used. Where the clay is good, a small oven may be built by it alone. Build two walls the required distance apart, about 6 inches high, with clay that has been well beaten and mixed, the back being joined to the walls ; then, with one hand on either side, gradually build the walls a few inches higher, the tops

slightly sloping towards each other, leaving a gap, in the form of a V, in the centre ; then mould a piece of the clay large enough to fill the gap, and place it in, care being taken to join well the edges with the walls both inside and out ; a small fire should then be lit and allowed to burn slowly until the clay is dry ; it will then become baked and quite firm, and may be used as other ovens.

10. Tin biscuit boxes filled with earth are a good substitute for material used in the construction of the Aldershot oven. They may be used as follows : melt one side of the solder and shape the tin into an oval ; lay it on the ground, and cover it with a few inches of clay or soil sufficient to retain the heat ; light the fire, and proceed as with the Aldershot pattern.

11. Ant-heaps can also be used as ovens, the insides being scooped out and the fire lighted as in the Aldershot oven.

12. Another method is to dig into the side of a bank or trench and improvise a door with any old sheets of tin or iron to hand, plugging up the crevices when cooking, as with the Aldershot oven.

13. The Aldershot ovens are, in many instances, so arranged that the flame from a specially constructed fire-place in front or at the side passes under the iron ground sheet with a chimney at the back or side, thereby, with the aid of fuel and stoking, providing a continual bottom heat. Bottom heat is, in other words, heat suitable for frying ; and, in the case of cooking meat by frequently turning, the results achieved are satisfactory. *See* Plates 29, 30 and 31.

(3.)

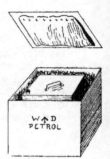

(4) 6lbs Cocoa Tin, containing
7lbs Jam Tin (4 pints)

(5) Tea Bucket, containing
6lbs Cocoa Tin (10 pints)

(6) Army Biscuit Tin, containing
4 Gall Petrol Tin (32 pints)

(7) 5 Gall Oil Drum,
containing
Stone S. R. D.
Bottle. (10 pints)
(for conveying hot
beverages to troops)

(8) 7lbs Jam Tin, containing
2lbs. Syrup Tin (1 pint)

12.

Table of Insulator Cookery.

Dish.	No men to each Container.	Boiling Time.	Min. Time in Insulator
Bacon & Beans. Tinned - Breakfast	120	30	1½ hrs.
Boiled Beef & Carrots.	50	30	3 hrs.
Salt. do. & do.	50	30	3 do.
Dumplings as Garnish	150	10	1 ..
Steak & Kidney Rolls.	60	30	2½ ..
Hams. 2 x 14 lbs.	100	30	4½ .
Braised Beef. 4 lb. joints	75	40	4½ ..
Brown Tomato Stew.	72	20	2½ ..
Curried Beef.	72	25	2½ .
Stewed Steak.	72	25	2½ ..
Braised Liver.	75	30	3 ..
Butter Beans.	150	30	3 ..
Haricot ..	150	30	3 ..
Rangoon ..	150	30	3 .
Blue Peas.	150	30	3 .
Carrots, Turnips, Parsnips, Swedes	100	15	2 ..
Stewed Cabbage.	120	5	1 ..
Potatoes Boiled.	80	5	1 ..
do. Savoury.	80	10	1 ..
Porridge - Rolled Oats.	120	5	¾ ..
Soups - Pulse. Vegt.	96	20	2 ..
Dried Fruit. Stewed.	100	5	1½ ..
Apple Rings. Fruit.	100	5	1½ ..
Salad, Prunes, Figs, Rice Pudding	100	5	1½ ..

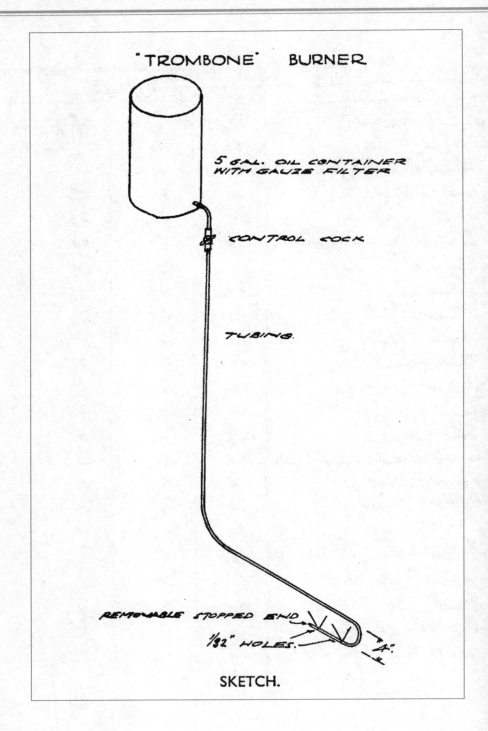

"TROMBONE" BURNER

5 GAL. OIL CONTAINER WITH GAUZE FILTER

CONTROL COCK

TUBING.

REMOVABLE STOPPED END

1/32" HOLES.

4"

SKETCH.

A more sophisticated system was made using a section of pipe which was curved and earned the nickname of a 'Trombone Oil Burner'.[41] Waste oil could be fed into the pipe and down flexible tubing, emerging at the end through vents in the pipe where it was ignited.

Throughout the war, tests were carried out on equipment mainly with the intention of saving fuel, and experiments were made with the American type of field cooker to compare with the British type. The American type was rejected because it was too delicate and required a fitter to ensure it was kept in working order. However, the Cooker Portable No. 1 was improved by fitting a windshield and the foot-pump was replaced with the hand-pump. A number of tests were carried out to find a small cooker suitable for mess-tin cookery and eventually a hexamine block (firelighter) was produced which was found to be extremely satisfactory; these blocks are still in use today.

Logistics

ALTHOUGH THE ROLE of the Army Catering Corps was the preparation of rations, supply was conducted by the Royal Army Service Corps. However, there was a close relationship between the two and the Lines of Communication (L of C) were long, and at times, threatened. Supplies were defined as including 'food, forage, fuel, light, disinfectants and hospital supplies which are provided, collected, distributed and accounted for by the R.A.S.C.'[42] In the case of the Second World War, the global nature of the conflict meant that the war effort was divided into a number of theatres of war, such as the Middle East and the Eighth Army, and the Far East and the Fourteenth Army. To ensure that supplies were adequate, albeit with minimum impact on shipping, it was necessary to obtain supplies locally in areas occupied by troops. In consequence the rations obtained varied from standard forms of supply, according to both location and distance. The main organisation was based on Supply Reserve Depots (SRDs). This abbreviation is the origin of the letters found on

41 *Manual of Army Catering Services, Part III – Cooking in the Field, including Improvised and Mess Tin Cookery* (1945), p. 15
42 *Royal Army Service Corps Training Pamphlet, Part 1: Supply Organisation in the Lines of Communication Area* (1942), p. 1

'rum jars' in both wars, which many soldiers believed stood for 'Service Rum Dilute' or 'Seldom Reaches Destination'. In time of war, Supply Reserve Depots dispatched overseas the various commodities required by the army to Main Supply Depots which were established in the theatres of war, (see diagram p.26 *Royal Army Service Corps Training Pamphlet, Part 1: Supply Organisation in the Lines of Communication Area* (1942)). It is worth adding, however, that supplies arriving overseas at a Main Supply Depot may have come from home but could also arrive from the empire or elsewhere in the world via convoy. For example, the pamphlet *Stowage Figures for Foods Ministry of Food* (1951) indicates that wheat arrived from Australia, Canada, the USA, India and South America; frozen mutton from New Zealand, Australia and South America; canned fruits from the USA, Australia and South Africa; peanuts from West Africa, linseed from India and sardines from Portugal.[43]

On arrival in an overseas base, supplies were received under supervision to the appropriate Base Supply Depot, Field Butchery, Cold Storage Depot and Field Bakeries. Supplies would normally be sent forward from there by rail or motor vehicle. One of the most remarkable features of this process is the amount of space taken up by even the most simple of supplies. It is laid down on p.20 of the *Combined Operations Pamphlet No.38, R.A.S.C. 1943* that supplies that were stacked should not exceed 50 tonnes each and in preference should be subdivided into a stack of half that weight. However, to reduce damage caused by enemy action there should be 40–50 yards (36–45 metres) between stacks.[44] The result is that nine stacks would require 5 acres (2 hectares) of ground even if the crates were stacked six high. This is the same size as three and a half football pitches. Some of these supplies would require dry storage, which would involve building structures, and every type of supply had different requirements for storage to prevent contamination or spoiling.

To put this into context, a single field bakery type 'A' consisted of four sections (eight sub-sections), each sub-section operating two steam field ovens. The capacity of each sub-section was 3,750lbs daily, the total of all eight sub-sections was 30,000lbs daily and the space required for this operation was about 3½ acres. In addition, 2,000 cubic feet (56m³) was needed for the storage of

43 Ministry of Food, *Stowage Figures for Foods* (1951), pp. 4–13
44 *Combined Operations Pamphlet No.38, R.A.S.C. 1943*, p. 20

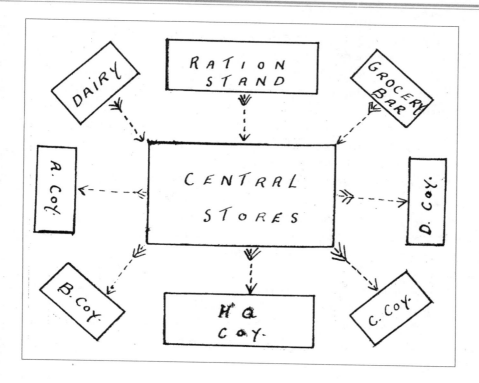

each 10,000lbs of bread.[45] This is the same amount of space as taken up by eleven elephants, just for one-third of a day's production in a field bakery. The situation is made worse by the size of the force required to be kept in the field, the need to camouflage the supplies, a virtual impossibility but important to prevent the enemy calculating the size of the army from its supply base, and the need to provide blast walls to provide some protection from aerial bombard-ment. It is therefore no coincidence that building up the resources required for an army took months, even if this operation had been planned well in advance. After D-Day (6 June 1944) it took until August before the resources in the 'Lodgement Area' were sufficient to supply an advance towards Germany.

In theory, at least, supplies were to be sent forward from the Base Area along the lines of communication to the formations in the field by rail, arriving at the Rail Head for collection by motorised transport and forward distribution to

45 *Royal Army Service Corps Training Pamphlet, Part 1: Supply Organisation in the Lines of Communication Area* (1942), p. 22

supply companies just behind the lines.[46] During the war this system worked in India, where the Japanese Army were not able to interfere with the railway network, but elsewhere bombing and systematic destruction by the enemy of rail routes meant that it was motorised vehicles that carried most supplies. This had the effect of increasing the amount of fuel needed, which in turn increased the requirement for petrol, oil and lubricants, leading to a further increase in the demands on shipping. To give an example of the magnitude of the task in sustaining one division in the field, the records of the 53rd (Welsh) Division in North West Europe are illuminating: between 27 June 1944 and 4 May 1945, 6,045,680 rations were issued, made up of 4,325,276 field service rations and 1,720,404 'compo' rations. This means that over 14,363 tons (13,029 tonnes) of food were transported to the divisional administrative area and during the campaign every man in the division ate 17 cwt of food (863kg), which amounts to fourteen times his own average weight or roughly the same weight as a cow! In the same period 1,030 portable cookers were issued.[47]

Although the British Army became almost fully motorised by 1941, draft animals remained in use in several theatres of war. These included the mountains of Italy, the jungles of Burma and the deserts of North Africa.

46 Messing Officers course No.16, November 1934, RLC 3046A8

47 Howard N. Cole, The Story of the Army Catering Corps and its Predecessors (Army Catering Corps Association: 1984), p.148

'Waste Not, Want Not': The Army Ration

BASIC REQUIREMENTS OF OPERATIONAL RATION DEVELOPMENT

An operational ration pack must be a self-contained, balanced ration. Therefore, several basic considerations must always be borne in mind.

(a) Acceptability – the ration must be acceptable to the troops in the field. Uneaten food results in loss of potential energy and lowered morale.
(b) Nutritional adequacy – the needs of the body must be satisfied in order that it can function properly.
(c) Military Utility – the ration must be developed to meet the requirements of modern war.
(d) Stability – will the ration keep for whatever period has been agreed for its turnover? The present minimum stability period accepted is two years, but it is anticipated that this period will be extended as research into storage methods and keeping qualities continues.

From: *Operational Ration Packs and their Development.*

On the outbreak of war on 3 September 1939, rationing on the Home Front became inevitable because of the demands on shipping created by the global conflict. Britain was far from self-sufficient and supplies for food stuffs from the empire and beyond were a necessity rather than a luxury. On the outbreak of war, the plans made by the Food Defence Plans Department of the Board of Trade assumed that the government would take control of all essential staple foods. However, when civilian rationing was introduced on 8 January 1940 for bacon, butter and sugar, this was not extended to servicemen and women because it was recognised that they would require a high level of calories to function under service conditions. In 1919 it was estimated that a working man needed 3,772 calories and that British rations in the Great War provided some 4,643 calories.[48] This situation continued to exist with servicemen and women receiving better nutrition than those people on the Home Front. A comparison of meat shows that one week's rations for a civilian is the equivalent of the amount provided for one day for a soldier. The Cabinet Food Policy Committee concluded early in the war that the total service ration should be 4,000 calories, although women would receive four-fifths of the male food ration.[49] However, it was not possible to discriminate between frontline and other soldiers because it was difficult to determine a dividing line between the two classes. By March 1941 the Home Service Ration was:

	Men (oz daily)	Women (oz daily)
Meat (bone in)	6	5¾
Bacon	1½	1 1/7
Offal or sausages	1 5/7	1 1/7 (sausages only)
Bread	10	7
Flour	2	2
Butter or margarine	1½	1½
Cheese	4/7	4/7
Milk, tinned	3	3¼
Sugar	2	2
Potatoes	13	12
Fresh vegetables	5 5/7	8
Tea	2/7	2/7

From: *The Story of the Royal Army Service Corps 1939–1945* (1955), p.468

2⅔

48 Dr. D. Noel Paton, *Army Rations: their Bearing on the Efficiency of the Soldiers* (1919), p. 8 and 20
49 *The Story of the Royal Army Service Corps 1939–1945* (G. Bell and Son Ltd: 1955), p. 463

Army Cooks Superior to Women

OLD ORDER CHANGED

Peace-time catering manager for Bournemouth and now the British Army's ace trainer of 6,000 messing officers, Major S. E. Sidwell, has one test for his trainees. It is this:

Does the food the British Tommy gets consist of the dishes he likes?

Does he get it when he wants it?

Does he get it how he wants it?

Does it give him the maximum amount of food value?

At the Cumberland Hotel, Scarborough, now headquarters of the Messing Officers' Training Centre, of which he is commandant, Major Sidwell gave answers to all sorts of questions fired at him at an Army food quiz by Press representatives.

Troops not afraid to complain

No complaints!—the old order has changed. When Tommy Atkins of this war feels that he is getting too much rice pudding or that he doesn't like the way the cheese is served, he is not afraid of being "pegged."

He takes his complaint to the Messing Committee, a body representative of all ranks of the unit and presided over by one of Major Sidwell's 6,000 messing officers.

That complaint cannot be ignored, because the minutes of every Messing Committee must be signed by the Messing Officer and the C.O. of the unit, and the Catering Officer of the Division must have access to those minutes whenever he pops in to see how things are going on.

There is no "come-back" on the private.

MEN BETTER COOKS

There is no doubt that men are the better cooks.

Major Sidwell has been in the catering business 35 years, but he has never heard of a famous woman chef. He feels that the reason is that a boy going in for catering is going to make it a career, but young girls don't. Their ambition is to get married.

Major Sidwell says the British soldier is much better fed than the German. There has been plenty of opportunity in recent months to study German rations and methods of cooking.

There is no doubt that the Germans are content with a mediocre standard of cooking.

Asked why the Tommy so often ignores the free Army supper and buys his meal in the canteen, Major Sidwell said it was because he likes a change of scenery—much the same as a civilian who has perfectly good meals at home, but occasionally prefers to go out for a meal at a hotel or restaurant.

Major Sidwell thinks that after war we are going to get a better standard of cooking country, because of the number of cooks that have in the Services.

This article tells it all! Army Cooks quickly became adept at a huge range of culinary tasks. Although, it is doubtful whether many women genuinely felt threatened! Taken from *Newcastle Evening Chronicle*, 1944.

Learning how to use a 'brew-up' oven.

The Ministry of Food aided in lectures to Army Cooks, teaching principles of 'waste not, want not'.

Lectures in butchery were vital to the Army Cook.

In the kitchen.

Inspecting the day's produce.

Army Cooks experiment with mess-tin cooking.

Army Cooks build a range of improvised ovens during their training.

Mid-way through creating an oil-drum oven.

Adding sand to an improvised oven, this technique was commonly used in the Middle East.

Covering an improvised oven in clay and mud.

Finishing off a brick and clay-covered oven.

Assessing the finished product.

Building the camp kettle oven.

Camp kettle cooking.

A sunken kitchen.

Checking how the potatoes are doing in this improvised oven.

One satisfied cook!

Enjoying the fruits of their labour.

CHART SHOWING RECOVERY AND UTILIZATION OF BY-PRODUCTS

Source	Explanation	Treatment	Classification	Utilization	Remarks
A.—Fats from Raw Meat—					Suet should, where possible, be used raw for suet puddings. It is better and more economical for that purpose than dripping. NOTE.—Fat is an essential article of diet. Meat and joints must not be spoilt by over-trimming.
1. Suet	... ...	Cut into small pieces, or put through mincer, rendered down and clarified.	1st class "white" dripping.	(i) For cooking purposes. (ii) For issue in lieu of margarine.	
2. Butcher's fat	Surplus fat from the carcase which a trade butcher removes in preparing meat for sale.				
3. Trimmings ...	Further surplus in cutting up meat for stews.				
B.—Fats recovered in process of cooking—					
4. Bacon rind ...	Remove before cutting up.	—	—	(i) Mince as an ingredient for rissoles, etc. (ii) For pastries, etc. Residue a valuable ingredient for rissoles, etc.	Bacon rind should be removed before serving bacon. It can be utilized in a variety of ways. After the extraction of the fat, the residue yields, after boiling, a jelly, valuable in making brawn. All stews, soups, etc., should be well skimmed.
		Boil up with water, skim, thoroughly clarify the fat.	Lard		
5. Skimmings ...	The grease which rises to the surface of stews, stock pots, etc., and which should be skimmed off.	Clarify, and, if discoloured, break into fresh water and clarify again.	1st class "white" dripping, or, if discoloured, "brown" dripping.	(i) "White"; as above. (ii) "Brown"; 2nd class cooking purposes or sale.	
6. Baking dishes residue.	The fat which a joint loses in process of cooking.	Clarify	Generally brown, through burning.	As above	If unburnt, this dripping has the flavour of the meat, and an admixture will improve dripping issued in lieu of margarine.
7. Bacon fat ...	The large amount of melted fat left after frying.	(i) Clarify and re-clarify. (ii) Clarify	(i) Lard ... ... (ii) "Brown" dripping.	(i) For pastries, etc. (ii) For sale as "brown" dripping.	
C.—Fat recoveries from refuse—					
8. Grease trap skimmings.	Skim daily, but do not attempt to treat sludge.			For sale	This material must not be treated in the cookhouse, but must be disposed of direct to the contractor.
D.—Bones—					
9. Marrow bones	Leg, buttock and shin bones.	(i) Untreated. Should be well stripped of meat. (ii) Break up, and add to stock pot.	(i) Marrow bones. (ii) "Other" bones.	(i) For sale ... (ii) For sale ...	
10. Green bones...	i.e. Uncooked ...	Well stripped of meat.	"Other" bones...	For sale	
11. Cooked bones.	From joints, from stock pots, and left on plates.	—	"Other" bones.	For sale	Bones should only be gently simmered; if violently boiled, the glue-contents are released, and the residue is fit only for manure, and will command a low price only.

The fact that servicemen and women were receiving a far larger ration meant that those on the Home Front had to make sacrifices in order to maintain the required level of nutrition for the army. This did create problems, particularly when a soldier returned home on leave. It was not unusual for parents of a soldier to go without so that when he returned home he was able to eat ample food despite the heavy rationing. There was a level of anxiety from soldiers abroad about the conditions on the Home Front with regards to food as they were aware that their families were not eating in the same style they were.

It must be recognised, however, that what was intended to be issued did not always arrive and that the conditions when training in the UK, in the field, behind the lines and in action, would vary depending on what could be issued and how it could be cooked. Another variable was climate and terrain; soldiers serving in the mountains of North Italy during the winter of 1943–44 faced restrictions of delivery even when pack ponies were used and freezing conditions made cooking virtually impossible. By contrast, soldiers in the deserts of North Africa faced conditions where tinned food melted even before it was opened and it was possible to fry an egg on a vehicle if such a commodity could be purchased or transported. On Home Service, the Rations Scale and system of distribution meant that the majority of food would be fresh and cooking conducted en masse by a combination of Army Catering Corps and sometimes civilian chefs. It was also possible to purchase additional items from the NAAFI or the civilian cafes, pubs and restaurants, and as some items were restricted a cash allowance was provided for this purpose.[50] This provided servicemen and women with a wide variety of food eaten normally in messes, which functioned like a canteen served by static kitchens using conventional kitchen equipment.

When troops were deployed overseas, conditions behind the lines would be similar, although there were potential complications with tented sites, the use of improvised or field cookers and proximity to the enemy. As far as possible the food issued was prepared in cookhouses suitable to feed hundreds, if not thousands, of soldiers and the food was consumed in huts or dining tents. One example can be provided from a rest-centre for 3,000 army and RAF personnel in the Normandy beachhead where each kitchen fed 1,000 men.[51] Closer to the

50 *The Story of the Royal Army Service Corps* 1939–1945 (G. Bell and Son Ltd: 1955), p. 466

51 Howard N. Cole, *The Story of the Army Catering Corps and Its Predecessors* (Army Catering Corps Association: 1984), p. 143

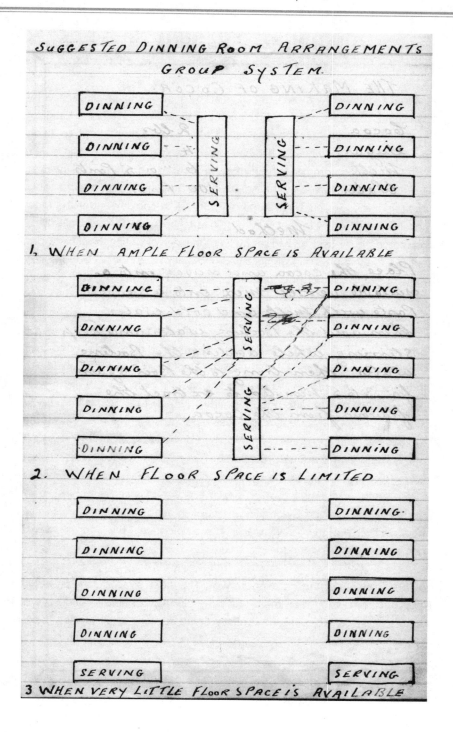

SUGGESTED DINNING ROOM ARRANGEMENTS
GROUP SYSTEM.

1, WHEN AMPLE FLOOR SPACE IS AVAILABLE

2. WHEN FLOOR SPACE IS LIMITED

3 WHEN VERY LITTLE FLOOR SPACE IS AVAILABLE

enemy, conditions were very different. This description is from the report of a Catering Advisor in the forward area of the Normandy battlefield:

> I visited a Unit where a jeep was placed at my disposal and an Officer accompanied me to the Forward Area. The first unit visited was an Infantry Battalion, and I believe their location was called 'Hell Fire Corner' and it certainly deserved the name. The unit had had some heavy fighting and casualties. The CO had been in command three days, the third in as many weeks. I walked around all accompanied by the Adjutant. The standard was good. The cooks had had a most trying time, and a difficult task in cooking under the most adverse conditions. Most of their time had to be spent for personal safety reasons in the slit trench. I had set out with the idea of visiting three Battalions, but realised that physical assistance was necessary. I therefore decided to stay the rest of the day with this Battalion. I arranged with the Adjutant to have all available cooks assembled in a vehicle pit and talked to them of my plans. These were to create a deep cook-house with a protective cover of soil and all equipment dug-in. Secondly the correct way of cooking compo and thirdly the protection of the cooks themselves. The cooks were then dismissed to their respective companies and I, with the assistance of the two ACC cooks and two Regimental Cooks proceeded to make the cooking point. A lot of digging was necessary but by later afternoon we had something to show for our efforts. A dug-out 6 feet long, 5 feet deep, 6 feet wide with long tree trunks along the top, some tin and corrugated iron over the trunks, twelve inches of soil on top of this. The sloping entrance protected by comp boxes filled with earth. It was a rough job, but would fulfil its purpose. I then went round all the companies again and found them all busy on similar erections. These cooks have really done a first class job of work. Having been in action with their units since D-day, with two of them badly shaken, I recommend that the latter be given a rest period, and this was done.[52]

Food prepared under these conditions would be eaten by soldiers in slit trenches or dug-outs using their own mess-tins. When in the frontline individuals would have to make do with mess-tin cookery or no cooking at all. During the First

---

52 Howard N. Cole, *The Story of the Army Catering Corps and its Predecessors* (Army Catering Corps Association: 1984), pp. 143–144

World War 'Iron Rations' had been introduced, consisting of biscuits and preserved food which could be eaten straight from the container. Rations provided during the Second World War were increasingly sophisticated and culminated in the 'Mess-Tin Ration', which provided all the food elements a soldier would require for forty-eight hours.

When frozen meat was issued this had to be stored at cold temperatures and improved meat stores were required. These meat stores served two purposes, to keep the temperature low while the frozen meat thawed and to ensure that air could circulate. There are examples from early in the war of meat arriving still frozen solid when it was required to be delivered to units as joints. In consequence, units who did not have a butcher were 'forced to chop up the frozen hard carcasses with axes and choppers in a somewhat hit and miss manner'.[53] In the *Royal Army Service Corps Training Pamphlet No.12: Cattle and Sheep; Fresh, Frozen and Chilled Meat* (1942) it takes eighty-nine pages to explain how meat is transported, classified and thawed to ensure that it arrives in prime condition for use. Defrosting and thawing is only encountered on p.87! The rest of the pamphlet deals with, in the highest detail, everything

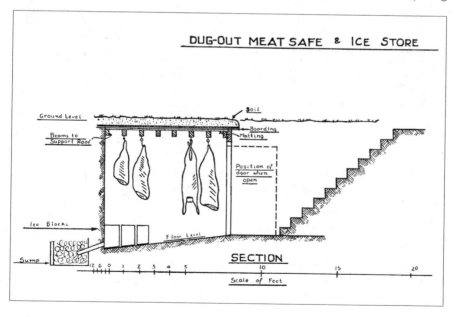

53 Howard N. Cole, *The Story of the Army Catering Corps and its Predecessors* (Army Catering Corps Association: 1984), p. 96

KOOLGARDIE MEAT SAFE

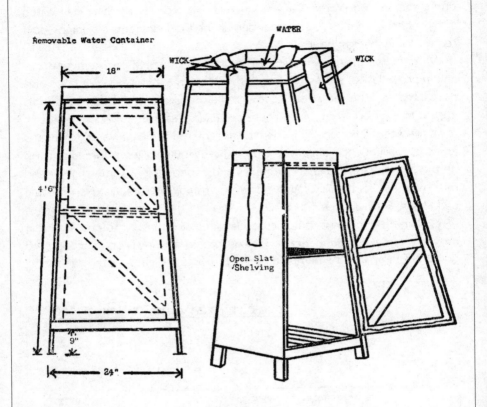

Removable Water Container

18"

WATER

WICK

WICK

4'6"

9"

24"

Open Slat
Shelving

NOTES

Cools by evaporation of water running down sides.

Keeps Milk, Butter, Meat cool in all weathers; should stand in the open air.

Splay shape essential to allow spread of water on sides.

Dimensions to suit local conditions.

Covering material on the four sides Hessian or other coarse canvas.

Wick of Lint or Cotton Bandages, etc., pinned to Hessian.

Joints can be halved or nailed.

Door preferably recessed to keep out flies.

Hook can be fixed to shelving to hang meat.

No special measures necessary for surface draining.

Made from timber, 2½" x ¼".

from diseases to the effects of mould and relative humidity. In these circumstances it is easy to see why, despite the weight and culinary limitations, tinned food overcame the natural preference of soldiers for fresh meat. For example, in the *Manual of Army Catering Services* a series of elaborate methods were suggested for keeping fresh meat, butter and other perishables cool and safe from contamination by insects. In the case of the 'Koolgardie Meat Safe', a wooden frame was covered with coarse canvas and fitted with a door that could keep out flies. On top of the meat safe was a container filled with water into which were placed a number of 'wicks', allowing the water to be drawn up and trickle down the sides of the safe. Even in hot conditions, evaporation would lower the temperature and these were used to store meat, milk, butter and other perishables. When this type of structure was not available it was advised to dig a pit in which products could be placed and covered with an insulated layer such as turf. In certain circumstances, specifically where the temperatures were very high or there was risk of being observed by the enemy, the manual advises that butchery and cooking is conducted in sunken cookhouses with a camouflaged roof. This both reduced the temperature and allowed for illumination as well as, if an elaborate system of pipes and flues were constructed, allowing smoke to diffuse.[54]

Today we are familiar with the idea of 'sell-by dates' and 'best before', however the *Royal Army Service Corps Pamphlet No.18, Part 2: Measures to be taken for the Preservation of Supplies* (1943) proves an interesting read in respect to this. It states that chilled beef can be stored for ten to fifteen days, frozen beef for up to ten months, figs for six months and turnips for one to two months. However, tinned cheese lasted for one to two years, tinned fruit for two to three years, meat extract cubes for up to five years and tinned sardines for up to ten years; someone was clearly planning for a very long war.[55]

Prior to 1939 very little thought was given to the feeding of small detachments of troops up to a platoon (forty-five plus in strength). The range of food available for feeding these men comprised of 'haversack rations' of tinned corned beef and biscuit, and when a hot meal was required a tinned

----

54 *Manual of Army Catering Services, Part III – Cooking in the Field, including Improvised and Mess Tin Cookery* (1945), pp. 41–43
55 *Royal Army Service Corps Pamphlet No.18, Part 2: Measures to be taken for the Preservation of Supplies* (1943), pp. 31–35

stew known as 'M and V' (meat and vegetable) was issued.[56] The outbreak of war demonstrated that greater sophistication was required to provide wider variety and to cater for different theatres of war. It was the experience of catering for the men and women of the Anti-Aircraft Command that led to the extensive use of canned food. This was proposed by the AA Command Catering Advisor following an experiment that ran from 1940–41. It was this experiment which led later in the war to the development of rations based on canned food. These proved to be an excellent method of introducing variety to the soldiers' diet. The initial introduction of the fourteen-man packs led to other composite packs being created.[57] The first tests were carried out with a pack designed to feed fourteen men for twenty-four hours or seven men for twice as long. These packs became known as 'Compo Packs' – the 'Compo' indicating composite. In order to cater for various sizes of unit the packs were later made up in quantity for two men, seven men and fourteen men.[58] During the war, no fewer than 40,000,000 packs were manufactured in different varieties.[59] The basic pack, known as the 'Landing or Assault Ration', was a twenty-four hour ration pack which was designed to provide the highest possible food value in the smallest possible space and weight; some 7,500,000 of these packs were produced during the war. The food was packed in a waxed cardboard container which was water and gas proof and fitted into the larger half of the mess-tin. One of the most remarkable items provided in this ration were tea, sugar and milk in block form, which could be crumbled into a pint of boiling water, and oatmeal blocks which included sugar and dried milk powder to make breakfast porridge.[60] The 'Compo' (fourteen-man pack) was produced for feeding troops over a period up to six weeks. It was made up entirely of tinned commodities with variations to allow for a daily

56 Howard N. Cole, The Story of the Army Catering Corps and its Predecessors (Army Catering Corps Association: 1984), p. 150

57 Howard N. Cole, The Story of the Army Catering Corps and its Predecessors (Army Catering Corps Association: 1984), p. 96

58 Howard N. Cole, The Story of the Army Catering Corps and its Predecessors (Army Catering Corps Association: 1984), p. 151

59 The Story of the Royal Army Service Corps 1939–1945 (G. Bell and Son Ltd: 1955), p. 469

60 Howard N. Cole, The Story of the Army Catering Corps and its Predecessors (Army Catering Corps Association: 1984), p. 150

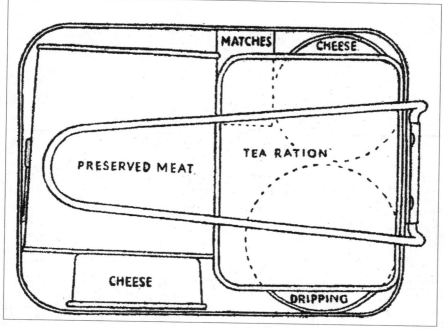

Mess Tin Ration

change of diet throughout the week. It was intended that cooking facilities under unit arrangement would be available when the 'Compo' ration was issued, however for some detachments improvised cooking would be necessary. Variations included 'Type A' to 'Type G' issued with biscuits and those identified 'Type 1' to 'Type 3' for issue when fresh bread was available.[61] One unintended result of providing so much tinned food was that vehicle crews found it possible to heat pierced ration tins by fastening them to hot engine parts, so producing a meal on the move. Tins also provided a variety of improvised cooking vessels and with the use of some basic tools a range of utensils could be created, which are illustrated in the War Office's *Manual of Army Catering Services: Part III*.[62]

61 *Operational Feeding: Use of Special Ration Packs* (1945)

62 *Manual of Army Catering Services, Part III – Cooking in the Field, Including Improvised and Mess-Tin Cookery, Static Cooking Apparatus and Cooking Equipment in the Field* (1945), p. 36

THE COMPOSIT

(A leaflet showing contents

Commodity	TYPE "A" No. and size of tins in each pack	TYPE "A" Approx. daily ration each man ozs.	TYPE "B" No. and size of tins in each pack	TYPE "B" Approx. daily ration each man ozs.	TYPE "C" No. and size of tins in each pack
Meat, preserved					
Meatstuffs (a)	11 × 16 ozs.	12½	10 × 16 ozs.	11½	14 × 16 ozs.
Sausages	2 × 28 ozs.	4	—	—	2 × 28 ozs.
Bacon	—	—	3 × 16 ozs.	3½	—
Luncheon meat	—	—	—	—	—
Beans, baked	3 × 16 ozs.	3½	—	—	—
Sardines	—	—	—	—	—
Fruits, tinned	2 × 30 ozs.	4	—	—	—
Soups, concentrated	—	—	2 × 30 ozs.	4	2 × 30 ozs.
Salmon, M.R.	—	—	—	—	—
Jam	1 × 21 ozs.	1½	1 × 21 ozs.	1½	—
Cigarettes	2 × 50 Nos.	7 No.	2 × 50 Nos.	7 No.	2 × 50 Nos.
Margarine	1 × 16 ozs.	1	1 × 16 ozs.	1	1 × 16 ozs.
Chocolate (Vit.)	14 × 2 oz. bars } In two tins	2	14 × 2 oz. bars } In two tins	2	14 × 2 oz. bars } In two tins
Sweets, boiled	16 ozs.	1½	16 ozs.	1½	16 ozs.
" "	2 ozs.		2 ozs.		2 ozs.
Matches, booklet	5 booklets } one tin	—	5 booklets } one tin	—	5 booklets } one tin
Salt	2 oz. pkt.	¼	2 oz. pkt.	¼	2 oz. pkt.
Tea, sugar and milk powder ...	3 × 15 ozs.	3	3 × 15 ozs.	3	3 × 15 ozs.
Vegetables	2 × 10 ozs. / 2 × 18 ozs.	4	2 × 10 ozs. / 2 × 18 ozs.	4	—
Biscuits	1 × 7¼ lb.	8½	1 × 7¼ lb.	8½	1 × 7¼ lb.
Puddings, sweet	—	—	1 × 14 ozs. / 2 × 28 ozs.	5	1 × 14 ozs. / 2 × 28 ozs.
Cheese	—	—	—	—	2 × 18 ozs.
Soap, tablets	1	—	1	—	1
Latrine paper, pieces	84	6	84	6	84

(a) The type of meat to be included in each type of pack will depend upon ava
Steak and Kidney Pudding; Steak and Kidney; Irish Stew; Stewed

NOTES.— (i) Calorific value of Types "A" to "G" is approximately 3,590 c
(ii) Weights and dimensions of packs.
Types "A" to "G" 21 ins. × 14 ins. × 11¼ ins. = 1·91 cubic feet

22029

TH BISCUIT)

ill be found in each case)

"D" size of each ck	Approx. daily ration each man ozs.	TYPE "E" No. and size of tins in each pack	Approx. daily ration each man ozs.	TYPE "F" No. and size of tins in each pack	Approx. daily ration each man ozs.	TYPE "G" No. and size of tins in each pack	Approx. daily ration each man ozs.
				12 × 12 ozs.	10		
	11½	12 × 16 ozs.	13½			14 × 16 ozs.	16
		2 × 28 ozs.	4			2 × 28 ozs.	4
	3½						
				3 × 12 ozs.	2½		
	2	8 × 3¼ ozs.	2				
	4			2 × 30 ozs.	4	2 × 30 ozs.	4
				3 × 16 ozs.	3½		
				1 × 21 ozs.	1½	1 × 21 ozs.	1½
	7 No.	2 × 50 No.	7 No.	2 × 50 No.	7 No.	2 × 50 No.	7 No.
	1	1 × 16 ozs.	1	1 × 16 ozs.	1	1 × 16 ozs.	1
ars } In two } tins	2	14 × 2 bars } In two tins	2	14 × 2 oz. bars } In two tins	2	14 × 2 oz. bars } In two tins	2
		16 ozs.		16 ozs.		16 ozs.	
	1½	1 × 12 ozs.	2	—	1½	1 × 12 ozs.	2
		2 ozs.		2 ozs.		2 ozs.	
-In one tin	—	5 booklets } one tin	—	5 booklets } one tin	—	5 booklets } one tin	—
	⅓	2 oz. pkt.	⅓	2 oz. pkt.	⅓	2 oz. pkt.	⅓
	3	3 × 15 ozs.	3	3 × 15 ozs.	3	3 × 15 ozs.	3
}	3		2½	2 × 18 ozs. } 2 × 10 ozs.	4	—	—
}	8½	1 × 7½ lb.	8½	1 × 7½ lb.	8½	1 × 7½ lb.	8½
	5	1 × 14 ozs. } 2 × 28 ozs.	5	1 × 14 ozs. } 2 × 28 ozs.	5	1 × 14 ozs. } 2 × 28 ozs.	5
	—	1 × 18 ozs.	1	—		—	—
	—	1	—	1	—	1	—
	6	84	6	84	6	84	6

one of the following :—
Meat and Vegetables ; Pork and Vegetables.

prox.).

THE COMPOSITE (14 MEN) PACK (WITHOUT BISCUIT)

(A leaflet showing contents and suggested menu will be found in each case)

COMMODITY	TYPE 1 No. and size of tins in each pack	Approx. daily ration each man ozs.	TYPE 2 No. and size of tins in each pack	Approx. daily ration each man ozs.	TYPE 3 No. and size of tins in each pack	Approx. daily ration each man ozs.
Meatstuffs...	(a) 14 × 12 ozs.	12	10 × 16 ozs.	11½	14 × 16 ozs.	16
Sausages ...	—	—	—	—	2 × 28 ozs.	4
Bacon ...	—	—	3 × 16 ozs.	3½	—	—
Luncheon meat ...	3 × 12 ozs.	2½	—	—	—	—
Beans, baked ...	—	—	2 × 32 ozs.	4½	1 × 16 ozs. } 2 × 32 ozs. }	5½
Sardines ...	9 × 3¼ ozs.	2	—	—	—	—
Fruits, tinned ...	—	—	2 × 30 ozs.	4	—	—
Soups, concentrated ...	2 × 30 ozs.	4	—	—	2 × 30 ozs.	4
Salmon, M.R. ...	—	—	—	—	—	—
Jam ...	(b) 1 × 21 ozs.	1½	1 × 21 ozs.	1½	1 × 21 ozs.	1½
Cigarettes ...	1 × 38 no. 1 × 60 no. }	7 no.	1 × 38 no. 1 × 60 no. }	7 no.	1 × 38 no. 1 × 60 no. }	7 no.
Margarine ...	1 × 16 ozs.	1	1 × 16 ozs.	1	1 × 16 ozs.	1
Sweets, boiled ...	3 × 5 ozs.	1½	3 × 5 ozs.	1½	3 × 5 ozs.	1½
Chocolate (vit) ...	(c) 10 × 2-oz. bars }	2	10 × 2-oz. bars }	2	10 × 2-oz. bars }	2
Chocolate (vit) ...	(d) 4 × 2-oz. bars }		4 × 2-oz. bars }		4 × 2-oz. bars }	
Matches, booklet ...	(c) 3 booklets		3 booklets		3 booklets	
Matches, booklet ...	(d) 2 booklets		2 booklets		2 booklets	
Salt ...	(d) 2-oz. packet	¼	2-oz. packet	¼	2-oz. packet	¼
Tea, sugar and milk powder ...	3 × 15 ozs.	3	3 × 15 ozs.	3	3 × 15 ozs.	3
Vegetables ...	3 × 18 ozs. 2 × 10 ozs. }	5	3 × 18 ozs.	4	—	—
Puddings, sweet ...	1 × 14 ozs. 2 × 28 ozs. }	5	—	—	1 × 14 ozs. 2 × 28 ozs. }	5
Soap, tablets ...	1	—	1	—	1	—
Latrine paper, pieces ...	84	6	84	6	84	6

(a) The type of meat to be included in each type of pack will depend upon availability and may be any one of the following :—

Steak and kidney pudding ; steak and kidney ; Irish stew ; stewed steak ; haricot oxtail ; preserved meat ; meat and vegetables ; pork and vegetables

(b) Or cheese 1 × 18 ozs. = 1 oz. each man a day approximately.

(c) Packed together in one tin with additional sweets as fillers.

(d) Packed together in one tin with additional sweets as fillers.

NOTES.—(i) Taken in conjunction with 14 ozs. bread each man a day—the calorific value of types 1 to 3 is approximately 3,520 each man a day.

(ii) Weights and dimensions of packs :—

Types 1 to 3, 20¾ ins. × 11½ ins. × 11 ins. = 1·52 cu. ft.

Gross weight 58 lb. (approximately).

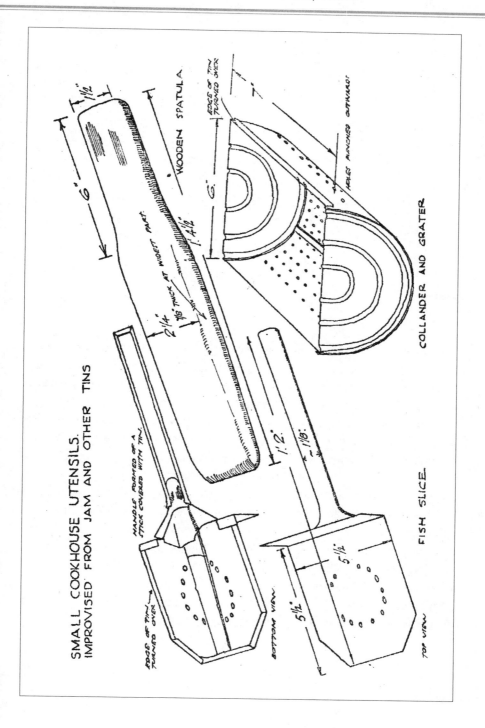

SMALL COOKHOUSE UTENSILS.
IMPROVISED FROM JAM AND OTHER TINS

WOODEN SPATULA.

COLLANDER AND GRATER

FISH SLICE.

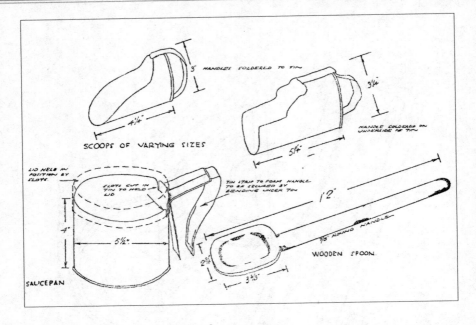

As a weight-saving measure dehydrated vegetables were introduced, although their use created problems not envisaged by the developers. Due to a shortage of water on the battlefield, soldiers frequently ate the vegetables only partially rehydrated. The consequence of this was severe constipation, which was noted in the Normandy campaigns as a problem but positively welcomed in the Burmese jungle where the opportunities to visit a latrine were limited! Perhaps the most unpopular dried produce was egg, especially when it was used to produce 'scrambled egg' rather than as a cake product. However, one unexpected outcome of food dehydration was a glut of dried carrot in American warehouses at the end of the war, which became the basis for the first-ever carrot cake. Another problem encountered was a dislike by the troops of 'Compo' ration sausages, the main ingredient of which was soya beans. In consequence, arrangements were made with three factories in Belgium and pork sent out from home. The improved sausages were manufactured under ACC supervision and were 78 per cent pork. These met the standard required by the consumers and are an example of what the corps did to improve feeding standards and boost morale.[63]

....

63 Howard N. Cole, *The Story of the Army Catering Corps and its Predecessors* (Army Catering Corps Association: 1984), p. 153

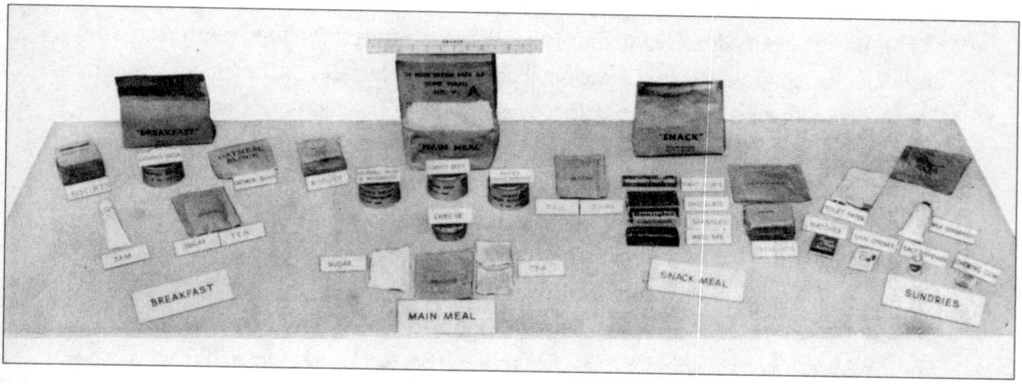

THE A.F.V. RATION PACK (NEW TYPE)

Size	Item	No. and size of tins in each pack	Ration (Approx.) ozs.	Description of package	Bulk packing
2-men	Sausages, tinned	1 × 16 ozs.	8	Fibreboard case measurement :— 8½ ins. × 5½ ins. × 5 ins. Gross weight 6 lb. 6 ozs.	8 packs in a Type 1 case. Measurements : 24½ ins. × 18¾ ins. × 5⅞ ins. (1·56 cu. ft.) Gross weight 64 lb. OR 6 packs in a Type 1 case. Measurements : 19⅝ ins. × 9⅜ ins. × 10⅞ ins. (1·16 cu. ft.) Gross weight 49 lb.
	M. and V. or Luncheon meat...	1 × 12 ozs.	6		
	Sardines	1 × 4½ ozs.	2¼		
	Cheese	3 × 1½ ozs.	2¼		
	Beans, canned	1 × 16 ozs.	8		
	Tea, sugar and milk powder ...	2 × 5 ozs.	5		
	Jam	2 × 4 ozs.	4		
	Boiled sweets	1 × 5 ozs.	2½		
	Latrine paper	12 pieces	6 pieces		
	*Biscuits, service	2 × 10 ozs.	10		
3-men	Preserved meat	1 × 12 ozs.	4	Fibreboard case measurement :— 9⅛ ins. × 7¼ ins. × 4⅞ ins. Gross weight 9 lb 3 ozs.	6 packs in a Type 1 case. Measurements : 23¾ ins. × 18⅞ ins. × 5⅞ ins. (1·52 cu. ft.) Gross weight 66 lb.
	Sausages, tinned	1 × 16 ozs.	5⅓		
	M. and V. or Luncheon meat...	1 × 16 ozs.	5⅓		
	Sardines	2 × 4½ ozs.	3		
	Cheese	2 × 3 ozs.	2		
	Beans, canned	1 × 16 ozs.	5⅓		
	Jam	3 × 4 ozs.	4		
	Tea, sugar and milk powder ...	2 × 5 ozs.	3⅓		
	Boiled sweets	1 × 5 ozs.	1⅔		
	Lemonade powder	1 × 5 ozs.	1⅔		
	Latrine paper	18 pieces	6 pieces		
	*Biscuits, service	3 × 10 ozs.	10		
5-men	Sausages, tinned	1 × 16 ozs.	3⅕	Fibreboard case measurement :— 9¾ ins. × 9⅝ ins. × 6 ins. Gross weight 14 lb.	4 packs in a Type 1 case. Measurements : 21 13/16 in. × 10 7/16 ins. × 12 1/16 ins. (1·59 cu. ft.) Gross weight 68½ lb.
	Pork and vegetable ration ...	5 × 16 ozs.	16		
	Bacon, tinned	1 × 18 ozs.	3⅗		
	Pudding, sweet	1 × 19 ozs.	3		
	Cheese	3 × 3 ozs.	1⅘		
	Beans, canned	1 × 20 ozs.	4		
	Tea, sugar and milk powder ...	3 × 5 ozs.	3		
	Boiled sweets	1 × 5 ozs.	1		
	Latrine paper	30 pieces	6 pieces		
	*Biscuits, service	5 × 10 ozs.	10		

**See* Note (ii) below.

NOTES.— (i) The nutritive values of the New Type A.F.V. packs are :—

2-men pack ... ... 3,570 calories approximately.
3-men „ ... ... 3,500 „ „
5-men „ ... ... 3,500 „ „

(ii) Biscuits, Service, are not contained in the A.F.V. ration packs, but are issued separately. Biscuits are packed in circular tins of 10 ozs. net. Bulk packing is either—

(*a*) 48 tins to a wooden case measurement :—20½ ins. × 15 ins. × 11¼ ins. (2.00 cu. ft.). Gross weight 55 lb.
or (*b*) 36 „ „ „ „ 22⅞ ins. × 11¼ ins. × 11 ins. (1·64 cu. ft.). Gross weight 45 lb.

(iii) For use in Mountain Warfare (without snow) the following packs are issued :—

A.F.V. 2-men packs ... ... 6 packs to a case.
„ Biscuits .... 36 tins to a case.

The basic twenty-four hour ration pack was designed for temperate climates and was not suitable for use in tropical and jungle warfare, or for Indian soldiers. Therefore a 'Pacific 24-Hour Ration' was developed which contained a supper of ham or beef, while the Indian packs contained curried fish.[64] There were varieties of these packs each containing a range of some thirty-nine foods. Between November 1944 and October 1945 approximately 15 million of these packs were produced.[65] Other developments included 'Pacific Compo', the 'Armoured Fighting Vehicle Pack', and the 'Airborne Pannier', which was developed to hold sufficient food for one company for one day and which could be air dropped.[66] The production of a special pack for use in the Arctic was in progress at the time the experiments for the provision of the forty-eight hour, 'one-man' ration were being held. This took the form of a circular tin into which was packed items with a high food value of a little over 5,000 calories, which was approximately 1,000 more than was required for high temperature climates. Pemmican (a concentrated mixture of fat and protein) was used in the place of meat, the rations also contained an anti-scorbutic in the form of ascorbic acid tablets and, in the place of normal matches, flare matches were inserted which could be handled easily and would remain alight even in a wind. The tin was also equipped with special fuel starters for lighting oil pressure stoves, which were the accepted means of heating to be used under Arctic conditions. During September 1941 and December 1942, 2,800,000 of these packs were produced.[67]

Once the United States entered the war in December 1941, British troops serving alongside Americans or participating in their operations found themselves supplied with 'K-Rations', so-called because they were designed by Dr Ancel Keys. Though initially the fact that the food stuffs within the K-Ration were high concentrate meant they were well received by British troops, there were concerns about the caloric and vitamin content of the K-Ration. British troops also reported that American rations rapidly became boring.

---

64 Howard N. Cole, *The Story of the Army Catering Corps and its Predecessors* (Army Catering Corps Association: 1984), pp. 152–153

65 *The Story of the Royal Army Service Corps 1939–1945* (G. Bell and Son Ltd: 1955), p. 475

66 Howard N. Cole, *The Story of the Army Catering Corps and its Predecessors* (Army Catering Corps Association: 1984), p. 151

67 *The Story of the Royal Army Service Corps 1939–1945* (G. Bell and Son Ltd: 1955), p. 475

It must also be remembered that, although cooking was not an issue, rations were provided by the army for horses, mules, dogs, pigeons and even guinea pigs.[68] Unfortunately some of these animals, supplemented by snake and, in Iceland, pony, also found their way into human rations as soldiers 'liberated' local food supplies. On one occasion the crew of a tank in Normandy found it impossible to service the engine during the nighttime 'leaguer' or 'laager' (a dense formation of vehicles in circular formation to prevent surprise attack) because the tank commander had stored a particularly large camembert cheese in the engine bay to ensure that it became 'ripe'.

THE MOUNTAIN (ARCTIC) PACK

(One man for two days or two men for one day)

(A leaflet giving details of contents, together with methods of preparation of the foodstuffs, is contained in each pack)

Item	CONTENTS	
	Number and weight of items in each pack	Approximate daily scale each man a day
		ozs.
Pemmican	2 × 6 ozs. slabs	6·0
Biscuits, service, sweet ...	2 × 8 ozs. packets	8·0
Tea, sugar and milk powder	1 × 5 ozs. tin	2·5
Chocolate, raisin	6 × 2 ozs. bars	6·0
Boiled sweets	4 ozs. loose	2·0
Cheese	1 × 9 ozs. tin	4·5
Margarine	1 × 4 ozs. tin	2·0
Sugar	2 × 2 ozs. placquettes	2·0
Salt ... ·	2 × ½ oz. packets	0·5
Bacon, chopped	1 × 8 ozs. tin	4·0
Rolled oats	1 × 4½ ozs. tin	2·2
Ascorbic acid tablets ...	4 tablets in a tin	2 tablets
Flare matches	6 matches in packet	3 matches
Fuel (starter)—for Primus stove	4 tablets in carton	—
Latrine paper	12 pieces	6 pieces

NOTES

(i) Calorific value—5,100 each man a day (approximately).

(ii) Each ration pack consists of a circular tin weighing approximately 6 lb. 11 ozs. gross.

(iii) For bulk packing six ration packs are contained in a type 1 wooden case measuring 22¼ ins. × 15½ ins. × 9 ins. (1·82 cu. ft.). Gross weight 47¼ lb.

(iv) High Vitamin B1 yeast—three tablets each man a day, will be issued separately.

68 The Story of the Royal Army Service Corps 1939–1945 (G. Bell and Son Ltd: 1955), p. 459

PACIFIC 24-H(

(An instructional leaflet is enclosed in each containe

COMPLETE RATION			**SEPARATE MEAL CONTAINE**				
			BREAKFAST				
Item	Number of pieces	Ration (approx.)	Item	Number of pieces	Ration (approx.)	Item	
Meat items	2 tins	7 ozs.	Ham and Egg	1 tin	3½ ozs.	—	
Biscuit	9	7¼ ozs.	Biscuit	3	2½ ozs.	Biscuit	
Meat biscuit	1	1 oz.				Meat biscuit	
Oatmeal blocks	4	5¼ ozs.	Oatmeal blocks	2	3½ ozs.	—	
Cheese blocks	2	1½ ozs.	—			—	
Fruit bar	2	2 ozs.				Fruit bar	
Tea Ration	2 tins	2½ ozs.	Tea ration	1 tin	1¼ ozs.	—	
Sugar	1 packet	1 oz.	—			Sugar	
Sweets, boiled	Loose	3¼ ozs.	Sweets, boiled	Loose	1¾ ozs.	Sweets, boiled	
Chewing gum	2 packets	2 packets	Chewing gum	1 packet	1 packet	Chewing gum	
Chocolate (HC)	1 packet (2 bars)	4 ozs.	—			Chocolate (HC)	
Lemon crystals	1 packet	¼ oz.				Lemon crystals	
Cigarettes	2 packets	10 Nos.	Cigarettes	1 packet	5 Nos.	—	
Matches, booklet	—	2 booklets	Matches, booklet	—	1 booklet	—	
Mepacrine tablet	—	1 No.	Mepacrine tablet	—	1 No.	—	
Compound vit. tab.	—	1 No.	Compound vit. tab.	—	½ No.	—	
Salt tablets	3 packets	24 Nos.	Salt tablets	1 packet	8 Nos.	Salt tablets	
Latrine paper	—	12 pieces	Latrine paper	—	4 pieces	Latrine paper	
Instruction leaflets	—	3 Nos.	Instruction leaflet	—	1 No.	Instruction leafle	

(i) The nutritive value of the ration is 4,160 calories (approximately).

(ii) The tea ration (tea, sugar and milk powder mixture) will produce 2½ pints of tea, e.g., 1¼ pints each for breakfast an

(iii) One solid fuel cooker (tropical) may be issued separately with the ration. The cooker comprises eight solid fue circular aluminium container. It is more economical in fuel to cook in pairs, and it is essential to use cook

(iv) On no account will rations be taken or accepted from wounded men,

H TROOPS)

ontents together with the methods of preparation.)

Ration (approx.)	Item		Number of pieces	Ration (approx.)	DESCRIPTION OF CONTAINERS	BULK PACKING
			SUPPER			
1¾ ozs.	Ham and Beef	...	1 tin	3½ ozs.	Three hermetically sealed aluminium containers :—	Nine complete rations to a flat camouflaged wooden case.
1 oz.	Biscuit ...	...	4	3½ ozs.		
	—				(Breakfast 5 × 5½ × 1½ ins.)	Measurement :—
	Oatmeal blocks	...	2	1¾ ozs.	(Midday 5 × 5½ × 1 in.)	19½ × 17 × 6¼ ins.
	Cheese blocks	...	2	1½ ozs.	(Supper 5 × 5½ × 1½ ins.)	
1 oz.	Fruit bar ...	...	1	1 oz.	nesting and strapped together.	(1·22 cu. ft.)
	Tea ration ...	...	1 tin	1¼ ozs.	Overall dimensions of complete ration 5 × 5½ × 4½ ins.	Gross weight 39¼ lb.
1 oz.	—				Weight of complete ration 3 lb.	(approx.)
½ oz.	Sweets, boiled	...	Loose	1 oz.		
1 packet						
4 oz.						
¼ oz.	—					
	Cigarettes ...	...	1 packet	5 Nos.		
	Matches, booklet			½ booklet		
	—					
8 Nos.	Salt tablets ...	...	1 packet	8 Nos.		
4 pieces	Latrine paper	...	4 pieces	4 pieces		
1 No.	Instruction leaflet	...	—	1 No.		

e taken as far as practicable during periods of greatest cold and fatigue.

o days), a three-legged stand, a disc on which to burn the tablet, and full instructions for use, all packed in a
ts—using a tin as a shield—or by making a small foxhole.

"K" RA

Complete ration			Breakfast unit		
Item	No. of pieces	Ration (approx.)	Item	Ration (approx.)	
Biscuits	6 pkts.	9 ozs.	Biscuits	3 ozs.	Bisc
Meat items ...	2 tins	7½ ozs.	(a) Meat and egg	3¾ ozs.	
Cheese	1 tin	4 ozs.	—	—	Che
Fruit bar	1 bar	2 ozs.	Fruit bar	2 ozs.	
Candy	1 pkt.	2 ozs.	—	—	(b)
"D" ration (chocolate)	1 pkt.	2 ozs.	—	—	
Coffee	1 pkt.	5 grammes	Coffee	5 grammes	
Lemon powder ...	1 pkt.	7 grammes	—	—	Lem
Bouillon powder ...	1 pkt.	10 grammes	—	—	
Sugar	8 lumps	1 oz.	Sugar	½ oz.	Sug
Chewing gum ...	—	3 pieces	Chewing gum	1 piece	Che
Cigarettes ...	3 pkts.	12 nos.	Cigarettes	4 nos.	Cig
Matches	1 bklt.	1 no.	—	—	Ma
Toilet paper ...	—	—	—	—	

NOTES.—(a) Tuna fish canned ... 3½ ozs. (tin)
      (b) Cereal ... ... 2 ozs. (packet)
      (c) Salmon... ... ... 3½ ozs.

–U.S.A.)

	Supper unit		Description of containers	Bulk packing
ation pprox.)	Item	Ration (approx.)		
ozs.	Biscuits	3 ozs.	Separate meal packing	
—	(*c*) Meat	3¾ ozs.		
ozs.	—	—		
—	—	—	—	
ozs.	—	—	Each 6⅜ ins. × 3⅜ ins. × 1½ ins. in waxed board containers and fibreboard outers Each 15 ozs. gross	36 cartons = 12 rations to fibreboard case
—	" D " bar (chocolate)	2 ozs.		
—	—	—		
grammes	—	—		
—	Bouillon powder	10 grammes		
oz.	—	—		
piece	Chewing gum	1 piece		
nos.	Cigarettes	4 nos.		
bklt.	—			
—	Toilet paper	—		

r the items stated, when the ration is provided for Indian troops.

Hospital Food

ONE INNOVATION OF the ACC was that, due to the importance placed on good catering in General Hospitals, a Specialist Messing Officer was appointed to each General Hospital. The Medical and Catering Services discussed in detail the requirements for military hospital diets and this resulted in a revised series of diet sheets being issued. This focus meant that the general standard of feeding in hospitals was high, and through the employment of technical experts the problem of getting hot food to the patients was overcome.[69] A crucial element was ensuring that the level of nutrition was appropriate for the sick or wounded and that the food was particularly appetising. This challenge was met in part by the training of specialist ACC Hospital Chefs.

The 'Mess-Tin Cook'

IN 1937 THE pattern of mess-tin provided for British soldiers changed for the first time since the Napoleonic Wars. The old D-shaped tin was replaced by a rectangular style in which the two halves fitted one inside the other. Originally made of tin-steel they were later made from aluminium. These new tins could be stored inside a soldier's haversack and provided protection against damp for ration items. As in previous conflicts, mess-tin cookery offered soldiers basic food on campaign and an improved Tommy Cooker began to be provided as an issue item, doing away with the need to gather fuel and light a fire which might betray the user to enemy aircraft. When a small unit of men were required to cook for themselves for any length of time, turns were taken for who had to undertake the cooking of food and the preparing of tea. This was a much disliked job, and the men often resented it when it was their turn to cook for their comrades.

The manual suggests:

> ... the only way to teach men to fend for themselves is to send them out into the blue in progressively difficult circumstances. On the first occasion they

---

69 Howard N. Cole, *The Story of the Army Catering Corps and its Predecessors* (Army Catering Corps Association: 1984), p. 140–141

INVALID PACK

(Hospital Supplies)

(200 men for one day)

For packing into Mark III (or Mark I) bomb-type container, supplies dropping apparatus

STRAW PACKING.

15"

8½"

9"

BRANDY 4½"

BISCUITS. 9¼"

16 ¾" SPACE FOR LOCKING DEVICE.

KEG.

51"

16 ¾"

KEG.

12½"

KEG No. 1

Meat extract (2 oz.) tins	72
Arrowroot (1 lb.) tins ...	2
Condensed milk (14½ oz.) tins ...	8
Sugar (1 lb.) tins	5
Cocoa (1 lb.) tins	1
Tea (2 lb.) tins	1
Boiled sweets (4 oz.) Bristol ...	2
Sweets, salt and matches (4 oz.) Bristol	2
Cigarettes, Magnum (60)	2
Chocolate, 2 oz. bars...	8

KEG No. 2

Meat extract (2 oz.) tins	72
Arrowroot (1 lb.) tins	1
Condensed milk (14½ oz.) tins ...	8
Sugar (1 lb.) tins	5
Cocoa (1 lb.) tins	2
Tea (2 lb.) tins	1
Boiled sweets (4 oz.) Bristol ...	2
Sweets, salt and matches (Bristol) ...	2
Cigarettes, Magnum (60)	2
Chocolate 2 oz. bars	8

ONE box containing two bottles Brandy.

ONE tin containing 9 lb. service biscuits and 14 (fourteen) × 2 oz. bars chocolate.

			lb.
Gross weight 2 kegs, each 43 lb. ...	86
,, ,, brandy in box ...	10¼
,, ,, tin of biscuits... ...	10¾
,, ,, of contents	107
,, ,, of cylinder, Mark III	93
TOTAL ALL-UP WEIGHT ...	200

(19252) 27093/2126 40,000 9/43 K.H.K. Gp. 8/8

MESS TIN COOKERY

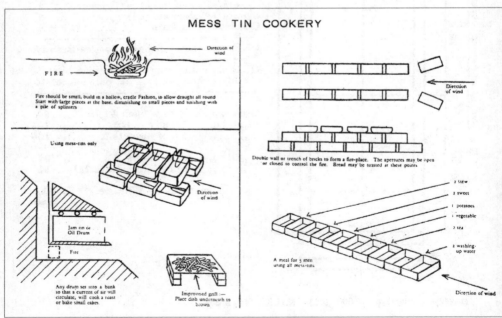

FIRE ⟶   Direction of wind ⟵

Fire should be small, build in a hollow, cradle fashion, to allow draught all round. Start with large pieces at the base, diminishing to small pieces and finishing with a pile of splinters

Direction of wind ⟵

Double wall or trench of bricks to form a fire-place. The apertures may be open or closed to control the fire. Bread may be toasted at these points.

Using mess-tins only

Direction of wind

Jam tin or Oil Drum

Fire

Any drum set into a bank so that a current of air will circulate, will cook a roast or bake small cakes

Improvised grill :— Place dish underneath to brown

2 stew
2 sweet
1 potatoes
1 vegetable
2 tea
2 washing-up water

A meal for 5 men using all mess-tins

Direction of wind

should be sent out with plenty of rations, and plenty of water, to cook one meal. They should work up to going out for 48 hours with barely adequate rations, and limited water supply, to live by their ingenuity. They should not take with them any apparatus or equipment except their mess-tins and jack knives, nor should they be allowed to remain in one place all the time.[70]

Although the type of rations became increasingly sophisticated as the war progressed, the ability for individual soldiers to cook their own meals was a basic skill. The men were trained how to use local materials such as straw and leaves to light the fire and dry wood as fuel. It was explained that this was made more efficient if the flow of air was directed under the mess-tin and that care had to be taken to remain concealed as both fire and smoke could give away a position. This could take the form of an excavated trench, bricks or even a pipe sunken into the ground.[71]

One of the most remarkable examples of rations developed during the war was 'self-heating soup' which was either oxtail, mock turtle or kidney. The outer tin contained soup, in the middle of which was a tube containing chemicals; once the tin was punctured and the seal over the chemical removed these could be a lit with a match or cigarette and would provide a hot meal within four minutes. A great danger was forgetting to pierce the soup tin as expansion caused the entire container to explode as a 'soup-bomb'. The pamphlet on *Operation Feeding: Use of Special Ration Packs* makes it clear that the value of these rations were as a 'hot drink' rather than for nutritional value.[72] Later in the war self-heating cocoa was also developed.

70 *Manual of Army Catering Services, Part III – Cooking in the Field, including Improvised and Mess Tin Cookery* (1945), p. 55
71 *Catering and Cooking for Field Forces*, RLCA 8373, p. 27
72 *Operational Feeding: Use of Special Ration Packs* (1943)

Food Wherever You Are

THE WORLDWIDE NATURE of fighting in the Second World War meant that consideration had to be given to conditions in Europe, the jungle, desert and the Arctic. Not only did the calorie requirements differ between these theatres of war, but so did the palatability of food and what was available locally. Consideration also had to be given to questions of religion and nationality. Moslem soldiers cannot eat pork; African troops expect to receive the tuber cassava, whilst British servicemen do not respond to a diet that lacks tea. So great was the British need to furnish their troops with an adequate supply of tea throughout the war that during one season in 1942–43 the Ministry of Defence bought India's entire crop of tea for use in the armed forces.

LIVING ON THE COUNTRY

Nature of Food.	How Obtained.	Preparation.
A. Coastal Areas.		
Fish.	Hook and line bottom fishing. Use bits of small octopus or pieces of shell fish or small fish for bait. Small rock pools may be baled out. Eels may be found in holes at low water.	
Shell Fish. oysters, mussels.	Found on the rocks.	Do not require cooking.
Crabs.	Abound along the shores: quite large ones are found in mangrove swamps.	Both small and large crabs are edible: boil the bodies after pulling off the legs.
Cocoanut.	Look for old nuts at foot of tree. Nuts on trees are found in various stages—the middle size are the best. To assist in climbing the tree tie the feet together with a length of strong rope or a belt about a foot long. Additional assistance is given by a loop of strong rope passed across the shoulders and around the tree trunk.	Remove husks by jabbing stick in pointed end. Inside find ball of coagulated milk which is very nutritious.
Edible birds Nests.	The birds resemble swifts. They live in caves along the foreshore and can be seen going in and out in thousands.	Wash the nest and boil down into soup. It is very nutritious.
B. Tropical Forest Areas.		
Roots.	The roots of most creepers are edible and the best method of approach is to dig out the roots and choose those that look and taste suitable. Descriptions of certain of them are however given below as a guide.	
(i) Ulsi.	The vine is dry and brittle and its leaves are dead in appearance and curled up. Follow the creeper down to the ground and locate the tuber some 4—6 inches below the surface. Looks like a long gnarled potato 2 to 8 inches long. At its best during the monsoon.	Boil for 15 minutes and then remove skin. Cut into small cubes and use in stews. Needs plenty of salt. May also be boiled or baked like potatoes.

Nature of Food.	*How obtained.*	*Preparation.*
(ii) Halander.	Leaves on the vine, which is otherwise similar to the Ulsi, are found tightly rolled at intervals. The tuber is small ½ to 2 inches and is soft and juicy.	Cook in the same way as the Ulsi.
(iii) Lundi.	The vine is similar to the other two but is recognised by the cluster of seeds and berries growing on it. The tuber is 5 to 12 inches long.	As above.
(iv) Taro.	The wild lily. Has big bulbous roots usually a mottled purple.	Roast in fire and boil tops as cabbage.
(v) Sweet Potato.	Tops look like potato. Tubers have purple skin with yellow flesh or brown skin with white flesh.	Roast.
The Plantain Trees. (i) Flower.	Discard the hard leaves and the hard fibrous parts of the flower.	Boil the floral part with condiments.
(ii) Main Stem.	Take out the centres and cut into fine slices.	Fry lightly with seasoning, add a little rice, flour or atta, wrap in a leaf and boil for an hour.
(iii) Roots.	Select the young and juicy ones.	Boil or roast.
Cane palm and Bamboo Shoots.	Select the young shoots. These are however only available during the early rains, i.e. March to June.	Boiled with plenty of salt, they resemble asparagus.
Meat Substitutes, i.e. food containing proteins.	(i) Grubs of bees and wasps, ants eggs, white ant queens.	First scald and then fry in a little fat. They are quite palatable and provide the proteins n o r m a l l y obtained in meat.
	(ii) Leguminous seeds, e.g. dhall, moong, peas, beans.	Soak the grain and pound it up into a paste. Add sufficient rice powder or atta to bind it, season to taste, wrap in a leaf and boil for half an hour. This will keep only for a week or so.

Fruit and Berries. A description of some of the many types is given below as a general guide. It must be remembered how ever that they are only available at certain seasons, viz: during the early rains, and that as some berries are poisonous it is safer to rely if possible on a local guide. As an alternative, eat only those you notice monkeys eating.

(a) Fruit. (1). Wild fig.	Tree somewhat similar to the crab apple ; trunk and limbs gnarled and twisted. Leaf dark green. Fruit grows in clusters, has colour of ripe peach and is soft to touch when ripe.	Can be eaten raw or stewed for half an hour in enough water to cover the fruit.

Name of Food.	How obtained.	Preparation.
(2) Wild Cherry	Tree similar to Mango tree: dark green leaf. Fruit red or yellow ripens in March-April, very juicy.	
(3) Almond.	Tree is 15—20 ft. high and branches spread flatly from crown umbrella-like. Fruit similar to peach in colour, size and shape, ripens in April-May.	Fruit useful as a purgative. Boil in water and drink resultant liquid. Nut inside the stone is oily and edible.
(4) Owli.	An egg shaped fruit, smooth and light brown.	
(5) Arvala.	A round yellow to reddish fruit. Tree has light, feathery fernlike leaves set on a strong central stem.	The fruit is acid to taste but if water is taken after eating, the acidity turns to sweetness.
(b) Berries. (1) Jambul.	A large black berry, grows in clusters on a long leafed creeper. Ripens May-June.	Can be eaten raw or stewed. It is very refreshing and thirst quenching raw.
(2) Karawand.	A soft, blue black berry, growing in clusters on an evergreen thorny shrub with wide spreading branches.	Very refreshing raw, and excellent stewed.
(3) Turna.	A white berry growing in large clusters on a low thorny tree. Unripe berries are red and not recommended as they dry the mouth.	Eat raw or stewed, preferably with other berries or fruits.

C. More open Forest and Grassland.

Game is more plentiful.
Chestnuts and acorns are to be found.
Seeds of most grasses are edible.

See previous note on trapping.

From: *Catering and Cooking for Field Forces, Allied Land Forces South East Asia 1945.*

India (including modern Pakistan and Bangladesh)

WHEN THE *MANUAL of Army Services* was first published in September 1945 (Part II – Recipes), there were fourteen pages applicable to India which included a detailed list of the many edible fruits and vegetables – certain of which were indigenous to types of country where jungle abounded – available, in India, and which the ACC Cook, in his everyday work, might well be called upon to prepare and cook. Among these were *bodi* and *suna* beans, *patrol* and *patrol* cucumbers, *brinjal/bainam* (or aubergine), the several types of gourds (*kaddu*), okra or 'ladies fingers', and *sag* (spinach). Detailed descriptions were also given to the Indian fruits – four types of Indian melons, guavas, papaya, pomelo, mangoes, *leechi* (lychees), *naspati* (Indian pears) and *sherefa* (custard apples). This section of the manual concluded with instruction on the methods of preparation and cooking of types of Indian vegetables, particularly *bakla* (french beans), *chuguandar* (beetroot), *mutter* (peas), *palak* (spinach) and *shalghan* (turnips).[73] In 1933 the standard ration provided for the Royal Indian Army Service Corps consisted of bread, flour, onions, sugar, salt (refined), meat, potatoes, fresh vegetables, tea and wood.[74] Breakfast dishes incorporated curried balls and special biscuits, including those flavoured with coffee and cocoanut [sic]. Accompaniments suggested consisted of fried, battered and stuffed *brinjals*, fried onions and stuffed tomatoes. However, due to the risk of tropical diseases, salads were liable to be forbidden by medical authorities in India at certain times of the year.[75] This was all in peacetime and conditions during the war were nothing like as luxurious. Rations issued to the Fourteenth Army were extremely poor, fresh meat was often unobtainable for long periods and eggs were a luxury. Sadly for the troops 'Soya Link', sausage, with a high content of soya, was issued as a substitute for a large number of ration items. Fresh vegetables were only available in the four months of the cold season, while for fresh fruit, oranges were issued from December to April, pineapples and little else in July and August, and plantains (small bananas) for the rest of the year. Eight months' issue of pumpkins and Indian vegetables, combined with preserved meat and Soya Link, for breakfast, dinner, lunch and tea made catering a problem

---

73 Howard N. Cole, *The Story of the Army Catering Corps and its Predecessors* (Army Catering Corps Association: 1984), p. 121

74 *Indian Military Manual of Cooking and Dietary,* 1933 (1936)

75 *Indian Military Manual of Cooking and Dietary,* 1933 (1936), p. 80

OPERATION RATION (TYPE IND O3) FOR INDIAN TROOPS (ORIGIN—AUSTRALIA)

Total ration			Breakfast		Dinner		Supper	
Item	No. of pieces	Ration (approx.)	Item	Ration (approx.)	Item	Ration (approx.)	Item	Ratio (appro
Fish items... ...	2 tins	8 ozs.	Fish	4 ozs.	—	—	Fish	4 ozs
Rice, brown ...	2 pkts.	8 ozs.	—		Rice	4 ozs.	Rice	4 ozs
Biscuit	2 pkts.	5¼ ozs.	Wholemeal biscuit	2¼ ozs.	Carrot biscuit	3 ozs.	—	—
Chocolate	1 block	3 ozs.	Chocolate	3 ozs.	—	—	—	—
Fruit and cereal block	1 block	3⅜ ozs.	—	—	Fruit and cereal	3⅜ ozs.	—	—
Wheat lunch block	1 block	3 ozs.	—	—	—	—	Wheat lunch	3 ozs
Peanut butter ...	1 tin	1½ ozs.	Peanut butter	1½ oz.	—	—	—	—
Potato powder ...	2 pkts.	2 ozs.	—	—	Potato powder	1 oz.	Potato powder	1 oz.
Curry powder ...	1 pkt.	½ oz.	—	—	Curry powder	½ oz.	—	—
Barley sugar ...	12 rolls	3 ozs.	Barley sugar	1 oz.	Barley sugar	1 oz.	Barley sugar	1 oz.
Fruit tablets ...	—	½ oz.	Fruit tablets	½ oz.	—	—	—	—
Sugar tablets ...	6 tabs.	1½ oz.	Sugar tablets	½ oz.	Sugar tablets	½ oz.	Sugar tablets	½ oz
Tea	3 pkts.	¼ oz.	Tea	1/12 oz.	Tea	1/12 oz.	Tea	1/12 oz
Salt tablets ...	18 tabs.	¾ oz.	Salt tablets	¼ oz.	Salt tablets	¼ oz.	Salt tablets	¼ oz
Skim milk powder	3 pkts.	¾ oz.	Skim milk powder	¼ oz.	Skim milk powder	¼ oz.	Skim milk powder	¼ oz

for the most experienced cooks. The most modern style of cooking apparatus was not available in India and wood continued to be the main fuel. The problems of cooking on a wood fire in the monsoon season can be imagined.[76]

Before the war there had been an Inspectorate of Catering in India and an Army School of Cookery at Poona. With the massive expansion of the forces in the country on the outbreak of war, it was clear that a larger organisation was required. This led to the expansion of the Inspectorate and the addition of two new schools of cookery. There was a steady expansion in the number of ACC officers serving in India, although there were never really enough. One issue was that British Army cooks had problems adapting to the climate, working with unfamiliar rations and coping with the shortages of almost every essential item of equipment. If the Fourteenth Army felt itself 'forgotten', its cooks certainly shared this feeling.[77] During the period 1942–45, 22,057 Indian and 3,052 British cooks were trained in India.[78]

76 Howard N. Cole, *The Story of the Army Catering Corps and its Predecessors* (Army Catering Corps Association: 1984), p. 121

77 Howard N. Cole, *The Story of the Army Catering Corps and its Predecessors* (Army Catering Corps Association: 1984), p. 121

78 Howard N. Cole, *The Story of the Army Catering Corps and its Predecessors* (Army Catering Corps Association: 1984), p. 122

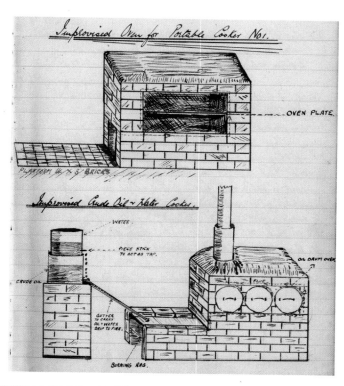

Sketch by E. Young of a Portable Cooker No.1, from her log book, 1941.

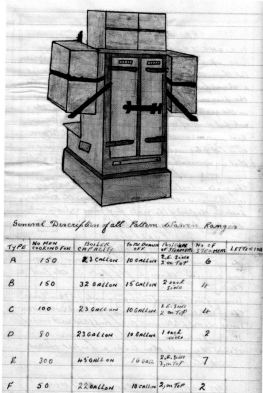

General Description of all Pattern Warren Ranges

TYPE	NO MEN COOKING FOR	BOILER CAPACITY	TO BE DRAWN OFF	POSITION OF STEAMER	No OF STEAMERS	LETTERING
A	150	23 gallon	10 gallon	2 E. side 2 on top	6	
B	150	32 gallon	15 gallon	2 each side	4	
C	100	23 gallon	10 gallon	1 E. side 2 on top	4	
D	80	23 gallon	10 gallon	1 each side	2	
E	300	45 gallon	16 gall	2 E. side 3 on top	7	
F	50	22 gallon	10 gallon	2 on top	2	

A colour sketch of a Warren Range, from the log book of Gnr Bell, Army School of Cookery, Poona, 1943.

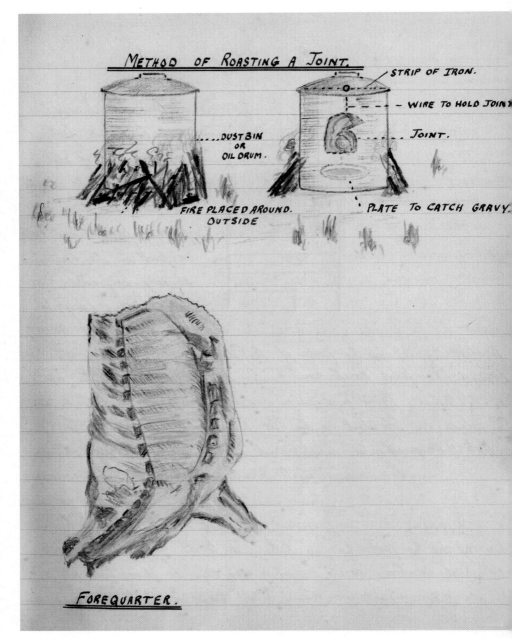

METHOD OF ROASTING A JOINT.

STRIP OF IRON.

WIRE TO HOLD JOINT

JOINT.

DUSTBIN
OR
OIL DRUM.

FIRE PLACED AROUND.
OUTSIDE

PLATE TO CATCH GRAVY.

FOREQUARTER.

Sketch by E. Young, from her log book, 1941.

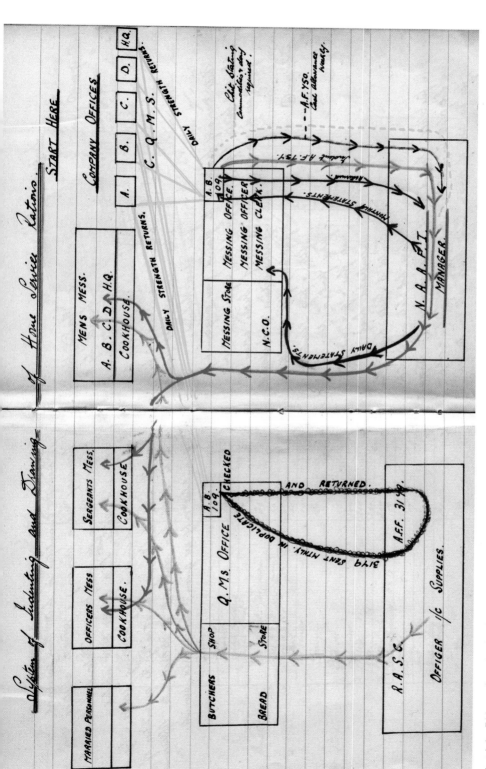

Sketch by E. Young, from her log book, 1941.

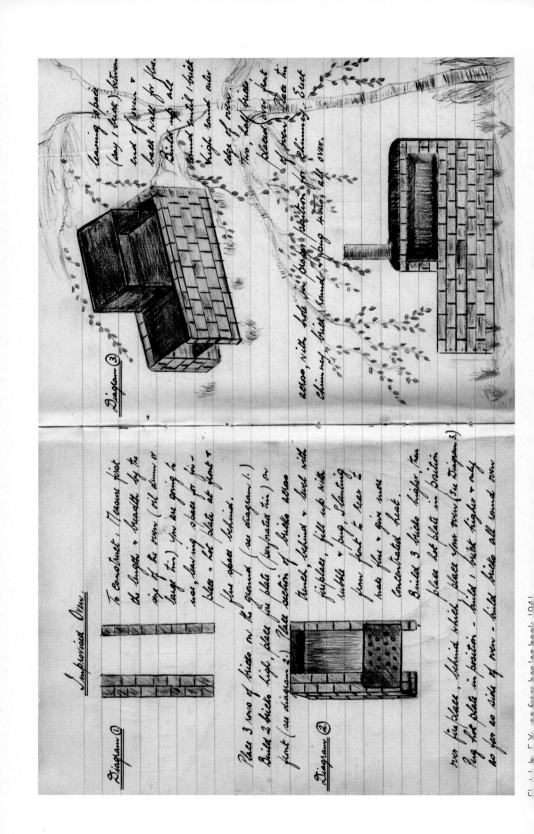

Improvised Oven

__Diagram ①__

To construct. Measure first the length & breadth by the size of the meal (oil drum or large tin) you are going to use, leaving space for fire-box, but slate at front & flue space behind.

Place 3 rows of bricks on the ground (see diagram 1). Build 2 bricks high, place the slate (perforated tin) on first (see diagram 2). Place section of bricks also

__Diagram ②__

first, behind & level with fireplace, fill up with rubble & png standing from front to rear 2 rows flue & fire into horizontal hut. Build 3 bricks higher, place hot plate in position.

oven fireplace behind which place your meal (see Diagram 3). Png hot plate in position. Build 1 brick higher & only so far as side of meal - build bricks all round oven

turning space (say 1 thick) between end of oven & back wall for flue. Build up all round.

Build until 1 thick above level & thick high round outer edge of oven. Two half bricks.

also, with hole for stovepipe together for chimney duct. Chimney only 1 brick thick. Smoke going through all over.

__Diagram ③__

Sketches from an unknown soldier's log book, 1949.

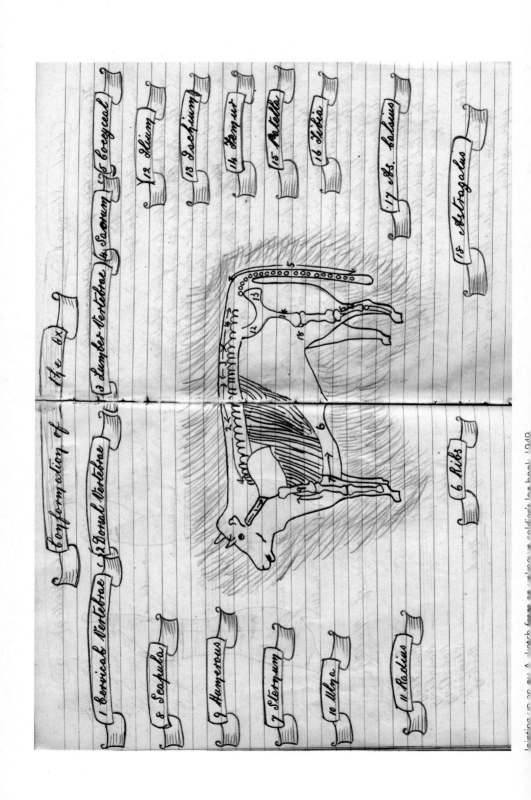

Conformation of the Ox

1 Cervical Vertebrae 2 Dorsal Vertebrae 3 Lumber Vertebrae 4 Sacrum 5 Co-cygeal
6 Ribs 7 Sternum 8 Scapula 9 Humerous 10 Ulna 11 Radius
12 Ilium 13 Ischium 14 Femur 15 Patella 16 Tibia 17 Os. Calcis 18 Astragalus

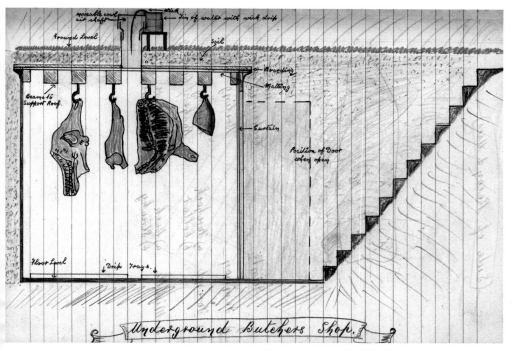

A sketch from an unknown soldier's log book, 1949.

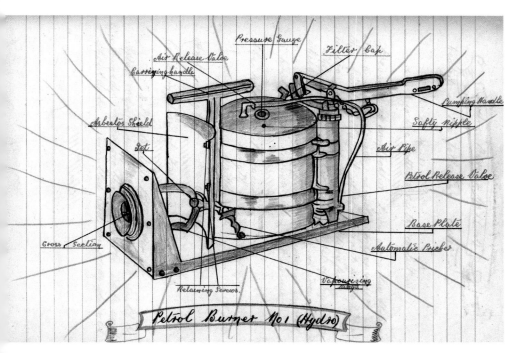

A more 'modern' version of No.1 Hydro burner, as of 1949. A sketch from an unknown soldier's log book, 1949.

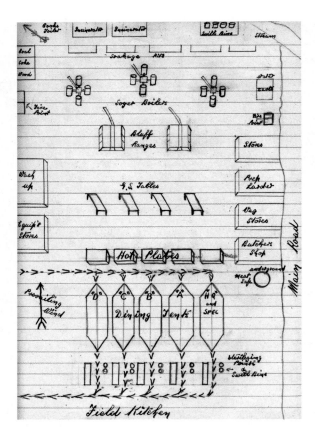

The arrangement of a field kitchen. A sketch from an unknown soldier's log book, 1949.

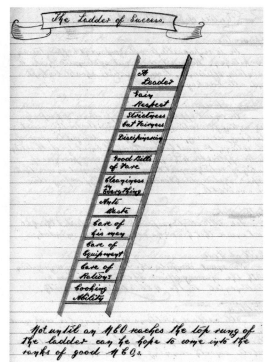

How to become the best Army Cook. A sketch from an unknown soldier's log book, 1949.

TYPES OF INDIAN VEGETABLES WITH METHODS OF PREPARATION AND COOKING—contd.

Dish.	Ingredients.	Method of Preparation.
LADIES FINGERS (BHINDI).		
Ladies Fingers fried.	33 lbs. Ladies fingers. 10 Eggs. Frying fat. 12½ lbs. Bacon. 2 ozs. Salt. 1 oz. Pepper. 6 lbs. Breadcrumbs.	Select such pods as are young and tender. There are two varieties, one white and the other green. Both can be tender or tough. When broken in two they should snap lightly apart, like a crisp French bean. Wash well and trim off the stem end, but be careful not to cut away so much of the pod that the juice can come out, cover them with boiling salted water and cook on a slow flame until tender. Then drain well. Season with salt and pepper, roll in a slightly beaten egg, then in crumbs, and fry in deep hot fat, drain and serve with rolls of crisply fried bacon or toast.
MARROW (SAFEDH KADDU).		
Marrow pudding.	50 lbs. Marrow (unprepared). 8 lbs. Flour. 3 lbs. Margarine. 18 pts. Milk. 25 Eggs.	Peel and cut the marrow in cubes, boil in small amount of boiling salt water till tender, then mash with a wooden masher to a smooth puree. Mix flour, butter, milk and cook like cream sauce. Add the yolks of eggs and the marrow, pepper and salt to taste; stir well together, put in buttered baking dish and grate cheese over it or scatter buttered baking dish and grate cheese over it or scatter buttered brown breadcrumbs over it. Bake for 15 minutes in a moderate oven.
Marrow vegetable and stuffing.	50 lbs. Vegetables Marrow unprepared. 3 qts. Brown Sauce. 6 lbs. Breadcrumbs. Bread stuffing as for beef olives. ¼ lb. Minced Meat. 4 lbs. Onions.	Peel marrows, cut in half lengthways, make an incision crossways with point of knife on the cut side and fry in deep fat until tender without taking colour. Remove from fat, drain and scoop out the centre pith with a spoon. Place into a greased baking tin, finely chopped onions stew breadstuffing and minced meat together. Bind with a little brown sauce. Stuff marrows, sprinkle with breadcrumbs and mark with the pack of a fort, sprinkle with a little melted dripping. Bake in oven until stuffing and marrows are cooked. When cooked cut into slices and serve mashed round with brown sauce.
Marrow vegetable with cheese.	60 lbs. Marrow (unprepared). 1 lb. Grated Cheese. 1 lb. Breadcrumbs. 1 lb. Margarine. 4 ozs. Salt.	Peel and cut marrow into even pieces, remove pith and seeds. Cook in boiling salted water and drain thoroughly. Place into greased baking tin, sprinkle with grated cheese, breadcrumbs and melted margarine. Place in hot oven and allow moisture to evaporate.
Marrow vegetable.		Wash, peel, cut into quarters and remove the seeds. Place the marrow into boiling water to which a little salt has been added, and boil until tender. After cooking, marrow may, if desired, be mashed with a little dripping, pepper and salt.

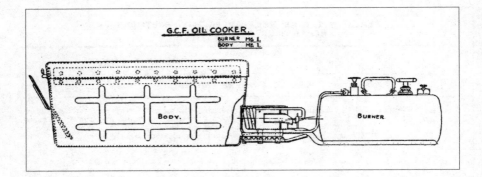

The Jungle

WHEN LIVING IN the jungle it was possible to live off the country and a small basic ration, which consisted of salt, tea, sugar and rice, to which was added everything available locally. In forest this ranged from birds and squirrels to wild pigs, snake and monkey, while in more open country buffalo and wild deer were available. Streams and lakes could provide fish but all water had to be boiled or sterilised, although water vines and coconuts provided sterile liquid. Most jungle berries are poisonous and instructions were given to avoid all unknown fruits, tubers and mushrooms. Some plants and fruits, especially the wild lily (Tarrow) being intensely irritating and if eaten could cause several hours of extreme discomfort. Another warning was against fruit that was similar in appearance to tomatoes, even if it looked and smelt attractive; generally in the jungle, red spells danger.

Good cooking was important in jungle conditions. The tastier the food the more efficiently it was absorbed. Dishes were made with the addition of suitable leaves, shoots and roots, such as ginger, turmeric and lily bulbs. A tin of curry powder and flavouring herbs were easily carried. The style of cooking in jungle warfare was limited to baking, roasting and boiling, and in the absence of any other utensils a large piece of bamboo could be cut, split and placed over a fire filled with water. This would provide sufficient hot water for shaving or a cup of tea, even though it did have a slightly woody taste. A similar technique could be employed using thin-walled bamboo – the hollow tube being filled with a combination of rice and water and once the water was steamed off the entire cavity of a bamboo was filled with cooked rice. Apart from poisoning, hygiene was of vital importance; in the jungle even a small amount of food left on a knife, fork or in a mess-tin could be the cause of food poisoning or dysentery. Emphasis was placed

THE JUNGLE RATION, MARK 2
(A leaflet showing contents and suggested menu will be found in each sealed food tin (*see* (iii) below)

Item	Pack	Daily Ration Each Man (approx.)			
		Type A	Type B	Type C	Type D
		ozs.	*ozs.*	*ozs.*	*ozs.*
(i) Fish and egg	1 tin	3½			
Breakfast pork ...	1 tin		3½		
Ham and egg	1 tin			3½	
Chopped liver and bacon	1 tin				3½
(ii) Preserved meat (beef) ...	1 tin	8			
Meat and kidney pudding	1 tin		8		
Stewed steak	1 tin			8	
Chopped ham and beef ...	1 tin				8
(iii) Oatmeal blocks	2 blocks	3½	3½	3½	3½
Biscuit	10 nos. film wrapped	8½	8½	8½	8½
Chocolate (vit.) H.C.	3 bars	6	6	6	6
Milk, sweetened, condensed ...	38 gramme tube	1½	1½	1½	1½
Tea tablets	12 tablet drum	½	½	½	½
Salt tablets	30 tablet drum	¼	¼	¼	¼
Compound vit. tablet ...		1 tab.	1 tab.	1 tab.	1 tab.
Sweets, boiled		2	2	2	2
Jam	1 tin	2	2	2	2
Cheese ... , ...	1 tin	1½	1½	1½	1½
Sugar tablets	8 tablets loose	1	1	1	1
Salt	1 packet	¼	¼	¼	¼
Chewing gum, sugar coated	1 packet	4 tabs.	4 tabs.	4 tabs.	4 tabs.
Fizz tablets	1 packet	12 tabs.	12 tabs.	12 tabs.	12 tabs.
Matches	1 booklet	1 bklt.	1 bklt.	1 bklt.	1 bklt.
Latrine paper	4 pieces	4 pcs.	4 pcs.	4 pcs.	4 pcs.
(iv) Cigarettes	1 tin ×20 (2 rations)	10 nos.	10 nos.	10 nos.	10 nos.

Packed in rectangular aluminium Container (6¾ ins. × 5¼ ins. × 2¾ ins.) lacquered dark green

NOTES.

(i) The nutritive value of the ration is 4,120 calories approximately.

(ii) Eight complete rations (each 3 lb. gross) are packed in a 4-gal. N/R tin : Measurements : 9½ ins. × 9½ ins. × 13½ ins. Gross weight : 30 lb.

(iii) Two 4-gal. N/R food tins (*i.e.*, 16 rations) are packed in a wooden case : Measurements : 21½ ins. × 10¾ ins. × 14¾ ins. Gross weight : 72 lb.

on avoiding smoke and glare during cooking. Suggestions to achieve this ranged from the idea of underground kitchens to using the tree canopy to diffuse the tell-tale smoke created by burning damp wood. This experience formed part of the information in the *1945 Manual* and would be vital to subsequent operations in the jungles of Malaya in the 1950s and '60s.[79]

Africa

FOLLOWING THE ESTABLISHMENT of the Army Catering Corps, the commander of the Sierra Leone area applied in May 1941 for a Command Catering Adviser to be posted to the area. However, General Headquarters Africa only asked the War Office for one officer for the whole command. When an ACC officer arrived in Freetown he was claimed by the commander of the Sierra Leone area. This officer, based in Freetown, found it impossible to supervise the entire command and subsequently an Area Catering Adviser was appointed for each colony whilst the Command Catering Adviser was established at GHQ at Accra in the Gold Coast (Ghana) dealing with that colony himself. Here at the command school of cookery, men from Nigeria, the Gold Coast, Sierra Leone and the Gambia undertook a course which accommodated fifty-six cooks. During the course of the war around 4,000 cooks were trained for the Royal West African Frontier Force.

During the war two schools of cookery were established in Nigeria: one school was for African cookery, while the other one taught African soldiers European cookery. At the African school the instructional staff consisted of twelve locally recruited women. At any one time they had as many as 150 students in training who undertook a two-month long course. Training consisted of the preparation of national dishes according to religion. It was for this reason that pork was never issued. Beef was the main meat supplemented with goat, sometimes dried Biltong, and smoked 'stink fish' as a delicacy. As in India the majority of cooking was done over open fires and these, together with the tropical heat, could be somewhat daunting. The European Cookery School ran courses aimed at students who had previously worked for government officials or the white business

---

79 Howard N. Cole, *The Story of the Army Catering Corps and its Predecessors* (Army Catering Corps Association: 1984), p. 126

community as cooks or stewards; twenty-five students were taken on for each three-month course and many made first-class cooks.[80] The two schools trained the cooks that would later serve with the 81st and 82nd West African divisions in Burma as part of the Fourteenth Army.[81]

One problem with supplying African soldiers was that they were used to locally grown food, with yams and cassava being a staple. Yams are heavy and bulky and a Yam ration for 100 soldiers weighed 300lbs for each daily issue, whereas an issue of rice or cassava weighed just 125lbs. The result was that the West African soldier's diet had to suffer in recognition of the shipping implications of a major food type. If Yams were sometimes in short supply, meat was fairly plentiful and this could be replaced or supplemented with fish, peanuts and palm oil. West African soldiers received a weekly issue of Kola nuts, which had a similar status as cigarettes in the British Army.

Middle East

FOLLOWING THE DUNKIRK evacuation, Italy seized the opportunity to strike at British positions in Africa, attacking British Sudan and Somaliland, as well as Italian forces in Libya invading Egypt. The British forces in this area became the Eighth Army and would fight through the Western Desert until the German Afrika Korps was defeated in 1943. Conditions in North Africa were harsh and varied from blistering heat during the day to freezing cold at night. The terrain was an example of geographic contrast and although sandy desert could be found, it was also rocky, mountainous and divided by gorges and ravines. With little natural fuel, petrol was readily used, in some cases even for washing clothes.

---

80 Howard N. Cole, *The Story of the Army Catering Corps and its Predecessors* (Army Catering Corps Association: 1984), p. 128

81 Howard N. Cole, *The Story of the Army Catering Corps and its Predecessors* (Army Catering Corps Association: 1984), p. 129

MIDDLE EAST FIELD SERVICE RATION SCALE.

To be brought into effect from midnight 15/16 May, 1942.

		ozs.	Ration equivalents to be issued when fresh rations are not available or under special G.H.Q. instructions.
1.	Bacon, M.C.	3	
	or Bacon, Tinned	2	
	or Sausages, Tinned	4	
2.	Bread	14	Biscuits 10½ ozs.
	or Flour	10⅓	
3.	Cheese	¾	
4.	Curry powder or Baking Pdr.	1/30	
5.	Dried Fruit	1	
6.	Fruit, fresh, when available or one Orange, in season whichever is the greater (Notes 1 and 2)		
7.	Herrings, Tinned	4/7	
	or Sardines, Tinned	2/7	
	or Salmon, Tinned	3/7	
8.	Jam or Marmalade, local	2	
	or Golden Syrup	1	
9.	Margarine (Note 4)	1½	
10.	Meat, frozen, with bone	8	Meat, preserved 6 ozs.
	or Meat, frozen, boneless	6	with Pickles 2/7 "
	or Meat, fresh, local with bone (Note 3)	10	or Chutney 1/14 "
11.	Meat, preserved	½	
12.	Milk, Tinned	2	or Milk, fresh, local 5 "
13.	Mustard	1/100	
14.	Oatmeal	1½	
	or Flour	2	
15.	Oil, cooking	5/7	
16.	Onions (Note 3)	2	
17.	Peas/Beans/Lentils, dried	1	
18.	Pepper	1/100	
19.	Potatoes, fresh	8	Potatoes, tinned 4 "
			and Rice 1⅓ "
			or Onions 1⅓ "
			or Onions 1⅓ "
20.	Rice	1	or Onions 1⅓ "
21.	Salt	½	and Rice 1.2/3
22.	Sugar	3	or Onions 1.2/3
23.	Tea	½	& Peas/Beans/Lentils 1⅓ "

24.	Vegetables, fresh (Note 3)	8oz	Vegetables, preserved	$3\tfrac{1}{3}$ oz
			comprising	
			Vegetables tinned	2.2/3 "
			and	
			Peas/Beans/Lentils	2/3 "
25.	Aso. Acid Tablets (Note 6)	1 tab.		

26. Tobacco or cigarettes

                        per week   2 ozs.

27. Matches   per week   2 boxes.

The above Ration Scale applies to :-

(a)   British Troops.
New Zealand Troops.
Union Defence Force (Europeans, Cape Coloured and S.A. Indians).
Free French Troops (Europeans, N. African and Pacific Units) (See sub-para (c) below).
Cingalese Troops.
Maltese Troops.
Mauritian Troops.
Seychellois Pioneer Coys.

(b)   The Union Defence Force (S.A.) (Europeans, Cape Coloured and S.A. Indians) will be issued with rations as laid down in the above-mentioned Order with the following ADDITIONS (provided by the Union Government) :-

Coffee 1 Oz. Sugar 2 Oz. Mealie Meal 2 oz - all daily.
Cigarettes - 2 oz. (50 cigarettes) weekly.

(c)   Free French Troops (European, N. African and Pacific Units) receive $\tfrac{3}{4}$ oz. coffee, when available, in lieu of $\tfrac{1}{2}$ oz. tea.
They also receive $\tfrac{1}{2}$ litre of wine, once per week, on repayment.

NOTES:

1. When Oranges are small, the 4 ozs. of Fresh Fruit may be made up either of Oranges alone, or of Oranges and other fruit.

2. When the distribution of Fresh Fruit is impossible, 2 oz. of Tinned Fruit in lieu of 4 ozs. of Fresh Fruit may be issued :-
   (a) In IKINGI-MARYUT and in areas WEST thereof.
   (b) In the SUDAN and ADEN Commands.

3. When frozen or fresh or boneless meat and fresh Onions and Vegetables are not available, 16 ozs. of M & V ration may be issued in lieu.

4. N.Z. Units in the Cairo Area receive 1½ oz. Butter in lieu of margarine (provided by the Government of New Zealand).

5. Units and detachments of units messing separately whose messing strength is under 50 will draw 10 per cent. extra rations, and those whose strength is 50 - 100 will draw 5 per cent. extra. Relevant indents for rations (A.B. 55) will be submitted by units concerned showing ACTUAL strengths. It is the responsibility of the R.A.S.C. Supply Officer concerned to issue the extra ration entitlement to such units.

6. To be issued in the case of an Army on the recommendation of the D.D.M.S., or

   (a) In the case of a Force, Division or Area on the recommendation of the A.D.M.S., or

   (b) In the case of the R.A.F. by the Senior Medical Officer, R.A.F. of an Area.

One aspect of the war in North Africa that deserves mention is the development of various forms of improvised cooker using petrol as fuel. This was not because the normal Cooker 1, 2, and 3 were not available, but because they often broke down due to sand and grit in the burners.[82] In an environment where there was more petrol than water, vehicle drivers in particular used empty petrol tins as suitable burners and petrol from vehicles as a means of cooking meals or brewing tea. These became known as 'Benghazi Burners' and normally consisted of a petrol tin with the lid removed, punched with holes using a pickaxe or entrenching tool, and then partially filled with sand.

Fuel was poured on to soak the sand and then lit, care being taken to be upwind from the result. Although it was possible to produce a quick 'brew' the fuel had a capacity to burn off before any more extensive cookery could be achieved. Unfortunately, because of the prevailing heat and bright light, many users assumed that the burner had gone out and added additional fuel, often directly from a petrol tin. The result can be all too readily appreciated and it has been suggested that more men were injured in this way than in tanks that were knocked out in action. With wonderful irony tank crews referred to vehicles that were hit and caught fire as having 'brewed up', and it was commonly believed that the Germans called British tanks 'Tommy Cookers'.[83] It's interesting to note that it was emphasised in the *Manual of Army Catering Services* that petrol was only to be used 'when no other type of fuel was available'. It also made it clear that 'Petrol is a vital munition of war and excessive quantities must not be poured into the sand or soil in the cookers.'[84]

82 Howard N. Cole, *The Story of the Army Catering Corps and its Predecessors* (Army Catering Corps Association: 1984), p. 114

83 *Manual of Army Catering Services, Part III – Cooking in the Field, including Improvised and Mess Tin Cookery* (1945), p. 15

84 *Manual of Army Catering Services, Part III – Cooking in the Field, including Improvised and Mess Tin Cookery* (1945), p. 15

IMPROVISED SAND AND PETROL COOKERS.

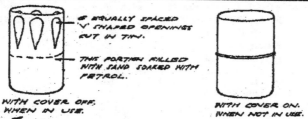

← 6 EQUALLY SPACED 'V' SHAPED OPENINGS CUT IN TIN.

← THIS PORTION FILLED WITH SAND SOAKED WITH PETROL.

WITH COVER OFF.
WHEN IN USE.

WITH COVER ON.
WHEN NOT IN USE.

FORMED OF FRUIT; MEAT ROLL OR JAM TIN.

EXAMPLE 1. COOKER FOR A.F.V. OR SMALL DETACHMENT.

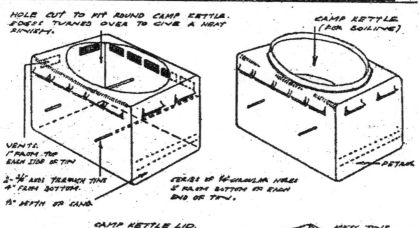

HOLE CUT TO FIT ROUND CAMP KETTLE.
EDGES TURNED OVER TO GIVE A NEAT FINISH.

CAMP KETTLE
(FOR BOILING).

VENTS.
1" FROM TOP
EACH SIDE OF TIN.

2 - 3/8" RODS THROUGH TIN
4" FROM BOTTOM.

SERIES OF 1/4" CIRCULAR HOLES
3" FROM BOTTOM OF EACH
END OF TIN.

1/2" DEPTH OF SAND.

PETROL.

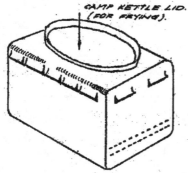

CAMP KETTLE LID.
(FOR FRYING).

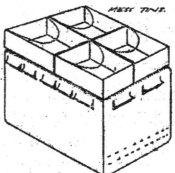

MESS TINS.

THE BOTTOM OF TIN IS FILLED WITH ABOUT 1/2" OF SAND. A CUP OF PETROL
POURED ON THIS WHEN IGNITED WILL BOIL A CAMP KETTLE OF WATER
IN ABOUT TWENTY MINUTES. THE SAND MAY HAVE TO BE STIRRED
WITH AN IMPLEMENT INSERTED THROUGH ONE OF THE VENTS.
CARE SHOULD BE TAKEN NOT TO REFILL THE COOKER WITH PETROL
WHILE HOT.

EXAMPLE 2.

THE "BREW-UP" COOKER

Experiments have been carried out with this cooker and have proved very satisfactory. It can be constructed in 20 minutes, has a petrol consumption of one pint per hour, and is suitable for ten men.

Equipment required:—

    1 x 4 gal. petrol tin.
    1 x 14 pound jam tin.
    Small quantity of absorbent brick pieces
    Mud filler (pug).

Construction:—

Petrol Tin.—Cut tin off at a height equal to that of the Jam Tin.

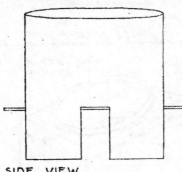

SIDE VIEW

TOP VIEW

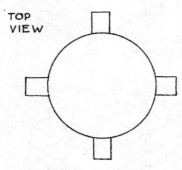

Jam Tin—Cut four 1" strips at an equal distance apart round the jam tin and half way up the side. Bend strips outwards and then double under to form four supports.

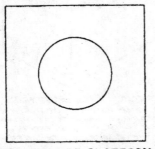

TOP VIEW OF PLATFORM

Petrol Tin—From the waste part of the petrol tin shape a platform, which will fit tight in the intact portion. Cut a hole in the centre of the platform large enough to enable it to be slipped over the jam tin and rest on the supports.

Erection

Place jam tin inside the petrol tin, fit the platform over until it rests on the supports. Fill space between the two tins, from the platform **upwards,** with mud (pug).

Fill the jam tin with absorbent brick or stone pieces.

Pour petrol through brick pieces until it finds its own level, up to the platform only.

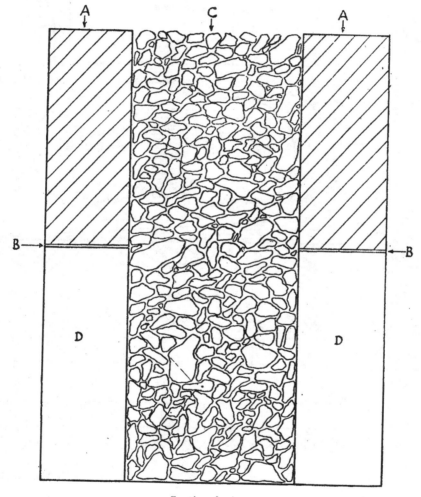

Sectional view
A. Mud (pug).
B. Platform.
C. Brick or stone pieces.
D. Petrol area.

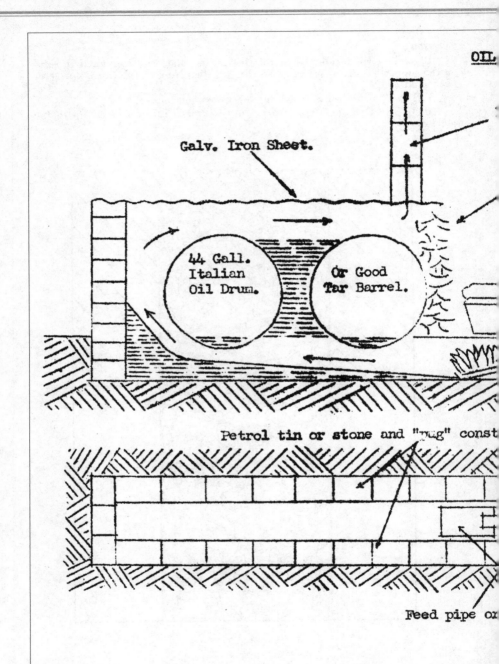

OIL

Galv. Iron Sheet.

44 Gall. Italian Oil Drum.

Or Good Tar Barrel.

Petrol tin or stone and "mug" const

Feed pipe or

OOKER.

himney.

e and "pug" wall.

NOTE:-

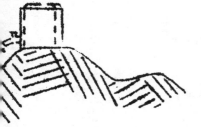

PREVAILING WIND.

1. Sloping Flue.
2. Sloping Flash Pan.
3. Long Chimney.
4. Prevailing Wind.
5. Flash Pan of Heavy
   Metal NOT Petrol Tin.
6. Get Pan Hot before Turning
   on Water.
7. Use Diesel Oil.
8. Pug Bottoms of Ovens.

lash pan.

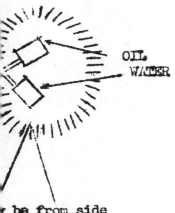

OIL.
WATER

be from side
desired.

Before the creation of the ACC, a school of cookery had been established at Safarand in Palestine. The Middle East School of Cookery was initially planned to take twenty students on a two-week course, but with the arrival of Australian, New Zealand, South African and Indian divisions it expanded and a new school, the Eighth Army ACC Training Centre and Depot, or the Western Desert School of Cookery, was created in Genifia, Eygpt in 1942.[85] Despite the existence of the Middle East and Western Desert schools of cookery, the widely dispersed nature of the forces meant that the standard of cooking varied considerably and there was a large shortage of trained cooks. At one time, reorganisation and expansion called for the training of over 5,000 cooks and the establishment of specialist Messing Officers and personnel in depots and elsewhere. Although training programmes were stepped up, demands were so great that the number of Army Catering Corps cooks and officers fell to less than a quarter of those required. As a result, Italian prisoners of war and civilians were trained to offset the deficiency and after VE Day German prisoners of war were trained to handle British rations and were posted to units instead of Army Catering Corps cooks. So great was the demand that the school at Genifa was reopened to train German prisoners of war as cooks and the results were recorded as being excellent.[86]

The conditions of desert warfare called for all sorts of improvisation including, underground bakeries at Tobruk and the creation of new recipes based on the limited availability of ingredients. One was the 'Dog Fritter' which was made of ration biscuits soaked till they expanded four times their normal size, they were then split, spread with jam and fried in fat. One particular problem was the feeding of armoured units because they were highly mobile and spent much of the hours of darkness in laager. During the brief hours available the crews of these vehicles had to rearm, refuel, and service their tanks and lorries, which left little time for cooking and the glare of cookers would draw enemy fire. To solve this, a range of mobile kitchens was created using standard lorries, equipped with petrol burners, hayboxes and large food containers. These gave good service in the desert and in subsequent operations.[87]

---

85 Howard N. Cole, *The Story of the Army Catering Corps and its Predecessors* (Army Catering Corps Association: 1984), p.115

86 Howard N. Cole, *The Story of the Army Catering Corps and its Predecessors* (Army Catering Corps Association: 1984), pp.118–119

87 Howard N. Cole, *The Story of the Army Catering Corps and its Predecessors* (Army Catering Corps Association: 1984), p.116

North Africa

AFTER THE ALLIED landings in North Africa the British First Army seized the ports of Algiers and Oran. The First Army Cookery School was established at Sidi Farouche, near to the Convalescent Depot at Algiers. The school was established to train Regimental Cooks and Messing Officers with the staff of one Warrant Officer and a Staff Sergeant from the ACC, plus four corporals from the infantry. Unusually, the Command Chief Instructor of the school was also responsible for the catering arrangements for 1,000 personnel at the Convalescent Depot.[88]

East Africa

AT THE TIME that the ACC was formed, British, Indian, Rhodesian (Zimbabwean) and East African troops were operating against Italian Forces in Somaliland and Abyssinia (Ethiopia). This vast area meant that the ACC was widely dispersed and an individual ACC cook could be found as far north as Addis Ababa (Ethiopia) and as far south as Lusaka (then Northern Rhodesia, now Zimbabwe), Mombasa or Nairobi. Despite the language difficulties, there was no shortage of work and individual members of the corps found themselves with a 'staff' of thirty or forty African cooks.[89]

Iceland

THE BRITISH GARRISON in Iceland and the Faroe Islands faced conditions which were a complete contrast to India or Africa. The Iceland force mainly consisted of the 49th (West Riding) Division and found itself facing isolation and the problem of a very cold climate. At the Winter Warfare School, tests were carried out in the development of appropriate Arctic Rations under the direction of the local Force Catering Advisor. These rations had to provide a very high calorific

---

88 Howard N. Cole, *The Story of the Army Catering Corps and its Predecessors* (Army Catering Corps Association: 1984), p. 132

89 Howard N. Cole, *The Story of the Army Catering Corps and its Predecessors* (Army Catering Corps Association: 1984), p. 131

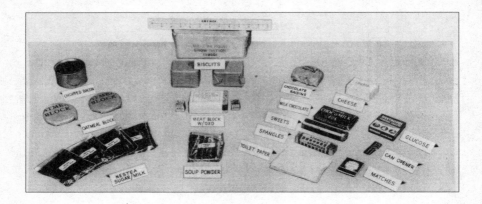

value and had to be easy and quick to cook. Porridge, oats, boiled sweets and additional hot beverages were added to the ration scale, and instruction given in the methods of producing hot and nutritious drinks in any weather conditions. Fortunately for the 49th Division, the entry of the United States into the war in December 1941 meant that British forces were, largely, replaced by US forces in 1942. Those that remained received American rations.[90]

90 Howard N. Cole, *The Story of the Army Catering Corps and its Predecessors* (Army Catering Corps Association: 1984), pp. 132–133

'If it's burnt, it's cooked':
Conclusion

THE MOTTO OF the Army Catering Corps was 'We Sustain'. This element of their cap badge was in 1993 incorporated into the cap badge of the Royal Logistic Corps, which was created by the amalgamation of the Royal Corps of Transport, Royal Army Ordnance Corps, Royal Pioneer Corps, Army Catering Corps and Royal Engineers Postal and Courier Service. Although there were complaints in the Second World War and later about the quality of rations produced by the ACC, they were always 'sustaining'. People rarely notice a good meal, sometimes recognise an excellent meal, but always comment on a poor meal. Under the circumstances of a global conflict it is not surprising that, either as a result of lack of ingredients, fuel, or the geographical and climatic constraints of the war, some meals were regarded as not acceptable by some of the consumers. The fact remains that the Army Catering Corps provided millions of meals every day for men and women all over the globe. For many the food was better than at home before the war and certainly the amount provided meant that most servicemen and women put on weight and improved in physical condition.

Corps troops have always been on the receiving end of jokes at their expense and the ACC was no exception. The least offensive are: 'Andy Capp's Commandos' and the 'Aldershot Concrete Company'. Others referred to them as 'Fitters and Turners' – taking food fit to eat and turning it into something inedible. It was added by some that the cooking technique normally employed by the ACC was 'if it is burning it's cooking, and if it's burnt it's cooked!' Perhaps

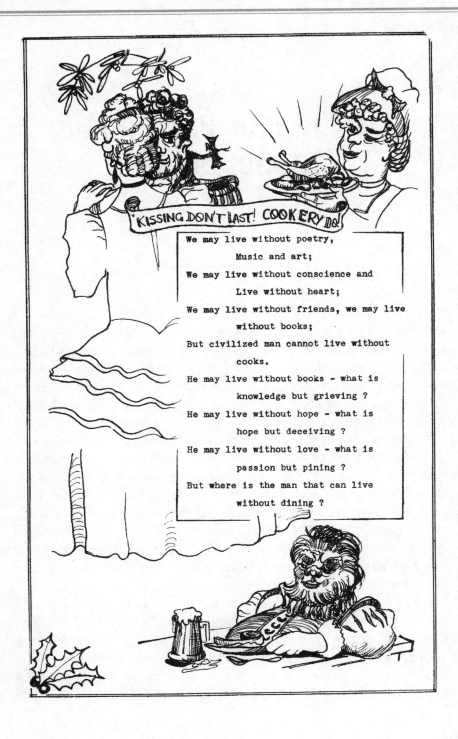

'KISSING DON'T LAST! COOKERY DO!'

We may live without poetry,
        Music and art;
We may live without conscience and
        Live without heart;
We may live without friends, we may live
        without books;
But civilized man cannot live without
        cooks.
He may live without books - what is
        knowledge but grieving ?
He may live without hope - what is
        hope but deceiving ?
He may live without love - what is
        passion but pining ?
But where is the man that can live
        without dining ?

these comments can be balanced by the nickname of the Royal Army Service Corps ('Run Away Someone is Coming!') or the Royal Army Medical Corps ('Run Away Matrons Coming!'). All of these demonstrate a robust sense of humour combined with the desire to denigrate non-combat troops no matter how vital their task in war and peace.

Perhaps a more fitting tribute to the memory of the men and women of the Army Catering Corps in the Second World War are the words of Colonel R.A.A. Byford CBE MVO, Controller ACC, who laid the foundation stone for the ACC Memorial Hall on 23 April 1955. The hall commemorates the known names of members of the Army Catering Corps who made the supreme sacrifice in the Second World War and subsequent conflicts:

> It is in their memory that this memorial is being erected, and it will be an inspiration to all members of the Army Catering Corps, past, present and future, to work for the cause and country which these men of the Corps so nobly gave their lives to save. In conclusion, I wish to quote two verses from the twenty fifth chapter of St Matthew's Gospel because those words will be inscribed on a plaque which will be placed on the wall of the shrine, together with the Book of Remembrance which will contain the Roll of Honour. The verses are 34 and 35. 'Then shall the King say unto them on his right hand, Come ye blessed of my Father, inherit the Kingdom prepared for you from the foundation of the world. For I was hungry and ye gave me meat, I was thirsty and ye gave me drink, I was a stranger and ye took me.'[91]

91 'ACC Soldiers Contribute to a War Memorial Hall of Remembrance', www.accassociation.org, accessed on 30 January 2012

Part Two

Battlefield Recipes

This section is made-up of recipes and tips from a wide variety of Army Cooks' personal log books from training and Army Manuals issued throughout the war. This is a mere snapshot of the wide breadth of recipes that the Army Cook was required to master and demonstrates the variety, that even in times of scarcity, troops 'enjoyed'.

Notes to the Army Cook

PRINCIPLES OF COOKING

Roasting

To roast, place the meat in a roasting tin, baste with dripping, and place in a very hot oven for just sufficient time to set the outside of the meat and prevent the loss of the juices. Then withdraw and cook at a temperature of approximately 350 deg. Fahr. Baste the meat frequently.

The time required is 15 to 18 minutes for each 1 lb. weight, but this must be judged by the thickness of the joint and the quality of the meat. Young and fat meat requires longer than old and lean.

Baking

Baking is a most convenient, economical and satisfactory method of cooking certain dishes, such as pastry, meat pies, pork, shoulder of mutton, etc., and it is popular with the troops.

In the baking of pies, etc., they should, at first, be placed in the hottest part of the oven. When the paste is cooked it can be left on the bottom to simmer until done.

Boiling

The boiling point of water is 212 deg. Fahr.

To boil joints of meat, they should be placed in boiling water and allowed to boil quickly for 10 minutes; then bring it to a simmer and allow it to cook slowly; garnish with fresh vegetables. The lid of the vessel should be kept on, care being taken that the scum rising to the surface of the stock is frequently skimmed off.

The time required to cook depends upon its weight and compactness: as a general rule 15 or 20 minutes for 1 lb. weight. If a piece of the flank weighing about 15 lb. were boiled as issued it would require about one hour or so, but if boned and rolled it would require from three to four hours, and would then be sent up to the table as a very substantial joint.

Vegetables

Cabbages, greens, etc., should be thoroughly cleaned and allowed to remain for a short time in salt and water; this will destroy any small insects that may remain. They should then be placed in boiling water with a little salt added, and boiled quickly until tender, then taken up and strained and served very hot. The boiler should be kept uncovered.

Stewing

Stewing is considered the most profitable method of cooking. If properly performed, tough meat is rendered tender and wholesome, and more nourishment is obtained than by any other process of cooking. It should be distinctly understood than stewing is not boiling; all that is required is a gradual simmering, and by this process the coarsest and roughest parts of the beast will become soft, tender and easily digestible.

Meat of a fibrous and course nature, such as legs, briskets, buttocks, clods or necks of mutton, should be issued for stewing.

Braising

Braising is half roast and half stew. Meat is coloured quickly in a very hot oven with sliced carrot and onion, moistened with brown stock, seasoned, covered with lid, and cooked in oven. Inferior cuts of meat are used in this method of cookery.

Steaming

Steaming is usually performed by steam passing from a close boiler to a close chamber, or by placing a steamer over a boiler containing boiling water, or by placing a few bricks or stones at the bottom of the boiler, covering them with water and placing on them the dish containing the articles required to be cooked.

The articles of food usually cooked by steam are meat puddings, potatoes, suet puddings, etc.

Frying

Frying is cooking with the aid of fats. With care the same fat should last a long time, but when it acquires a dark brown colour it is no longer fit for use, and should be put aside and sold with the by-products.

For shallow frying, place in a pan only sufficient fat to cover the bottom of it. When deep frying, use sufficient fat to cover the food to be cooked.

The heat required for frying purposes is from 350 deg. to 400 deg. Fahr. A simple way to ascertain when the fat is sufficiently hot is to place in it a piece of bread for a few seconds; if this becomes a golden brown colour, the fat is ready; if the bread assumes a light yellow, it is not hot enough, but if the bread be burnt a dark brown colour, it is too hot.

Grilling

Grilling is cooking over or in front of a fire, a gridiron being generally used. Care should be taken to see that it is perfectly clean and free from grease. It should be placed on the fire slantways, the lower part in front; this prevents the fat falling into the fire and causing it to smoke. The fire must be clear, bright and tolerably strong.

Meat for grilling should be cut in thin and even slices. The meat will then be equally cooked throughout.

Previous to cooking, the meat should be sprinkled with pepper and salt. It should be frequently turned, and when firm to the touch on being pressed with the flat part of the knife it is done.

MAKING OF TEA

Ingredients (for 100 men).

Tea 12oz.
Sugar 3 lb.
Milk 2 tins or 3 Pints.
Water 12 gallons.

Method.—Weigh or measure the tea and sugar, a measure is easily made by cutting down a tin. **Don't use your hand as a measure: this results in waste.** Place the dry tea into muslin bags and tie loosely. Tea bags tied tightly will not allow sufficient room for expansion of the tea during the infusion. Rinse out the tea buckets or dixies with boiling water to ensure cleanliness and to heat the buckets, then place the tea bags in the buckets and fill with boiling water. Stand for 10 minutes, remove bags, squeeze, add sugar and milk. Serve.

DON'TS

DON'T put handles of knives in hot water.
" waste or throw away food that may be used again.
" leave until known preparation you can do to-day.
" smoke yourself, or allow others to do so in kitchen.
" slam the oven door when baking cake.
" forget that purity is essential in good feeding.
" leave nails taps running.

" use cooking utensils for cleaning purposes.
" peel potatoes thickly to boil half to own to skin.
" forget to baste frequently when roasting v braising.

DON'T forget that stewing is not boiling.
" forget that stewing is most economical way of cooking meat.
" attempt to fry fish unless fat is smoking hot.
" forget to boil pulses overnight.
" hide dirt.

" purchase which makes you have the proper ingredients
" forget to boil suet puddings in boiling water.
" use more fuel than is necessary.
" serve up any thing unless properly cooked.
" forget to boil joints in the hottest part of oven.
" be afraid to acknowledge mistake. This can often be rectified.

DON'T forget that vegetable scraps are nourishing.

DON'T allow a fire to burn too low before replenishing.
" leave bones in stockpot overnight.
" leave scum on stock pot.
" use a fork to turn joints.
" leave anything until the last minute.
" forget that sour bones must not be placed in
(contd.

DON'T.

DON'T.

DON'T.

Tips.

Eggs poached in vinegar & water only, no salt. To save time can be left in the vinegar & water overnight & just brought to the boil in morning.

Fry Eggs in thick pan. To hard boil, always place in hot water.

To improve Welsh Rarebit, place a walnut in centre.

Scotch Woodcock - Cut anchovys in strips & place as diagram on scrambled eggs on rounds of toast.

Dianne. Bacon & fried mushroom.

Canape Ivanhoe. Bone & skin smoked haddock — Chop finely - mix with white sauce. Pile dome shape on rounds of toast, also slice pickled walnut, heat gently in oven - as previous recipe.

Use bath brick for cleaning.

- fat to preserve stoves.

Caustic Soda & fat to make soap.

When stirring heavy mixtures stir away from you.

Nitrogenous Foods.

Proteins. Organic Substances containing Carbon - Hydrogen, nitrogen & sulphur. Nourish & repair.

Non Nitrogenous: Fats Contain Carbon Hydrogen & Oxygen, body heat, & deposit of reserve energy.

Cooking for 100 Troops

Cooking for 100-plus troops at a time could pose a logistical nightmare. Throughout the following recipe section are a number of recipes that pose the challenge of mass catering in the field. You will be able to denote these by the quantities involved!

FOOD QUANTITIES FOR 100 PORTIONS

Apple rings (apple charlotte)	8 lb.
,, ,, (apple pie)	8 lb. (or 30 lb. fresh)
,, ,, (apple pudding)	6 lb.
,, fresh (apple fritters)	12½ lb.
,, ,, (apple baked)	35 lb.
,, ,, (apple dumplings)	25 lb.
Bacon with (bubble and squeak, egg and chips, bacon and potato pie, beans in tomato sauce, egg, sausage, beans, mashed potatoes, liver, sausage cake, scrambled eggs, poached egg)	12½ lb. prepared (or approximately 15 lb. unprepared)
,, with tomatoes	12½ lb. prepared
,, plain	25 lb. unprepared
,, with fried bread	15 lb. prepared
Beans, haricot or butter	10 lb.
Brawn	25 lb.
Beef (croquettes, minced, Vienna steaks, cold pressed brisket, cottage pie)	25 lb. cooked and prepared
,, olives	37½ lb. unprepared
,, curried, braised, hot pot, boiled salt ...	37½ lb. unprepared
,, braised with rice, braised steak	37½ lb. unprepared
,, roast	37½ lb. unprepared
,, steak and kidney pudding	37½ lb. unprepared
,, fried steaks	25 lb. prepared
,, Hamburg roast	25 lb. prepared
Butter or margarine (per meal)	3½ lb.
Beetroot	28 lb. prepared
Carrots	40 lb. unprepared
Cabbage	50 lb. unprepared
Curry powder	1½ lb.
Celery	25 heads
Cheese	6¼ lb.
Cocoa	2 lb.
Fruit salad (dried fruits)	12½ lb.
Figs	12½ lb.
Fish kedgeree or fish salad	20 lb. cooked
,, pies	26 lb. cooked
,, cakes	12 tins or 12 lb. fresh fish

Flour (apple fritters, rock cakes)	6	lb.
,, (apple puddings, baked jam roll, sultana roll, golden roll, suet pudding, currant roll, marmalade roll, jam roll, short paste ...	16	lb.
,, (baked apple dumplings, fruit puddings, apple turnover, slab cake)	12	lb.
,, banana fritters	4	lb.
,, (Baroness pudding, treacle pudding, College pudding, flour paste, fruit tart, Banburys fruit pies, mock mince pie, jam pancakes)	8	lb.
,, Yorkshire pudding	14	lb.
,, fruit cake	9	lb.
,, trifle	2¼	lb.
Golden syrup, in lieu of jam or marmalade ...	12	lb.
,, ,, for puddings	6	lb.
,, ,, with porridge	4	lb.
Jam, tea meal	12	lb.
,, for puddings	7	lb.
,, for sauce	3	lb.
Liver, breakfast, with bacon	12½	lb.
,, dinner	25	lb.
Marmalade, breakfast	7	lb.
Milk, fresh for tea, coffee or cocoa	6¼	pts.
,, fresh for porridge	5	pts.
,, (baked rice pudding and dates, baked rice and sultana pudding, baked rice and raisin pudding)	4	galls.
,, (fruit cakes, scones)	4	pts.
,, (chocolate fruit pudding and sauce) ...	8	pts.
,, white sauce	2	galls.
,, rice and fruit fritter	3	galls.
,, Yorkshire pudding	16	pts.
,, jam pancakes	1	gall.
Mutton, boiled, braised, stuffed, roast	37½	lb. unprepared
,, cassoulet	37½	lb. unprepared
,, curried, haricot, Lancashire hot-pot stewed, Irish stew, white stewed	37½	lb. unprepared
Mustard, for table use	2	oz.
Onions, fried or braised	33	lb.
Oatmeal or Oats, breakfast porridge	8	lb.
Peas, blue	10	lb.
Pepper, for table use	2	oz.

Potatoes, dinner (old)	65	lb. unprepared
,, dinner (new)	56	lb.
,, breakfast or supper	32	lb. unprepared
Salmon (tinned), cutlets, fish cakes	12	tins
,, (tinned), mayonnaise	19	tins
,, (tinned), tea meal	19	tins
Sausages with bacon and potatoes	12½	lb.
,, as meat for sausage cake	25	lb.
,, for sausage rolls filling	12½	lb.
Sugar (tea, cocoa or porridge)	3	lb.
,, (apple charlotte, apple fritters, apple pie, baked bread pudding, Baroness pudding, Cabinet pudding, College pudding, fruit pudding, jam sauce, open fruit tart, sultana roll, stewed figs, stewed prunes, white sauce)	2	lb.
,, (apple pudding, baked apple dumplings, fruit salad, fruit tart)	3¼	lb.
,, (baked rice pudding, rice and fruit fritters, apple turnover, syrup)	3	lb.
,, (baked rice and sultana pudding, chocolate fruit pudding, slab cake, fruit cake) ...	5	lb.
,, (sultana scones, rock cakes, tea scones) ...	1½	lb.
,, chocolate sauce, fruit pies	2½	lb.
,, (flan paste)	1	lb.
,, jam pancakes	1	lb.
,, trifle	2¼	lb.
Tea, breakfast or tea	12	ozs.
Turnips	50	lb. unprepared
Tomatoes (fresh with bacon)	25	lb.
,, (fresh with green salad)	4	lb.
,, (tinned) with bacon	10	(large size)
Vinegar with salads or salmon	5	pts.

Breakfast from Preserved Meats — For 100 Men — Ingredients

Description	Faggetts	Sausage	Savoury Balls	Meat Croquetts	Rissoles	Potatoe Cutlets	Curried Balls	Pres. Meat Fritters	Lorne Sausage
Tins	16¾ 3lb	33¼	33⅓	33¼	33⅓	33⅓	33⅓	33⅓	33¾
Flour (lbs)	3	3	3	3	3	3	3	3	3
Mixed Herbs pkt				1					1
Bread (lbs)	8lb 1	8	8	8	8	8	8		8
Sage (pkt)	1								
Thyme (pkt)	1								
Nutmeg	1								
Spice (pkt)	2	2							
Onions (lbs)	3lb	3	3 fry	3 fry	3	6 fry	3		3
Potatoes (lbs)	36lb					25			
Salt oz.	2	2	2	2	2	2	2	2	2
Pepper oz	1	1	1	1	1	1	1	1	1
Cayenne Pepper						1	1		
Dripping (lbs)	3	3	3	3	3	3	1	3	3
Bkg. Powder oz							3¾		
Cracklings (lbs)	2	2	2	2			24		2
Eggs									
Liver (lbs)	12½								

127

Breakfast Menus

1	TEA,	BREAD,	BUTTER.	MILK.	PORRIDGE.	FISH & MASH

SUGGESTED BREAKFAST DISH

1 TEA, BREAD, BUTTER. MILK. PORRIDGE. FISH & MASH
2 " " " " " SAUSAGE AND MASH
3 " " " " " FRIED STEAK AND CHIPS
4 " " " " " SALMON AND RICE CURRIED EGGS
5 " " " " " "
6 " " " " " FISH KEDGERIE
7 " " " " " SAUSAGE AND FRYED EGGS
8 " " " " " POTATOE CUTLETS
9 " " " " " FISH CAKES AND MASH
10 " " " " " MEAT CUTLETS FRYED ONIONS
11 " " " " " PRESERVED MEAT FRITTERS
12 " " " " " BATTERED STEAKS & MASH

BREAKFAST MEALS

PORRIDGE

Ingredients

Oatmeal	8 lbs
Sugar.	3 "
Milk	6 "
Salt	2 ozs
Water	30 Pints

Method

Bring Water to Boiling Point sprinkle oatmeal in to Boiling Water and mix thoroughly until all ingredients are mixed allow the Porridge to simmer for 20 minutes in steamer or over a fire during the simmering process the mixture should be frequently stirred add milk and Sugar.

CURRIED EGGS.

Ingredients

Eggs	25 DOZEN
Curried Powder	1 lb
Dripping	1 "
Onions	3 "
Salt	2 oz
Pepper	1 "
Stock or Water as required	

Method

Make a curried gravy. Boil eggs hard.
for about 6 minutes Place the eggs into
cold running Water then remove the
shells cut eggs into halves length
ways and arrange neatly into
Baking trays cover with curried gravy
then Place into a moderate oven.

TIME 45 MINUTES

Dinner Menus

SUGGESTER DINNER DISHES

1/ TEA, BREAD, ONION SOUP, ROAST MEAT, YORKSHIRE
    PUDDING, POTATOES, VEGETABLES, RICE FRITTERS + JAM

2/ TEA, BREAD, VEGETABLES SOUP, BEEF OLIVES, RICE
    MOULDS AND JAM.

3/ TEA, BREAD, PEA SOUP, MEAT PIE, POTATOES, VEGETABLES
    RICE AND OATMEAL PUDDING

4/ TEA, BREAD, ALL IN STEW AND BREAD PUDDING

5/ TEA, BREAD, POTATOE SOUP, CORNISH PASTIES
    POTATOES VEGETABLES AND FRUIT FRITTERS

6/ TEA. BREAD, BEAN SOUP, TURKISH PILLAU,
    POTATOES VEGETABLES AND BAKED JAM ROLL

7/ TEA, BREAD, MULLIGATARNEY SOUP, MEAT PUDDING
    POTATOES, VEGETABLES AND RICE AND FRUIT PUDDING

8/ TEA, BREAD, CURRIED STEW RICE AND JAM ROLL

9/ TEA, BREAD, LENTIL SOUP, PRESERVED MEAT FRITTERS
    POTATOES VEGETABLES AND STEWED FRUIT

10/ TEA, BREAD, CURRIE SOUP, GATEAU-DE-RIT, POTATOES
    VEGETABLES, PLAIN PUDDING AND JAM SAUCE

11/ TEA, BREAD, SEA PIE, POTATOES, VEGETABLES.
    RICE MOULDS AND JAM SAUCE

12/ TEA, BREAD, SOUP, SCOTCH EGGS POTATOES
    VEGETABLES AND FRUIT PUDDING.

Tea Menus

SUGGESTED TEA DISHES

1 Tea, Bread, Butter and Jam

2 Tea, Bread, Butter and cheese

3 Tea, Bread, Butter, and cold meat

4 Tea, Bread, Butter and Fish Paste

5 Tea, Bread, Butter and Rock Cakes

6 Tea, Bread, Butter and meat Paste

7 Tea, Bread, Butter and Sausage Rolls

8 Tea, Bread Butter and Scones

9 Tea, Bread, Butter and oatmeal cheese cakes

10 Tea, Bread, Butter and Welsh Rare bit

11 Tea, Bread, Butter and Fruit

12 Tea. Bread, Butter, and Cornish Pastie.

TEA DISHES FROM PRESERVED MEAT.

X = TO COLOUR
A = AS REQUIRED

DISCRIPTION	FISH PASTE	MEAT PASTIES	SAUSAGE ROLLS	POTTED MEAT
BKG POWDER OZ		4	4	
DRIPPING LB		3	3	1
PEPPER OZ	1	1	1	A
SALT OZ	1	2	2	A
POTATOES LB	2			
ONIONS LB		1½		
SPICE PKT			½	½
BREAD LB		2		
MIXED HERBS (PKT)		¼	½	
FLOUR (LB)		12	12	
TINNED MEAT (LB)	16 2/3	16 2/3	16 2/3	16 2/3
COCHINEAL	X			
VINEGAR				
TINNED FISH LB	3			
COLD WATER	A	A		

Supper Menus

Suggested Supper Dishes

1 Tea Bread   AND   Steak and chips

2 Tea Bread   "   Stew

3 Tea Bread   "   Stewed Steak & onions

4 Tea Bread   "   Roast meat Potatoes & Vege

5 Tea Bread   "   Sausage and Mash

6 Tea Bread   "   Sausage Rolls

7 Tea Bread   "   Meat cutlets & onions

8 Tea Bread   "   Cheese and Onions

9 Tea Bread   "   Soup

10 Tea Bread   "   Egg and Chips

11 Tea Bread   "   Cornish Parties

12 Tea Bread   "   Potatoe cutlets

Puddings & Cakes

THE USE OF OATMEAL

Dish	Ingredients	Method
OAT CAKES.	12½ lb. oatmeal. 3 lb. dripping. 1 lb. sugar. Salt.	Place meal in a mixing bowl and add pinch of salt, dripping and sugar; mix well together and leave for 2¼ hours. Shape into three-cornered cakes of 2 oz. each and bake until brown. Serve two for each man.
OATMEAL CHEESE CAKES.	12½ lb. oatmeal. 12½ lb. cheese. A little dry mustard. Pepper and salt to taste.	Cut up cheese into small pieces and pass through mincer; add meal and work into a stiff dough; roll out into a paste, and cut into circular cakes; bake in hot oven for 15–20 minutes.
SCOTCH CAKES.	6¼ lb. oatmeal. 20 oz. milk. 5 lb. flour. 2 lb. dripping. 2 lb. sugar. Salt. 9 oz. baking powder.	Sieve the flour and mix in the oatmeal, then thoroughly rub in the dripping. Add the remaining dry ingredients and mix well with milk to attain the correct consistency. Roll out and shape into rounds. Mark each round into 4 scones.
RICE AND OATMEAL PUDDING.	7 lb. rice. 7 lb. oatmeal. 2 lb. currants. 2 lb. sugar. 3 nutmegs (if desired) or mixed pudding spice. 1 lb. dripping.	Wash the rice and pick out discoloured grains. Wash and pick over currants. Place oatmeal, rice, sugar, currants and dripping into mixing bowl and mix thoroughly. Place into well-greased baking dish and cook in moderately heated oven for 1½ hours.
PORRIDGE.	7 lb. oats (rolled) or oatmeal. 4 lb. sugar. 21 pts. milk (or 8 tins). 2 oz. salt.	Bring water to boil, add the salt, and sprinkle in the oats or oatmeal, stirring well to prevent lumps. Allow to simmer for 1 hour, if using oatmeal. If rolled oats, 20 minutes simmering will be found sufficient. SPECIAL NOTE.—Milk and sugar may be added, or served separately. Golden syrup may be used if prepared, in which case both sugar and milk can be dispensed with.

135

VARIOUS METHODS OF USING UP SPARE BISCUITS

Dish	Ingredients	Method
*PLAIN SUET PUDDING.	16 lb. biscuits. 4 lb. suet or dripping. 1 oz. salt.	Powder or soak the biscuits, add the salt and chopped suet, and mix well. Add sufficient water to make into fairly stiff dough, tie in cloths and boil for 2½ hours. Serve hot with jam or marmalade. The above, if desired, may be placed in a greased baking dish and baked in a moderate oven for 1¾ hours. The same mixing should be used for jam rolls.
*FRUIT AND BISCUIT PUDDING.	As above, with the addition of dried fruit.	Thoroughly clean and cut the fruit into small pieces and proceed as above.
*DUMPLING.	As for a plain suet pudding.	Proceed as for plain suet pudding, but make the dough into small balls, and place in the stew 40 minutes before serving.
*BISCUIT PASTRY.	12 lb. biscuits. 3 lb. dripping. ⅜ oz. salt. 6 lb. jam.	Powder the biscuits, add salt and pinch in the dripping. Mix lightly into a medium paste with cold water. Roll out to a thickness of ¼ inch and place in well-greased dixie lids or baking dishes. Partly bake, then spread on sufficient jam and return to oven to finish baking. Time about 35 minutes. This pastry without the jam can be used for meat pies and puddings.
*SCONES.	16 lb. biscuits. 4 lb. dripping. 4 lb. sugar. 8 oz. baking powder. 3 tins milk.	Powder the biscuits, add the baking powder and sugar, shred in the dripping, and mix well. Add sufficient milk to make a pliable paste, and break into 1 lb. pieces. Roll out and divide into 4 pieces. Bake in a moderate oven for 20 minutes. Scones should be served hot. They are improved by adding a little dried fruit.
*ROCK CAKES.	16 lb. biscuits. 4 lb. dripping. 3 lb. sugar. ⅜ oz. salt. 6 oz. baking powder. 3 tins milk. 2 lb. currants.	Powder the biscuits, wash and pick the currants. Place dripping and sugar into a bowl and beat it up until it becomes soft and light. Add the remainder of the ingredients, and use sufficient milk to make a stiff paste. Divide into small rock cakes, and bake from 10 to 15 minutes in a fairly hot oven.

VARIOUS METHODS OF USING UP SPARE BISCUITS—*continued*

Dish	Ingredients	Method
* GOLDEN PUDDING.	16 lb. biscuits. 4 lb. suet or dripping. 6 lb. marmalade. 2 tins milk.	Crush the biscuits. Shred in the dripping. Mix in part of the marmalade, a little milk and baking powder, until all becomes a stiff dough. Cut up into 5-lb. pieces. Tie up tightly in a wet cloth. Place in boiling water and boil for 2¼ hours. When taken out, allow to remain in the cloth for 10 minutes. Make a sauce with the remainder of the marmalade by adding hot water and letting it simmer. Serve with pudding.
BISCUIT PORRIDGE.	12 lb. biscuits. 1¼ lb. sugar. 3 tins milk. 30 pints water.	Boil the water in the camp kettle. Crush the biscuits, and add to the boiling water, stirring until it becomes quite thick. Remove from the fire. Stir in the sugar and milk. Time required, 20 minutes.
* BISCUIT AND RICE PUDDING.	12 lb. biscuits. 6 lb. rice. 1 lb. sugar. 2 tins milk. 8 tins jam.	Cook rice in usual way, and sweeten to taste. Soak, squeeze and pass biscuits through mincer. Well grease a baking dish and put in a layer of rice, a layer of jam and a layer of biscuit. Add sugar to the milk and barely cover the whole. Place in a moderate oven until milk is absorbed and pudding brown. Cut into squares and serve.
* BISCUIT DOUGH-NUTS.	12 lb. biscuits. 3 lb. dripping. 2 lb. sugar. 1 tin milk. ½ oz. salt. Lime-juice to flavour. A little flour.	Powder the biscuits, and add salt, dripping, sugar and flour, and mix well together. Make a hollow in centre, and add milk and lime-juice flavouring. Mix into a stiff dough Roll out and cut into round cakes. Fry in hot fat till brown. Jam should be served with them for tea meal.
YORKSHIRE PUDDING.	12 lb. biscuits. Stock. Pepper.	Strain off some good stock, bring to the boil and pour over biscuits, and allow to soak for 1 hour. Pass through mincer twice, adding a little more stock as required, to reduce the consistency to batter. Mix in pepper and pour into well-greased baking dish and bake till brown.

* Flour may be used instead of biscuits.

For specimen bills of fare, *see* "Management of Soldiers' Messing."

ECONOMICAL PUDDING RECIPES

Utilising Bread and small Fruit Content.

Boiled and Steamed Puddings Quantities for 100 Men	Base of Recipes	Date Pudding	Fruit Do.	Raisin	Fig.	Baroness	Syrup	Marmalade	College	Ginger	Chocolate	Chocolate & Fruit
Suet, Chopped	6 lb.	6 lb.	6 lb.	6 lb.	6 lb.	6 lb.	6 lb.	6 lb.	6 lb.	6 lb.	4 lb.	4 lb.
Sugar	2 lb.	2 lb.	2 lb.	2 lb.	2 lb.	2 lb.	2 lb.	2 lb.	2 lb.	6 lb.	4 lb.	4 lb.
Breadcrumbs	8 lb.	8 lb.	8 lb.	8 lb.	8 lb.	8 lb.	8 lb.	8 lb.	8 lb.	8 lb.	12 lb.	12 lb.
Flour	8 lb.	8 lb.	8 lb.	8 lb.	8 lb.	8 lb.	8 lb.	8 lb.	8 lb.	8 lb.	4 lb.	4 lb.
Milk or water	8 pt.	8 pt.	8 pt.	8 pt.	8 pt.	8 pt.	4 pt.	4 pt.	8 pt.	4 pt.	8 pt.	8 pt.
Baking Pdr.	8 oz.	8 oz.	8 oz.	8 oz.	8 oz.	8 oz.	8 oz.	8 oz.	8 oz.	8 oz.	8 oz.	8 oz.
Salt	2 oz.	2 oz.	2 oz.	2 oz.	2 oz.	2 oz.	2 oz.	2 oz.	2 oz.	2 oz.	2 oz.	2 oz.
Dates		6 lb.										
Sultanas		2 lb.										
Currants		2 lb.								4 lb.		
Spice			1½ oz			4 oz.			2 oz.			
Figs					6 lb.							
Stoned Raisins			2 lb.	6 lb.		6 lb.						6 lb.
Treacle / Syrup							6 lb.					
Marmalade								4 lb.				
Peel									1 lb.			
Ginger										4 oz.		
Cocoa											1 lb.	1 lb.
											12	12

If breadcrumbs are not available increase flour to 16 lbs.

V.—SWEETS

67 Apple Charlotte

8 lb. Apple rings
4 lb. Breadcrumbs
2 lb. Sugar
10 lb. Bread

1½ lb. Margarine
4 qts. Syrup sauce

Method.—Soak the apple rings for 24 hours; drain and chop. Heat the margarine and fry on the apple rings, without taking colour, until tender. Add the sugar and breadcrumbs and a little mixed spice if available.

Cut the bread into slices after removing the crust. Pass through melted margarine and line a baking tin, each slice overlapping by half. Place the apple puree in the centre, cover with the crusts and bake in a moderate oven for approximately one hour. Turn out on a dish and serve with syrup sauce.

68 Apple Fritters

12½ lb. Apples (fresh) or large soaked apple rings
2 lb. Sugar
7 lb. Flour
1 oz. Salt

1 oz. Sugar
2 oz. Baking powder
½ pt. Oil or melted dripping

Method.—Make a batter (see Recipe No. 35).

Peel and core the apples and cut into slices approximately quarter inch thick, sprinkle with sugar. Heat the fat, or frying oil, pass each slice of apple through the batter, wipe off surplus and drop into the hot fat. Allow to fry approximately five minutes till tender and a golden brown. Drain, sprinkle with sugar and serve with sauce.
N.B.—Oranges and bananas can be used if apples are not available.

69 Apple Pie

8 lb. Apple rings
2 lb. Sugar
12 lb. Flour

4 oz. Baking powder
4 lb. Margarine or dripping
2 oz. Salt

Short Paste for Cover

Method.—Mix flour, baking powder and salt, work in the margarine or dripping and make a bay. Add the water and make into a fairly stiff dough. Allow to rest. Divide into 16 pieces (if using steel plates), or into five if using the baking dishes (i.e., 20 portions). Soak the apple rings for 24 hours. Place on to boil, together with the sugar, and cook.

Roll out the paste to approximately one-sixth inch in thickness. Line the plates or baking dishes, which should be slightly greased. Prick the bottom, place in the apples and cover with paste. Brush over with a little water or milk, sprinkle with sugar and mark the top with a point of a knife to define portions. Place in top of oven (350 deg. Fahr.) and bake approximately 40 minutes to one hour until paste and apples are cooked. Care must be taken to see that the bottom of paste is cooked.

70 Baked Apple Dumplings

25 lb. Apples (four to 1 lb.) (or rings)	4 oz. Baking powder
	Water for paste
3¼ lb. Sugar	1½ oz. Salt
12 lb. Flour	
4 lb. Margarine or dripping	

Method.—Prepare a short paste as for apple pie and roll out quarter inch thick. Cut into sections approximately four inches square and place a peeled and cored apple in the centre of each. Sprinkle sugar in the centre of each apple, wet edges of paste and cover the apple. Place on a baking sheet and egg wash. Bake 'at the top of the oven for approximately 40 minutes.

71 Baked Bread Pudding and White Sauce

10 lb. Bread (soaked)	2 lb. Sugar
2 lb. Sultanas	2 lb. Margarine
2 lb. Golden Syrup	
2 lb. Currants	

Method.—Soak stale bread in water, press out the water and pass through a mincer. Cream the margarine, sugar and warm treacle. Add bread, a little at a time, and thoroughly mix. Add the fruit and place into greased baking tins. Smooth the tops and sprinkle with a little sugar. Bake for one hour in a slow oven. Cut into portions and serve with a sweet white sauce.

72 Baked Jam Roll and Sauce

16 lb. Flour	6 lb. Margarine or dripping
4 oz. Baking powder	7 lb. Jam
2 oz. Salt	Jam sauce

Method.—Prepare a short paste (see Recipe No. 97). Divide into eight pieces, roll out each one quarter inch thick to form a two-foot square. Spread with jam within an inch all round, wet edges and roll up.

Place on baking trays and put into hot oven (400 deg. Fahr.). to start. Reduce heat to 300 deg. Fahr. and cook for one hour. Cut each roll into 12 portions slantwise and serve with jam sauce.

73 Creamed Rice Pudding

4 gallons Milk	½ lb. Margarine
3 lb. Sugar	5 lb. Rice

Method.—Bring the milk and sugar to boil, wash and pick over the rice and rain into the boiling milk. Allow to simmer for 20 minutes, stir constantly. Grease the pie or baking dishes with a little margarine. Divide the rice into the baking dishes, sprinkle with melted margarine and bake on top shelf of oven approximately one hour.

74 Baked Rice and Sultana Pudding

4 gallons Milk	2 lb. Sultanas
3 lb. Sugar	5 lb. Rice
½ lb. Margarine	

Method.—See Recipe No. 73, using sultanas which are added after the rice has simmered for 20 minutes.

278 Bath buns.

6 lb. Flour.	7½ oz. Margarine.
2½ oz. Yeast.	⅝ oz. Salt.
12 oz. Sugar.	1 lb. Currants.
8 oz. Peel.	Egg colouring.
1 lb. Crushed loaf sugar.	2 pts. Milk.

Method.—Dilute the yeast with luke-warm water and a little flour, stand for ¼ hour. Sieve the flour and rub in the margarine. Make a bay, place the sugar and salt in the bay and dissolve with the milk, water and egg colouring. Break in the ferment and work into a fairly stiff dough. Work until it comes away clear from the hands. Add the fruit, allow to stand for ½ hour, fold, allow to stand for another ½ hour, scale off (½ oz. pieces) and place on baking tray. Allow to prove, and egg wash. Place a few nobs of sugar on each and bake in a hot oven.

279 Chelsea Buns.

6 lb. Flour.	⅝ oz. Salt.
12 oz. Sugar.	¼ oz. Cinnamon.
8 oz. Margarine.	Egg colouring.
2½ oz. Yeast.	2 pts. Milk.

Method.—Dilute the yeast with luke-warm water and a little flour, stand ½ hour. Sieve the flour and rub in margarine. Make a bay and place in the sugar and salt. Dissolve with the milk, water, egg colour and bun spice. Break in the ferment and work into a fairly stiff dough, work until it comes away clear from the hands.

Let stand for ½ hour, fold in again, allow to stand for a further ½ hour and then roll out. Brush melted margarine over top, sprinkle with the currants a little sugar and cinnamon mixed, make into a roll, cut into portions, place upright on baking tray, allow to prove and bake in a hot oven.

280 Cherry Cakes.

9 lb. Flour.	1 lb. Broken glacé cherries.
5 lb. Sugar.	Egg colouring.
4 lb. Margarine.	4 pts. Milk.
12 Eggs.	
6 oz. Baking powder.	

Sift together baking powder, flour and salt.

Method.—Cream margarine and sugar together until light, add the eggs two at a time, beating continually. Add a little egg colour to the milk, and gradually beat into the mixture, alternatively with the flour, until both are absorbed. Fold in the broken cherries. Place into paper-lined hoops, or serving dishes, smooth the top with a little milk and bake for about 2 hours in a moderate oven.

281 Coco-nut Buns.

6 lb. Flour.
1½ lb. Margarine.
1¼ lb. Sugar.
3 oz. Baking powder.

1 lb. Desiccated coco-nut.
2 pts. Milk.

Method.—Cream margarine and sugar together. Sieve flour and baking powder, rub creamed margarine and sugar into it, until a sandy mixture is obtained. Add desiccated coco-nut. (Retain a little for decoration.)

Add egg colour (if desired) to the milk. Make a bay with other ingredients, add the milk and make into a fairly stiff paste. Divide into portions, mould into balls and flatten out ½-inch thick on the remainder of the coco-nut. Turn over, place on lightly greased baking trays, and bake in a normal oven for 20 minutes until a golden colour.

282 Coco-nut Cake.

8 lb. Flour.
5 lb. Sugar.
6 oz. Baking powder.
4 lb. Margarine.
12 Eggs.

4 lb. Coco-nut.
½ oz. Salt.
Egg colouring.
4 pts. milk.

Method.—*See* recipe No. 280, using coco-nut in place of cherries.

283 Currant Buns.

6 lb. Flour.
2½ oz. Yeast.
1½ lb. Currants.
8 oz. Margarine.

12 oz. Caster sugar.
1 oz. Salt.
Egg colouring.
2 pts. Milk.

Method.—Prepare the bun dough (*see* recipe No. 278). Add the currants, cover, and allow to stand in a warm place. Fold, and leave to stand again. Scale off in

3-*oz.* pieces, divide each in two and roll into balls. Place on a lightly greased baking tray. Allow to stand again for approximately 20 minutes. Bake in the top of a hot oven (approximately 20 minutes) and brush over with bun wash while hot.

284 Doughnuts.

See recipe No. 244.

Method.—Prepare a bun dough. Scale off into 100 pieces, and mould into balls. Allow to prove in a warm place (not in steam prover) for approximately 20 minutes. Drop into hot fat (not too hot) and allow to fry for 20 minutes, turning over with a wire slice from time to time, until a golden colour. Well drain on a cloth and roll in sugar and cinnamon. Currants may be added before moulding. If desired a small hole can be made after frying and jam inserted with a paper cavet. Afterwards roll in sugar. Can also be split on one side and filled with butter cream, afterwards rolled in sugar and cinnamon.

285 Fruit Cakes (Small).

9 lb. Flour.	12 Eggs.
4 lb. Margarine.	4 lb. Mixed fruit.
5 lb. Sugar.	4 pts. Milk.

Method.—Prepare a cake mixture (*see* recipe No. 280), add the mixed fruit and fill greased and papered cake tins (6 or 12 pattern). Smooth the top and bake in moderate oven for approximately 1 hour.

286 Fruit Pies (Individual).

8 lb. Flour.	6 lb. Dried fruits (or
3 lb. Margarine.	18 lb. fresh fruit).
1 oz. Salt.	Water for paste.
2¼ lb. Sugar.	

Method.—Prepare a short paste (*see* recipe No. 268) and the fruit (dried or fresh). Roll out paste ¼ inch thick and cut in rounds 2½ inches diameter. Place the fruit on half the rounds, wet the edges, cover with the remaining rounds of paste, press round the edges and notch with the back of a knife. Place on a baking tray, brush over with a little milk and sprinkle with sugar. Allow to relax ½ hour then bake in a hot oven for 35–40 minutes.

287 Ginger Cake.

9 lb. Flour.	12 Eggs.
5 lb. Sugar.	1½ lb. Peel.
6 oz. Ground ginger.	2 oz. Salt.
4 lb. Margarine.	8 pts. Milk.
6 oz. Baking powder.	

Method.—Mix flour, baking powder, salt and ground ginger. Cream the margarine and sugar, add the eggs one at a time, add milk and flour alternately, finish with flour, and add the crystallized ginger. Fill into buttered and prepared tins, smooth top with a little milk and bake in a normal oven for approximately 2 hours.

288 Gooseberry Pie.

25 lb. Gooseberries.	3¼ lb. Sugar.

Short Paste, recipe No. 268.

Method.—*See* Apple Pie, recipe No. 220, same preparation, using gooseberries (topped, tailed and washed) in place of the apples.

289 Jam Puffs.

See Puff Paste, recipe No. 256. Filling, 3 lb. plum and apple jam.

Method.—Prepare the puff paste. Roll out approximately to ¼-inch thickness and cut into 5 to 6-inch triangles. Place a spoonful of jam in the centre, wet the edges and bring the points towards the centre, sealing them. Turn over and place on a baking sheet, brush over with a little milk, sprinkle with sugar and bake in fairly hot oven for approximately 25–30 minutes.

290 Queen Cakes.

4 lb. Flour.	4 Eggs.
1¾ lb. Sugar.	Vanilla essence.
2½ oz. Baking powder.	Egg colouring.
1 lb. Currants.	1½ pts. Milk.
1¾ lb. Margarine.	

Method.—Prepare a cake mixture (*see* Cherry Cake) with the ingredients. Grease and flour the patty tins, place a spoonful of mixture in each (about the size of an egg) and bake in a moderate oven for 20 minutes.

Yeast (Cont)

Effect of wrong treatments in Doughs.

If yeast used in liquor which is to hot (eg over 120°F)
  a) Yeast plant is killed
  b) Yeast losed fermenting power.

If yeast used in liquor which is to cold (Best fermentation 90°F)
  a) Action of yeast is retarded
  b) Rope may occur (bacteriological changes)
  c) Sour dough may result.

If too must liquor is used
  a) The dough will be to slack
  b) The dough will have no stability
  c) The dough will be sticky and unworkable
  d) Flat buns will result.

If too little liquor is used
  a) The dough will be to stiff
  b) The dough would lack elasticity
  c) Small buns would result

If the dough is to little worked
  a) The dough will be sticky.

If the dough is to little proved
  a) The dough is termed "green"
  b) Buns will be small
  c) Buns will go stale very quickly

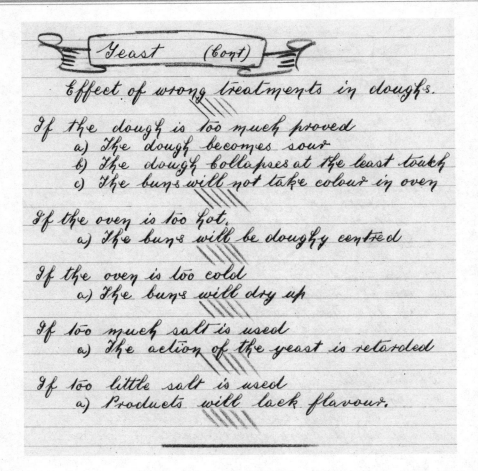

Yeast   (Cont)

Effect of wrong treatments in doughs.

If the dough is too much proved
a) The dough becomes sour
b) The dough collapses at the least touch
c) The buns will not take colour in oven

If the oven is too hot.
a) The buns will be doughy centred

If the oven is too cold
a) The buns will dry up

If too much salt is used
a) The action of the yeast is retarded

If too little salt is used
a) Products will lack flavour.

Basic Small Cake Mixture

Ingredients:-

Flour   - 6 lbs
Baking Pdr   - 3 oz
Marge   - 1½ lb
Sugar   - 1½ lbs
Salt   - ⅛ oz
Milk   - 2 Pts
Sprayed Egg   8 oz.

Method

a) Mix the B Pdr & Flour & sift
b) Rub in Marge finely.
c) Make a bay & place in sugar & salt
d) Pour in the milk & reconstituted egg
   and disolve the sugar and salt
e) Mix to a smooth dough

Chocolate Scones.:- In addition to basic ingredients
                    1 lb cocoa Pdr

Cheese Scones.:- In addition to basic ingredients
                 1½ lb cheese Pinch cayenne Pepper (No Sugar)

Chocolate Buns:- Substitute 6 oz of cocoa for 6 oz of
                 Flour in basic ingredients

Milk Scones :-

Rock Cakes :- In addition to basic ingredients
              1 lb currants, 6 oz chopped Peel

80 Suet Pudding and Syrup

8 lb. Flour	2 lb. Sugar
8 lb. Breadcrumbs	8 pts. Milk and water
6 lb. Suet	6 lb. Golden syrup (heated and
2 oz. Salt	thinned down with water)
8 oz. Baking powder	

Method.—Prepare the suet pudding in a similar manner to that shown in Recipe No. 91. Place the prepared mixture into floured pudding cloths, or greased empty jam tins, and either boil or steam for two to three hours. Remove, cut into sections and serve with the golden syrup sauce.

81 Marmalade Roll

8 lb. Flour	4 pts. Milk or water
8 lb. Breadcrumbs	2 oz. Salt
6 lb. Suet	8 oz. Baking powder
2 lb. Sugar	6 lb. Marmalade

Method.—Mix flour, baking powder and salt, add the chopped suet and breadcrumbs. Make a bay in the centre, add the milk or water and make into a fairly stiff dough. Allow to rest for half hour, cut equally into eight or nine pieces and roll out each one in a square, approximately half inch thick, spread with marmalade, wet edges with water, fold in the two outer edges, and roll up. Place into floured pudding cloths and tie up. Steam or boil for three hours. Serve with a marmalade sauce.

The sauce is made similarly to jam sauce, using marmalade instead of jam.

82 Bread and Jam Fritters

12 lb. Bread	Batter
6 lb. Jam	1 oz. Sugar
7 lb. Flour	½ oz. Salt
2 oz. Baking Powder	Water for batter as required

Method.—Slice bread, spread with jam. Make into sandwich cut into fingers, dip in batter (Recipe No. 35) and fry in deep fat. Serve with jam sauce or custard.

83 Oatmeal Golden Pudding

4 lb. Oatmeal	4 lb. Suet
4 lb. Flour	7 lb. Marmalade
4 lb. Breadcrumbs	Water as required

Method.—Mix together dry ingredients. Mix 3 lb. marmalade with the water. Stir into the dry ingredients to make a thick batter. Grease the basins or jam tins. Place ¼ lb. marmalade in each basin or tin. Two parts fill with the mixture. Cover securely with greased paper. Steam or boil for 2½ hours.

84 Currant Roll and White Sauce

8 lb. Flour	8 oz. Baking powder
8 lb. Breadcrumbs	6 lb. Suet
6 lb. Currants	2 lb. Sugar
2 oz. Salt	8 pts. Milk

75 Baroness Pudding with White Sauce

8 lb. Flour
8 lb. Breadcrumbs
6 lb. Suet
2 lb. Sugar

4 qts. Milk
6 lb. Sultanas or stone raisins
2 oz. Salt
8 oz. Baking powder
4 oz. spice (if available)

Method.—Remove all skin from suet and chop finely or pass through a mincer. Mix all dry ingredients together. Dilute the milk to make one gallon, with water. Make a bay with dry ingredients, add the milk and water and mix all together to form a fairly stiff paste. Place the mixture into floured pudding cloths to form a roll. Tie either end and one loose string round the centre. Steam, or boil, for three hours; or three-parts fill greased basins with the mixture and cover with greased paper to seal, place in boiling water. Leave uncovered and simmer gently.

If placed in cloths, put into boiling water and allow to simmer. Can also be made into puddings by using empty fruit tins or jam tins. Turn out and serve with white sauce.

76 Flan Paste

8 lb. Flour
1 lb. Sugar
3 lb. Margarine

Water for paste
1 oz. Salt

Method.—Sieve the flour and salt, make a bay and mix sugar and margarine together in the centre, add water and work lightly to make a fairly stiff paste. Care must be taken not to overwork the paste on account of the sugar.

77 Fruit Pie and White Sauce

20 lb. Fruit
12 lb. Flour
4 lb. Margarine or dripping

6 lb. Sugar
2 oz. Salt
4 oz. Baking powder

Method.—Make a short paste (Recipe No. 97). Prepare fruit, wash well. Fill the baking dishes, add the sugar, half-fill with water, wet edge, cover with short paste, thumb up, and bake for 30 minutes in a moderate oven. Serve with white sauce.

78 Open Fruit Tart

16 lb. Dried mixed fruits
2 lb. Sugar
Flan paste for cover (see Recipe No. 76).

Method.—Prepare the fruit, allow to cool. Line greased steel plates, or baking dishes, prick the bottoms and bake until half cooked. Fill in the fruit and finish baking. Brush over with hot syrup sauce and serve.

79 Stewed Figs or Prunes and White Sauce

16 lb. Figs or Prunes
2 lb. Sugar
2 gallons White sauce

Method.—Wash the figs and soak in plenty of water to allow for swelling overnight. Place on to boil, allow to simmer approximately for one hour together with the sugar until tender. Drain off the liquor and reduce by half. Pass on the figs and allow to cool.

Alternative Recipe

12 lb. Flour	2 lb. Sugar
4 lb. Breadcrumbs	6 lb. Suet
6 lb. Currants	1 lb. Mixed peel
2 oz. Salt	4 qts. Milk or water
8 oz. Baking powder	

Method.—Remove all skin and chop suet finely. Mix flour, baking powder and salt, add dry ingredients, mix together, make a bay in the centre, add the milk or water, and mix together to form a fairly stiff mixture. Steam or boil the mixture in basins, cloths or empty jam tins. Cook for three hours. Cut into sections and serve with a sweet white sauce.

85 Jam Roll and Jam Sauce

6 lb. Jam	2 oz. Salt
8 lb. Flour	8 oz. Baking powder
8 lb. Breadcrumbs	2 lb. Sugar
6 lb. Suet	4 pts. Milk or water

Method.—Similar preparation to Marmalade Roll using jam instead, see Recipe No. 81.

86 Sultana and Apple Roll

6 lb. Apple rings	6 lb. Suet
2 lb. Sultanas	2 lb. Sugar
8 lb. Flour	1 oz. Salt
8 lb. Breadcrumbs	8 oz. Baking powder

Method.—Soak the apple rings for 12 hours. Cook for one hour in short liquid together with the sugar. Drain and chop coarsely. Prepare the suet paste (see Recipe No. 84). Roll out into eight or nine squares. Cover each square with apple and sultanas, wet edges and roll up. Steam or boil, and serve with custard sauce.

87 Short Paste

For covering.

12 lb. Flour	4 oz. Baking powder
4 lb. Margarine or dripping	2 oz. Salt
	Water for paste

Method.—Mix the flour, baking powder and salt together. Rub in fat lightly and mix quickly to a stiff dough with water, Keep in a cool place and use as required.

88 Biscuit Golden Pudding

16 lb. Biscuits	6 lb. Marmalade
6 lb. Suet or dripping	2 tins Milk
8 oz. Baking powder	6 pts. Water

Method.—Crush the biscuits. Shred in the dripping or suet, add baking powder. Mix in half of the marmalade, milk and water, until all becomes a stiff dough. Cut up into 5 lb. pieces. Tie up tightly in a wet cloth. Place in boiling water and boil for 2½ hours. When taken out, allow to remain in the cloth for 10 minutes. Make a sauce with the remainder of the marmalade by adding hot water and letting it simmer. Serve with pudding.

Note.—After adding the water to the mixture, the pudding must be put on to boil as soon as possible.

Hospital Food

SECTION XIX

INVALID DIETARY

Simple Recipes for light diets which may be useful pending the admission to Hospital of a sick or wounded soldier.

Barley Water

Two ozs pearl barley boiled in 1 qt. of water for 20 minutes and afterwards allowed to stand until it becomes cold. Strain through a sieve into a jug, add a small piece of lemon peel. Should be kept covered.

Toast Water

Boil 1 qt of water and pour it on a good sized round of toast which has been well browned before a clear fire. Allow to steep for half an hour. It is then ready.

Sugar Water

To one pint of cold spring water add 1 oz of lump sugar and 1 tablespoonful of orange or lemon juice.

Arrowroot

To ½ pint of boiling water add rather more than ½ oz of arrowroot previously mixed in a teacup with a small quantity of cold water. Stir this on the fire until it boils for a few minutes. Pour into a basin. Flavour with a little sugar and a small spoonful of brandy, a little red or white wine, or a small piece of orange or lemon peel, which may be boiled with the arrowroot.

Sago or Tapioca

Boil 2 ozs of either in 1 pint of water for 20 minutes as directed for arrowroot. Sago may also be boiled in mutton, chicken or veal broth, or in beef tea.

Gruel

Take one teaspoonful of oatmeal and mix with a little water, and having poured this into a stewpan containing 1 pint of boiling water, stir the gruel on the fire for 10 minutes boiling. Pour into a basin, and add salt and butter. If preferred, rum, brandy or wine and sugar may be added.

Oatmeal Porridge

Boil one qt of water in a saucepan, as soon as it boils sprinkle in slowly a cupful of coarse oatmeal, stirring gently until it is thick and smooth enough, pour it at once into plates, and serve with milk and syrup.

Calves Foot Jelly

Put an ox foot into 2 qts of water, and gently simmer all day. The following day, remove the fat, strain, and cut the foot into four parts. Place altogether in a saucepan with ¾ lb of moist sugar, the juice and peel of 2 lemons, or oranges if preferred, and 2 eggs (whites, yolks and shells beaten up together). Bring slowly to boil, and boil quickly for eight minutes. Remove the foot, add ½ pint of cold water. Allow to stand for a little, then strain through a sieve or muslin.

Beef Tea

To each pound of beef allow 1 qt of water. Remove all fat and cut the meat (which should be rump or shin) into very small cubes. Put this into a clean stewpan, add the water and set on the fire to boil, remembering that as soon as the scum rises to the surface, it should be skimmed off with a spoon. A small quantity of cold water and salt should be poured in at the edge of the stew pan, in order to facilitate the rising of the albumen in the form of scum. Unless the skimming is properly done, the broth instead of becoming clear and bright, will be thick, muddy and unappetising.

When the beef has boiled gently for about ½ an hour, and is reduced to about half the original quantity, strain through a clean sieve or cloth into a basin, and serve with dry toast and salt.

If broth of a stronger character is required, double the quantity of meat which will produce a stimulating extract.

When the broth is required in a hurry, the meat should be chopped as fine as sausage meat, or passed through a mincing machine, put into a stewpan with boiling water, stirred on the fire for 10 minutes, and then strained through a cloth for use. The latter method should only be used in an emergency.

Mutton Broth

To each 1½ lbs of stewing mutton allow 1 qt of water, a little salt, 2 ozs of pearl barley. Chop the mutton into small pieces and place with the water in a stewpan, set to boil, skimming well, add a little salt and the barley. Boil gently for one hour. Strain off the broth through a sieve into a basin and serve with dry toast. A turnip and half a head of celery may be added where vegetables are not objected to.

Chicken Broth

Clean the chicken, scale the legs and remove the cuticle which covers them. Cut up into joints, leaving the breast whole, put the pieces into a clean stewpan with 1 qt of water, a little salt and 2 ozs of washed rice. Boil very gently for one hour, and when done, serve the broth with or without rice according to taste. The broth may also be garnished with some of the white meat cut into small dice if desired.

Onion Porridge

Take a large Spanish onion, peel and split into quarters, put these into a small saucepan with a pint of water, a pat of butter and a little salt. Boil gently until cooked, add a pinch of pepper. Thicken with flour, sago or cornflour and reboil.

Egg Flip

Break 2 eggs, beat the white to a froth, then add the yolks and rebeat. Fold into a cupful of hot milk, add one tablespoonful of brandy, a little sugar and a pinch of nutmeg.

Baked Egg Custard

Break up four eggs and one pint of milk, add two ozs of sugar and a little flavouring essence. Pour into a slightly greased mould, place this in a tin dish containing water and bake in a moderate oven until set; approximately 45 minutes. May be served hot or cold.

Junket

Heat up one pint of milk and 3 ozs of sugar to blood heat. Stir in ½ oz of essence of rennet. Run into serving dishes, sprinkle with grated nutmeg and allow to cool. Serve cold. Can be served with stewed fruit if desired.

Hospital Diet for Invalids.

__Horlicks__   2ozs. Horlicks Milk Powder.
        1pt. milk.

__Method.__ Cold: whisk horlicks powder into the milk
vigorously add sugar if required. Hot: Put powder
in jug add hot milk slowly, stirring well to prevent
lumps. Ovaltine: as above, half water can be used
where diluted milk diet is necessary.

All patent foods adhere rigorously to directions on
this unless a doctor prescribes different prescription
using any of the foods as used for invalids.

__Egg Blancmange.__   2ozs. Cornflour. 1½oz. sugar.
        1pt. milk.   1 egg.
        pinch of salt. 1 strip lemon rind
        Few drops of Essence as required.

Mix Cornflour to a paste with milk bring milk to boil
with lemon rind. When boiled remove rind add to
the paste stirring well, add sugar, essence, salt,
reboil, allow to cool for a few minutes - seperate yolk
from white, add yolk, whisk stiffly, then fold into
mixture, fill into a wet mould.

Left-Overs

LEFT-OVERS

Their Source, Composition and Uses

The great value attached to "left-overs" is in using them to supplement later meals and to save waste.

By "left-overs" is meant those portions of the cooked rations which are left after all the men have been served with their requirements.

It is most important that any such left-over food should be used as soon after its initial cooking as possible. Dishes made from left-overs should be supplied as adjuncts to the main dish or for the supper meal, the same day.

It is found, as a general rule, that foods which are fried are most popular; consequently, recipes for a number of fritters and rissoles will be found among the following suggestions:—

Recipes

Frying Batter may be made with yeast or eggs, or baking powder, but if none of these is available, a good batter may still be made with flour and water only. Any batter can be improved by the addition of frying oil or melted dripping at the rate of half pint per gallon mixture.

Ingredients: 7 lbs. flour
5 pts. water (approx.)
1 oz. salt.
1 oz. sugar
2 oz. baking powder

Left-over Bread

1 Dry in hotplate cr slow oven, make into brown crumbs and use for coating fish cakes, rissoles, tops of cottage pie, fish pie, etc. Will keep in this state for several weeks.

2 Fresh white crumbs can replace a percentage of flour inside boiled and steamed puddings, and may replace potatoe inside fish cakes, rissoles, etc. May also be used as a thickening medium for soups.

3 Dice and fry and serve with soup. Slice and fry and serve with sausages or bacon.

4 Use for bread and jam fritters.

5 Use for bread pudding, bread and butter pudding. Stuffings.

6 Use as a base for Welsh rarebit.

Left-over Cooked Potatoes
1 Mix with left-over cabbage as bubble and squeak.
2 Mix with cooked or tinned fish for fishcakes, rissoles, croquettes, fish pie, shepherds pie, etc.
3 Fry and serve with bacon or sausages.
4 Use as a thickening for soup.
5 Mix with minced meat for rissoles.
6 Fresh mashed potato may be used in pastry (75% flour, 25% potato).
7 Coat sausage with potato, dip in frying batter and fry in fat.

Left-over Vegetables
1 Cooked root vegetables can be cut up and used to garnish stews and soup.
2 Use for bubble and squeak.
3 Cooked green vegetables can be added to Hamburg roast.
4 Cooked root vegetables will warm up satisfactorily placed in boiling water, again brought to boil and drained off.

Left-over Puddings
1 Sultana Roll and similar puddings can be cut in half slices, sprinkled with a little sugar and fried gently in a little dripping and served as a tea meal.
2 Steamed puddings can also be satisfactorily reheated if a steamer is available.
3 Left-over puddings can also be minced into crumbs and added as fillings for fruit cakes.

Left-over Porridge (Unsweetened)
1 Drop spoonful into hot shallow fat and serve as fritters with bacon or sausage.
2 Mix with sausage meat and fry—"Sausage Cake".
3 Mix with next morning's issue.
4 Use as a thickening medium for soups.

Left-over Porridge (Sweetened)
1 Fry as a fritter and serve with a little jam sauce.
2 Australian flap-jack.

Left-over Corned Beef or Meat Roll
1 Dip in frying batter and serve as a fritter.
2 Use in the same manner as left-over fresh meat.

Left-over Fresh Meat
1 Stew or soup or any liquid should be brought to boil then rapidly cooled before putting in the larder.
2 Use for Cottage pie, rissoles, Cornish pasties, Toad-in-the-hole.
3 Stew can be added to meat for meat and potato pie, can also be minced and added to prepared mince.

Left-over pieces of Cheese
1 Welsh rarebit.
2 Cheese and potato pie (covered with crust or potato).
3 Cheese and potato paste for spreading on bread—50% grated cheese. 50% dry mashed potato.

Left-over Sausages—Cooked

1. Mince and use in croquettes, rissoles, pasties, Shepherds pie.
2. Cut into thick slices, reheat in some good brown sauce and serve with savoury rice (supper dish).
3. Sandwiches (haversack ration).
4. Fried in batter (serve with tomato sauce).

Cooked, Stewed Beef

1. Reheat and serve with savoury rice (supper meal).
2. Put on for curry, cooking less meat accordingly, serve with rice.
3. Mince and use for croquettes fried in batter, Shepherds pie, mix with dry mashed potatoes, season well and treat as bubble and squeak for breakfast. This could be served with a rasher of bacon.

N.B.—During the hot months perishable left-overs such as meat, fish, etc.. will on no account be kept overnight.

STOCK POT

Where bones are available a stock pot will be kept in all cookhouses—Stock is the basis of Soups, Gravies, Stews, Meat Pies, and Braising.

White Stock

40 lb. Beef bones.
5 lb. Onions.
5 lb. Carrots
2½ lb. Leeks.

Produces 38 qts. of stock.

Method.—Chop bones into pieces about four inches in length. Place in a large pot. Cover the bones with nine gallons of fresh, cold water and bring quickly to the boil on a good fire. Scum must be removed from the surface as it rises. Add another gallon of cold water and bring the pot to the boil again. **Frequently remove all fat by skimming.** (This should be placed in a receptacle containing clean cold water.) After fat is removed allow pot to simmer for four hours. Peel and add vegetables, seasoning, and allow pot to simmer for a further two hours. (Carrots and onions should be added whole.) Remove all vegetables (these can be used as a vegetable garnish) and finally remove any further fat which may have formed on the stock. Pass liquid from pot through a clean fine cloth into another clean pot, return to fire and reboil. Stock is now ready to be used as required.

Special Note.—Sides of pot, owing to' reduction by evaporation, should be kept clean.

Brown Stock

Quantities as for White Stock.

Method.—Bones for brown stock should be meaty, chopped and roasted (without the addition of dripping), gaining colour evenly and quickly. Proceed as for white stock. The vegetables, when peeled, must be cut into approximately 1-inch dice. In hot, shallow fat, fry on the vegetables to an even brown colour, and after straining off any fat add to bone stock (as in the case of white stock). The process is the same in all stocks.

Meat

5 Bacon and Haricot Stew

8 lb. Bacon (pieces will do)
10 lb. Haricot beans
1 lb. Flour
1 lb. Onions
Stock
4 oz. Margarine
1 lb. Celery if available

Method.—Soak the beans overnight with boiling water. Wash them, cover with stock, add the bacon and bring to boil, allow to cook for about one hour. Chop the onion, fry it lightly in a little stock skimmings and add to the beans, allow to cook for about another hour until the beans are cooked. Remove the bacon and cut into slices. Mix the flour into a very smooth paste with the margerine, add some of the hot stock gradually, then return it to the beans shaking vigorously and mixing well together without breaking the beans. Simmer for a few minutes to cook flour. Correct seasoning and serve hot with the slices of bacon.

N.B.—**If tinned bacon is used,** do not add to the beans, but serve separately.

6 Bacon and Potato Stew

8 lb. Bacon pieces
50 lb. Potatoes
Stock
2 lb. Onions
1½ lb. Flour
4 oz. Dripping or Stock Skimmings

Method.—Slice or separate the bacon, fry until tender or warm through, grease the serving dishes or baking tins and place a layer of sliced potatoes on the bottom; follow with a layer of sliced carrots, then bacon, then carrots and finally a thick layer of potatoes, brush with melted dripping, sprinkle with breadcrumbs, brush with stock. Bring to the boil, bake to a golden brown, serve with good brown gravy.

Bacon and Potato Pie

65 lb. Potatoes	1 lb. Flour
12½ lb. Bacon (prepared) or	2 lb. Dripping
tinned bacon	2 lb. Breadcrumbs
10 lb. Carrots	Stock

Method.—Chop the onions fine, fry them in the dripping for a few minutes (without colour) add the bacon pieces, cut into small cubes and continue to fry for a further few minutes being careful not to colour the onion, add the flour, stir well and cook slowly for five minutes. Add the potatoes even sized (large potatoes should be cut in quarters) cover with stock, season, stir and bring to the boil. Cook for 30 to 35 minutes and serve hot.

N.B.—**If tinned bacon is used** add after the potatoes are cooked.

8 Pease Pudding

Soak peas overnight in plenty of cold water. Wash well, place into saucepan, cover with cold water, add salt, bring to the boil. Skim, add whole carrots, onions and knuckle of bacon. Allow to simmer until tender. When cooked remove garnish and knuckle of bacon and strain, keeping the liquor. Pass through sieve and return to saucepan. Add margarine, pepper, correct the seasoning and mix in sufficient of its own liquor to make it a mashed potato consistency.

9 Bacon and Sausage Cake

12½ lb. Bacon (prepared) or tinned
12¼ lb. Sausage cake

Method.—Form sausage meat into 2-oz. cakes, dust with flour, fry in shallow bacon fat until the blood percolates through. Turn over and fry the other side a nice golden colour. Can be fried lightly either side and finished off in a slow oven until they are firm to the touch. Fry the bacon and serve.

10 Braised Bacon and Cabbage

40 lb. Cabbage (unprepared)	2 qts. Stock
1 lb. Carrots	1 qt. Fat from stock pot
1 lb. Onions	2 qts. Brown sauce
12½ lb. Bacon prepared or tinned	1 oz. Salt
1 lb. Bacon trimmings	

Method.—Clean the cabbage, cut into quarters, cook in boiling salted water for 5 minutes. Drain in a colander. Peel and slice carrots and onions, place into saucepan, add bacon trimmings, fry on lightly. Place quartered cabbage on sliced carrots, onions, etc., half cover with stock and white stock-pot dripping, and bring to the boil. Cover with lid, and braise in oven until tender. (Time approximately one hour.) Remove cabbage, strain stock, remove all fat, reduce stock and add to the brown sauce. Serve with the cabbage.

N.B.—**If fresh bacon is used** cook the bacon underneath the cabbage.

If tinned bacon is used prepare and heat separately.

Care must be taken in adding salt as the bacon may be salty in itself.

11 Spinach

Remove coarse stalks from spinach. Wash the leaves thoroughly in plenty of salt water. Cook in boiling salt water until tender, using only sufficient water to well cover the bottom of boiler. Allow to cook until stalks are tender, drain well, and press between two plates, cut into portions. Serve with bacon.

28 Vienna Steak

20 lb. Minced Beef (raw) (prepared)	¼ oz. Pepper
6 lb. Breadcrumbs	2 lb. Dripping
6 lb. Cooked savoury rice	1 gallon Brown sauce
3 lb. Onions	
2 oz. Salt	

Chop and stew onions and allow to cool

Method.—Prepare steaks by mixing the minced raw beef with the onions, breadcrumbs, salt, pepper, add cooked rice. Mould into a 100 portions, medallion shape, with a little flour. Fry off in hot dripping and finish cooking in the oven. Serve with brown sauce and fried onions.

29 Meat and Potato Pie

50 lb. Potatoes	Salt
37½ lb. Meat (unprepared)	Pepper
4 lb. Onions if available, or	
2 lb. Leeks	

Short Pastry

12 lb. Flour	4 oz. Baking powder
4 lb. Margarine or dripping	Water for pastry
2 oz. Salt	

Method.—Cut the beef into one inch pieces, slice the onions and potatoes, season with salt, pepper, fill the serving dishes, baking dishes or pie dishes with alternate layers of meat, onion and potato, barely cover with water, correct the seasoning, make a short paste (see Recipe No. 87) and cover the dishes with pastry, bake in a moderate oven for two to three hours before serving, fill up with gravy if necessary.

30 Cottage Pie

37½ lb. Meat (unprepared) (or 20 lb. cooked and prepared meat)	1 lb. Dripping
	50 lb. Potatoes
6 lb. Onions	4 qt. Brown sauce
1 lb. Margarine	2 lb. Breadcrumbs

Method.—Chop the onions finely, heat the dripping and fry the onions lightly without taking colour. Add the meat (cut into small dice or coarsely minced), season with salt and pepper. Bind with a little of the sauce and bring to the boil. Place in baking-tins, or frying pans from No. 1 cooker, cover them with dry mashed potatoes, smooth over, sprinkle with breadcrumbs, melted margarine and bake a golden brown in a quick oven. Serve the rest of the sauce separately.

N.B.—If raw meat is used, allow to cook.

31 Curried Beef and Rice

37½ lb. Beef (unprepared)	1½ lb. Curry powder
8 lb. Onions	7 lb. Rice
4 lb. Flour	1 oz. Pepper
1 lb. Sultanas	4 oz. Salt
1 lb. Apple Rings. Cook the Apple Rings.	

Method.—Chop the onions finely, fry to a light golden colour. Add the beef cut into small dice and colour also. Add curry powder. Allow to cook five minutes, add flour and allow this to cook to a sandy texture. Add sultanas, chopped apple rings, cover with boiling stock and season. Bring to boil and simmer for 1½ hours. Meanwhile, plain boil the rice in plenty of boiling salt water (time approximately 15 minutes), refresh and reheat in boiling salt water. Drain and serve with curry.

32 Steak Pie

37½ lb. Beef (unprepared)	4 oz. Baking powder
3 lb. Onions	Seasoning
12 lb. Flour	Stock
4 lb. Dripping or margarine	

Method.—Cut the beef into half-inch dice. Chop onions, mix with the meat, and well season with salt and pepper. Place into baking tins or frying pans (No. 1 cooker), cover with stock or water. Make a paste from flour, dripping, baking powder and water (see Recipe No. 42), cover dishes and bake in moderate oven two to three hours. Fill up with gravy.

N.B.—Meat can be stewed first, but must be cold before covering with pastry.

33 Brown Stew

37½ lb. Meat (unprepared)	2 lb. Dripping
3 lb. Flour	6 lb. Haricot beans
6 lb. Onions	2 oz. Salt
6 lb. Carrots	Stock

Method.—Cut meat into large cubes. Season. Heat dripping in pan. Fry on meat quickly to seal pores, add carrots and onions cut into half-inch cubes. Fry on together. Dust with the flour and cook in oven for 10 minutes.

Cover with stock or water and bring to boil, add the salt and skim. Cook slowly in oven for two hours.

Soak the beans overnight, cover with hot water, bring to boil, skim, season, add two onions and two carrots and simmer until cooked.

Drain off liquor. Remove stew from the oven. Skim, correct colour, consistency, add seasoning and beans. Serve.

PRESERVED MEAT

34 Savoury Steaks

25 lb. Preserved meat	Pepper
6 lb. Breadcrumbs	2 lb. Dripping
3 lb. Onions	1 gallon good Brown sauce
2 oz. Salt	

Method.—Pass preserved meat through mincing machine. Fry the onions, allow to get cold. Mix the meat, cooked onions, breadcrumbs, salt and pepper. Mould into round shapes with a little flour and breadcrumbs. Fry off in hot dripping and finish cooking in the oven. Serve with brown sauce.

35 Preserved Beef Fritters

35 lb. Preserved meat	1 oz. Sugar
Batter for frying	1 oz. Salt
7 lb. Flour	Water as required
2 oz. Baking Powder.	½ pt. frying Oil or dripping

Batter for frying :—

Method.—Sieve the flour, add the salt and sugar, mix well. Place in a basin, make a bay in the middle, mix all together with sufficient water, making a paste, add oil or melted dripping. Paste to be thick enough to well coat the back of a spoon, add baking powder just before using.

Cut the meat into thick slices, pass through prepared batter, fry in hot fat until brown.

N.B.—If baking powder is not available, proceed as follows :—

Make a smooth batter with flour and water, cut the meat into thick slices, prepare some breadcrumbs, dip the meat into the batter and pass through the breadcrumbs. Fry in hot fat until brown.

36 Meat and Vegetable Roast

20 lb. Preserved beef (prepared)	6 lb. Dry mashed potatoes or rice
10 lb. Carrots	
10 lb. Turnips	1 lb. Dripping
3 lb. Onions	Salt and pepper to taste

Method.—Chop the onions, carrots and turnips and fry them in the dripping without taking colour. When cooked allow to get cold. Pass the meat through a mincer, add the cooked vegetables and dry mashed potatoes or rice (it is important that the vegetables and potatoes are cold when mixing with raw meat), season well, salt and pepper to taste. Mix thoroughly then divide into sections each sufficient for 12 persons. Roll out into the shape of a large roll. Place in greased baking tins and baste with a little dripping. Bake in a moderate oven for about one hour. Roll in breadcrumbs or oatmeal and colour off in the oven. Slice and arrange neatly on dish, serve with a good brown sauce or thickened gravy.

37 Preserved Meat and Vegetable Pudding or Roll

Filling   20 lb. Preserved beef
10 lb. Carrots
6 lb. Turnips
1 lb. Onions
5 pts. Water
Salt and pepper to taste

Suet Paste 16 lb. Flour
6 lb. Suet
8 oz. Baking powder
2 oz. Salt
Pepper
Water to make a light dough

Method.—Chop the onion, carrot and turnips. Cut the meat into one inch dice, place in a bowl, add chopped vegetables, water, season well with salt and pepper.

Make a fairly stiff dough as follows:—Place the flour into a bowl, add the chopped suet, salt and baking powder, mix well, make a well, add water and mix into dough. If pudding basins are available—grease the basins, line with dough. Fill with the prepared filling, wet the edge of the dough, cover with dough. Thumb up the edges, cover with greased paper and steam for four hours.

If pudding basins are not available, proceed as follows:—Place a pudding cloth in a G.S. baking tin, divide the dough into 18 equal pieces, roll out to a square, lay the dough on the pudding cloth previously floured. The G.S. tin acts as a mould. Divide the filling into 18 equal parts, place the filling on the dough, fold over the ends of the dough, wet the edges, and fold over, then the cloth; and holding the ends firmly remove from the G.S. baking tin and roll lightly. Tie the ends firmly and tie lightly in the middle. Place in a saucepan or soyer of boiling water and simmer for three hours. Serve with a good thickened gravy, each roll is sufficient for six men.

N.B.—Puddings can be cooked in empty fruit or similar tins, if pudding basins or cloths are not available.

38 Preserved Beef Pie

30 lb. Preserved meat
3 lb. Onions
1 gallon Brown sauce
8 lb. Flour

1 oz. Salt
3 lb. Dripping or margarine
Water for paste
2 oz. Baking powder

Method.—Chop the onions as for stew, fry to a golden colour. Carefully slice the meat, arrange in pie dish or baking tins. Add sufficient sauce to cover. Make the pastry with the flour, baking powder and salt, rub in the fat lightly and mix to a stiff dough. Cover the pie with the pastry. Bake until brown.

No. 7 SAVOURY SAUSAGES.

Ingredients—

12 lbs. Soya Link Sausage.

12 lbs. Tinned Meat.

4 lbs. Tinned Bacon (if available).

Potatoes, Biscuits or Bread for binding.

1 oz. Mixed Herbs.

A little Curry Powder may be added if desired.

Method.—Pass all ingredients twice through the mincer or knead well together. Make into sausage shapes, pass through thin batter and brown breadcrumbs. Fry shallow fat.

No. 9 SCOTCH EGGS.

Ingredients—

100 Eggs.

20 lbs. Tinned Meat.

3 lbs. Potatoes.

Pepper to taste.

Brown Sauce.

Method.—Hard boil the eggs, Mince the beef or well knead, season and add sufficient sauce to make the mixture workable. Shell, wash and dry the eggs, wrap a portion of the meat round each egg (approx. 4 ozs.), and pass through batter and breadcrumbs. Fry in deep or shallow fat. Serve hot or cold with suitable sauce.

No. 10 FRITTERS.

Ingredients—

    25 lbs. Tinned Meat.

    3 lbs. Onions.

    6 lbs. Breadcrumbs.

    1 oz. Mixed Herbs (if available).

A little Curry Powder or Pepper.

Brown Sauce to moisten.

Batter—

    7 lbs. Flour.

    1 oz. Salt.

    2 ozs. Baking Powder.

Milk or Water as required.

Method.—Boil the onions. Pass the meat and onions twice through the mincer or knead well. Add the breadcrumbs, herbs, curry powder, well mix together with sufficient brown sauce to the required consistency. Mould croquette shape, pass through batter and fry deep fat.

No. 12 OMELETS (suitable for Officers & Sgts. Messes).

Ingredients.—Meat mixture as for Fritters excluding mixed herbs and curry powder. Allow 2 eggs per man.

Method.—Beat the eggs, season and pour into an omelet pan containing very hot fat. Stir briskly with a fork in order to heat the whole mass evenly. Add the garnish before rolling up. The whole process should be done speedily.

No. 17 " EASTCOM " PASTRY ROLL (originated by Catering Section, H.Q. Eastern Command).

Ingredients—

25 lbs. Tinned Meat.

3 lbs. Onions.

5 lbs. Carrots.

3 lbs. Rice.

25 Eggs.

2 ozs. Mixed Herbs.

2 lbs. Margarine.

Pepper.

Stock.

16 lbs. Short Paste.

Method.—Boil the rice in a good stock with 1 lb. of onions—allow to cool. Boil the carrots and allow to cool. Chop and fry the remainder of the onions. Pass the tinned meat through the mincer, add the onions, pepper, herbs, moisten with stock and well mix. Roll out the pastry 12″ square and wash the edges. Place the rice down the centre of the pastry. Place hard boiled eggs (quartered) along the centre of the rice with a row of carrots either side. Cover with the meat mixture, fold over the pastry, seal the edges shaping into a roll. Eggwash and bake in moderate oven. Serve with a little hot melted margarine or a good Espagnole Sauce.

No. 34 AMERICAN HOT POT.

Ingredients—

    25 lbs. Tinned Meat.

    40 lbs. Potatoes.

    3 lbs. Onions.

    10 lbs. Tomatoes.

    Seasoning.

    Brown Stock.

    2 ozs. Chopped Parsley.

Method.—Cut the meat into half inch cubes. Shred onions parboil in stock. Boil potatoes in jackets, skin and cut into $\frac{1}{4}$ inch slices, arrange a layer of potatoes in bottom of baking dish, then layer of meat and sliced onions, season, sprinkle with chopped parsley. Repeat until dish is $\frac{3}{4}$ full. Top layer should be of sliced tomatoes (if unavailable potatoes), barely cover with stock and finish cooking in a moderate oven for 15 minutes.

Fish

73   Fried Codsteak and Chips.

    50 lb. Cod (Headless).
    40 lb. Potatoes.
    Batter (*See* recipe No. 72.)

Method.—Clean, wash and cut the cod into steaks. Season with salt and pepper, pass through frying batter and place into a pan of hot deep fat. Allow to cook for 8 minutes. When cooked they should be a golden brown colour. Drain on a cloth and serve with fried chips. Fried chips, *see* recipe No. 178.

74   Codsteak Meuniere.

    As for recipe No. 79. Using codsteaks instead of fillets.

75   Codsteak Lyonnaise Sauce.

    37½ lb. Cod (Headless).   2 oz. Salt.
    3 lb. Dripping.   1 gallon lyonnaise sauce.
    2 lb. Flour.

Method.—Clean, wash and cut the cod into steaks. Season with salt, pepper. Pass through flour. Heat the dripping in a frying pan, add the steaks and let them fry until a golden brown. Turn steaks over and repeat the process. Remove from the pan and serve with lyonnaise sauce.

76   Steamed Cod and Egg or Parsley Sauce.

    37½ lb. Cod fillets.   1 gallon egg or parsley
    2 oz. Salt.   sauce.
    4 Lemons.

Method.—Skin the fillets and cut them into 6-oz. individual portions, place into a clean steaming tray, sprinkle with salt and lemon juice. Cover with grease-proof paper and steam until cooked. Dish up and serve with 1 gallon of egg or parsley sauce.

77   Fried Curled Whiting.

    100 × 6 oz. Whiting.
    4 lb. Breadcrumbs.
    Batter for crumbing.

Method.—Clean, wash and skin the whiting without removing the head. Curl by placing tail into mouth. Pass through flour, a thin flour and water batter and then into fresh white breadcrumbs. Place on a wire frying grill and fry in hot deep fat until a golden colour, approximately 5 minutes. Drain and serve.

78 Fish Cutlet, Robert Sauce.

10 lb. Cooked fish, free from bones.	2 oz. Salt.
	¼ oz. Pepper.
1 bott. Anchovy essence.	Batter for crumbing.
25 lb. Potatoes.	4 lb. Breadcrumbs.

Method.—Flake the fish and add to dry mashed potatoes. Add the anchovy essence and necessary seasoning. Heat up together to boiling point. Lay out on a clean table or trays, and allow to cool. Mould into 1 × 4 oz. piece, or 2 × 2 oz. pieces, pass through flour and a thin batter made of flour and water, also fresh breadcrumbs. Shape into cutlets. Fry in hot deep fat.

79 Fillets of Cod fried in Butter.

37½ lb. Cod fillets.	4 oz. Chopped parsley.
2 lb. Flour.	½ pt. Vinegar.
1 oz. Salt.	3 Lemons.
3 lb. Margarine.	

Method.—Cut the fillet into 6-oz. portions, season and pass through flour. Heat the margarine in a frying pan, and sauté the fish until a golden colour, turn it over and finish the cooking. Place the fish on a dish with a slice of peeled lemon on top, sprinkle with vinegar and pour the hot melted margarine over the fish. Sprinkle with coarsely-chopped parsley.

80 Fillet of Fish Fried.

37½ lb. Fillets of fish.

As for recipe No. 73. Using filleted fish in place of codsteaks.

81 Fish Cakes.

12 tins Salmon.	1 bott. Anchovy essence.
25 lb. prepared potatoes.	4 oz. Cayenne pepper.

Method.—As for recipe No. 78, shaped as medallions in place of cutlets.

Soups

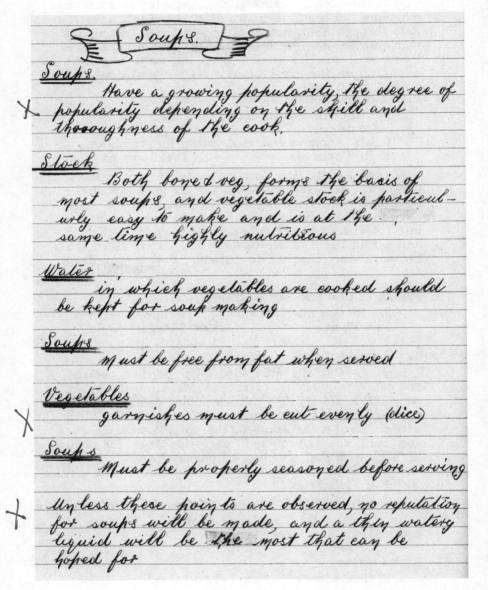

Soups.

Have a growing popularity, the degree of popularity depending on the skill and thoroughness of the cook.

Stock

Both boned veg, forms the basis of most soups, and vegetable stock is particularly easy to make and is at the same time highly nutritious

Water

in which vegetables are cooked should be kept for soup making

Soups

Must be free from fat when served

Vegetables

garnishes must be cut evenly (dice)

Soups

Must be properly seasoned before serving

Unless these points are observed, no reputation for soups will be made, and a thin watery liquid will be the most that can be hoped for

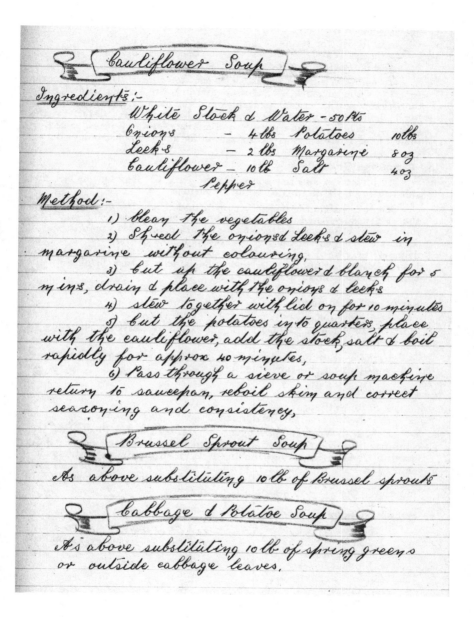

Cauliflower Soup

Ingredients:-

White Stock & Water — 50 Pts
Onions   — 4 lbs   Potatoes   10 lbs
Leeks   — 2 lbs   Margarine   8 oz
Cauliflower   — 10 lb   Salt   4 oz
                 Pepper

Method:-

1) Clean the vegetables
2) Shred the onions & leeks & stew in margarine without colouring.
3) Cut up the cauliflower & blanch for 5 mins, drain & place with the onions & leeks
4) Stew together with lid on for 10 minutes
5) Cut the potatoes into quarters, place with the cauliflower, add the stock, salt & boil rapidly for approx 40 minutes,
6) Pass through a sieve or soup machine return to saucepan, reboil skim and correct seasoning and consistency,

Brussel Sprout Soup

As above substituting 10 lb of Brussel sprouts

Cabbage & Potatoe Soup

As above substituting 10 lb of spring greens or outside cabbage leaves.

II.—SOUPS

12 Butter Bean Soup

10 lb. Butter beans	2 lb. Onions
25 qts. Water or stock	Bacon trimmings
2 lb. Carrots	4 oz. Salt

Method.—Wash the beans and soak overnight. Drain and cover with the water or stock, add the salt and bring to boiling point. Skim thoroughly, add the diced vegetables and the bacon trimmings. Simmer for 1½ hours, and if possible pass through a strainer. Return to the boiler and reboil. Skim carefully and simmer for 10 minutes, removing the scum as it rises. Correct the seasoning and the consistency. Serve.

13 Carrot and Bread Soup

As for carrot and rice soup (Recipe No. 16), leaving out rice and substituting 6 lb. diced fried bread as garnish.

Method.—Melt the margarine or dripping, add the diced onion and the thinly sliced and blanched carrots. Cover with a lid and stew slowly until tender. Add the stock and bring to boiling point, Season with salt. Cut the bread into squares and bake in the oven in a little dripping to a light golden colour, add to the soup and simmer for one hour. Mix thoroughly to a good consistency. Just bring to boil, correct the seasoning and consistency. Serve.

14 Carrot and Rice Soup

25 qts. Stock	4 lb. Onions
4 lb. Rice as garnish	½ lb. Margarine or dripping
14 lb. Carrotts	4 oz. Salt

Method.—Similar preparation to carrot and bread soup (Recipe No. 13) substituting rice for grilled bread.

15 Pea Soup

10 lb. Split peas
Other ingredients as for lentil soup. (Recipe No. 25.)

Method.—Wash and pick over the peas, then soak. Place them into saucepan, cover with water, add salt and bring to boiling point. Skim carefully, add the aromates, the diced vegetables. Simmer until tender, skimming when necessary. If possible, pass the soup through a strainer or mix thoroughly and reboil. Remove the scum and simmer for 10 minutes. Correct the seasoning, consistency, and serve.

16 Household Soup

25 qts. Stock	½ lb. Dripping
4 lb. Onions	5 lb. Lentils or peas (soaked)
4 lb. Carrots	1 lb. Celery
1 bunch Leeks	Salt and seasoning
10 lb. Potatoes	

Method.—Cut the onions, carrots, leeks, and celery into small squares. Melt the dripping, add these vegetables and stew until tender. Moisten with the stock, add the seasoning, and bring to boiling point. Add the lentils and the potatoes, cut into small pieces. Simmer very gently until cooked. Remove any fat. Correct the seasoning and serve.

17 Lentil Soup

14 lb.	Lentils	4 oz. Salt
25 qts.	Water	
2 lb.	Onions	
2 lb.	Carrots	
Bacon trimmings		

Method.—See Recipe No. 12.

18 Vegetable Soup

25 qts.	Stock	1 Large cabbage
4 lb.	Carrots	8 oz. Margarine or dripping
1 bunch	Leeks	Seasoning
7 lb.	Potatoes	If with rice add 2 lb. rice as
3 lb.	Onions	garnish
2 lb.	Turnips	

Method.—Melt the margarine or dripping, add the diced carrot, leeks, onions, cabbage and turnips, cover with a lid and stew until tender. Moisten with stock, add the cubed potatoes, bring to the boil and skim. Simmer until tender and pass through a strainer, or mix thoroughly, reboil, remove the scum, correct the seasoning and consistency and serve.

19 Beef Hot Pot

50 lb.	Potatoes	Salt and pepper to taste
37½ lb.	Beef (unprepared)	
6 lb.	Onions or	
6 lb.	Leeks	

Method.—Shred the onions and slice the potatoes ¼-inch thick, grease the frying pan or baking tins, place a layer of potatoes and onion in the bottom, cut the meat into one-inch pieces, season with salt, pepper, add the meat, fill up with onions and potatoes arranged in slices, half fill with well seasoned stock, bring to the boil, place in a moderate oven, cook slowly, press down occasionally with a slice. When cooked skim off all fat from the surface, correct the seasoning.

20 Braised Beef with Vegetables

37½ lb.	Meat (unprepared)	5 qts. Brown Sauce
14 lb.	Onions	5 qts. Brown Stock
14 lb.	Carrots	1 lb. Dripping
12 lb.	Turnips	Salt.

Method.—Fry joints in shallow fat until brown. Remove, and quickly colour the vegetables, previously cut into suitable sizes. Strain vegetables, replace joints and vegetables in tin. Add stock and Brown Sauce—boil; remove fat; cover with lid, and place in moderate oven until cooked. Slice meat against the grain, arrange in dishes with the vegetables. Boil up gravy, remove all fat; add to meat, and serve.

21 Braised Steaks and Carrots

37½ lb.	Beef (unprepared)	2 lb. Flour
	cut into 4-oz. steaks	2 lb. Dripping
33 lb.	Carrots	
4 lb.	Onions	

Method.—Cut beef into steaks and dust with flour and fry in hot shallow fat. Place steaks in baking dishes, add carrots and onions which has been sliced and lightly fried in dripping, sprinkle with flour, brown, cover with stock, bring to boil, simmer and cook till tender.

Liver Soup.

25 qts. brown Stock.
2 lbs. carrots.
2 lbs. onions.
1 lb. flour.
2 lbs. dripping.
2 lbs. liver minced or cut up.
4 ozs. salt.
1 faggot.

Method. Melt dripping till smoking hot, fry vegts. to a golden brown, brown the flour. gradually add the stock. Seasoning & faggot. Simmer gently 2 hrs., Strain & add the liver, (browned) if not previously cooked and Simmer for another hour. Season & serve.

Kidney same as above.

Sauces

SAUCES.

No. 35 ESPAGNOLE (24 hrs. production).

Ingredients.—1st Stage.

16 Gallons Beef Stock.
8 lbs. Braised Carrots.
8 lbs. Braised Onions.
4 lbs. Browned Flour.
16 lbs. Crushed Bones.
1 Small Garlic.
Pinch Thyme.
2 Bay Leaves.
$\frac{1}{4}$ oz. Peppercorns.
12 Cloves.
12 ozs. Salt (approx.).
4$\frac{1}{2}$ lbs. Ham Bones.
14 lbs. Tomatoes.
Pinch Pepper.

Produces 6 gallons.

Method.—Measure 15$\frac{1}{2}$ gallons of beef stock into stock pot, add braised carrots, onions and braised bones, also boquet of garni, salt, pepper, ham bones and tomatoes. Dilute browned flour with $\frac{1}{2}$ gallon of stock and add to mixing. Simmer for 24 hours. Strain.

Ingredients.—2nd Stage.

8 Gallons Beef Stock.
9$\frac{1}{2}$ lbs. Braised Bones.
4$\frac{3}{4}$ lbs. Braised Carrots.
9$\frac{1}{2}$ lbs. Braised Onions.
Pinch of Thyme.
2 Bay Leaves.
Salt and Pepper (to taste).
2 Cloves of Garlic.

Produces 1$\frac{1}{2}$ gallons.

Method.—After the last stage has been cooking 18 hours, prepare the 2nd stage as follows. measure into a clean stock pot 8 gallons of beef stock, add braised bones, carrots, onions and boquet of garni, season to taste. Simmer for 6 hours.

Ingredients.—3rd Stage.

6 Gallons, 1st Stage Stock.
1$\frac{1}{2}$ Gallons, 2nd Stage Stock.
6 lbs. Tomatoes.

Produces 6$\frac{1}{2}$ gallons.

Method.—Pound the tomatoes. Transfer 6 gallons of 1st stage into a stock pot, then add 1$\frac{1}{2}$ gallons of 2nd stage bring to boil, add tomatoes, cook 45 minutes. Strain and serve.

309 Lyonnaise.

4 qts. Espagnole sauce.	½ pt. Vinegar.
1 lb. Onions.	3 oz. Dripping.

Method.—Peel and finely shred the onions ; melt the dripping and lightly fry the shredded onions. Add the vinegar and boil until reduced by half. Add the espagnole sauce, bring to the boil, season well with salt and pepper, skim before using.

310 Gravy for roast joints.

This should be made from residue in roasting tins when joints are cooked.

Method.—When joints are being roasted, certain meat juices escape and mix with the melting fat. Remove the joint and heat the contents of the pan to a temperature which will evaporate the moisture and leave behind when strained, a substance resembling meat extract ; care must be taken not to burn. To this, brown stock should be added to make a sufficient quantity of gravy.

Approximate quantity 1½ gallons for each 100 men— ½ gill a man.

SPECIAL NOTE.—Season if necessary.

311 White.

1 lb. Flour.	4 qts. Milk.
¾ lb. Margarine.	Salt to taste.

Method.—Melt margarine in saucepan without frying. Add the flour, stirring to form a smooth paste, care being taken to keep the mixture from sticking to the sides of saucepan. Allow the mixture to cook without taking colour until it attains a sandy texture then allow to cool slightly. (This is technically known as a white roux). Boil the milk and add gradually to the roux, mixing well to prevent lumpiness. When all milk is absorbed, add the salt and allow to boil gently for ½ hour. The sauce is now ready for use.

SPECIAL NOTE.—It should not be necessary to pass this sauce if it is correctly mixed at the beginning. This recipe is one for a foundation white sauce. More milk or other flavouring must be added as required.

312 Anchovy.

Proceed as for White Sauce, adding twelve table-spoonfuls of anchovy essence.

313 Caper.

4 oz. Margarine.	2 qts. Mutton stock.
8 oz. Flour.	8 oz. Capers.
2 oz. Salt.	

Proceed as for White Sauce and work in the strained-off mutton liquor little by little, working with a wooden spoon and keeping smooth. Allow to simmer 20 minutes and add the capers. Correct seasoning.

314 Mustard.

1 lb. Margarine.	2 qts. Milk.
1 lb. Flour.	2 qts. Water.
4 oz. Mustard.	Salt.

Method.—Proceed as for White Sauce. Add the boiling milk and water little by little, until all is absorbed, stirring briskly to prevent lumps forming. Allow to simmer 20 minutes. Mix the mustard and add; correct the seasoning and pass through a strainer.

315 Onion.

Proceed as for White Sauce, adding 10 lb. of cooked and finely-chopped onions.

316 Parsley.

Proceed as for White Sauce, adding chopped parsley.

317 Egg.

1 gallon of white sauce to which is added 12 coarsely chopped hard-boiled eggs.

Purée type of Sauces :

318 Tomato.

4 tins Tomatoes.	$\frac{1}{2}$ lb. Margarine.
12 ozs. Cornflour.	Pepper.
2 gallons brown stock.	Salt.

Method.—Pound the tomatoes. Mix the cornflour to a smooth paste with water. Place tomatoes, pepper, salt and stock into a saucepan and bring slowly to the boil; then add the margarine. When boiling, add the cornflour and cook for a further 20 minutes. Bacon bones make a good flavouring for this sauce.

319 Mexicaine.

2 lb. Chopped onions.	1 qt. Vinegar.
1 oz. Sugar.	½ oz. Salt.
+1 Faggot.	24 Peppercorns.
1 tin Tomato purée.	

Method.—Place vinegar, faggot, peppercorns and chopped onions to cook and allow a reduction to half quantity. Pass through a fine strainer, add salt, sugar and stir in the tomato sauce. (This is a cold sauce for cooked meats, etc.)

320 Bread.

4 qts. Milk.	½ lb. Margarine.
1 lb. Onions.	Pepper.
¼ oz. Cloves.	Salt.
2 lb. Breadcrumbs.	

Method.—Place in a saucepan the milk, onions and cloves, and bring slowly to the boil. Simmer for 15 minutes. Remove the onions and cloves and add the breadcrumbs. Stand in a warm part of the stove for 15 minutes so that the breadcrumbs may absorb some of the milk. Bring to the boil again and stir in the margarine.

321 Apple.

12 lb. Apples or 4 lb. Apple rings.	3 Cloves.
2 lb. Sugar.	½ gallon Water.

Method.—Soak apple rings overnight. Place in a stewpan, add sugar and cloves, cover with water, allow to boil for ˊ30 minutes until cooked, pass through a sieve and keep in Bain Marie.

322 Curry.

1 gallon Brown stock.	8 oz. Chopped apple rings.
½ pt. Diluted tomato purée.	2 oz. Salt.
1 lb. Chopped onion.	3 oz. Curry powder.
4 oz. Soaked coco-nut.	4 oz. Fat.
12 oz. Flour.	

Method.—Lightly fry onions, add curry powder, cook 5 minutes ; add flour, cook further 5 minutes ; add apples, stock, purée gradually, coco-nut, and salt and bring to boil. Cook for 1 hour.

Pass the sauce—season and boil up to the correct consistency (to well coat back of a spoon).

Cold Sauces :

323 Mayonnaise.

12 yolks of Egg.	$\frac{1}{2}$ oz. Pepper.
1 qt. Vinegar.	8 qts. Water.
44 Peppercorns.	2 oz. Salt.
2 oz. Mustard.	1 qt. Oil.
1 lb. Cornflour.	

Method.—Place the yolks of eggs into a basin. Add a good teaspoonful of salt and $\frac{1}{2}$ teaspoonful of pepper. Gradually work the yolks into the condiments to set the yolks. Work in 1 gill vinegar, stirring continually. Add the oil very slowly continuing to stir vigorously. If the sauce should curdle, place a tablespoonful of vinegar or warm water in another basin and gradually work on the sauce until it begins to thicken up. Finally, having worked in all the oil, finish the sauce with a little made mustard and tablespoonful of boiling water, or vinegar, to set the sauce.

Boil remainder of the water and vinegar together with the peppercorns, and thicken with the diluted cornflour. Strain and allow to cool, then incorporate into the other emulsion.

324 Mint.

2 pts. Vinegar.	1 pkt. Mint.
12 pts. Water.	1 lb. Sugar.

Method.—Warm the vinegar, add the sugar, then place in the mint. Pour on boiling water and allow to cool.

325 Tartare.

As for Mayonnaise Sauce with the addition of finely-chopped gherkins and capers.

Custard type Sauces :

326 Custard.

2 lb. Sugar.   2 lb. Custard powder.
2 gallons Milk.

Method:—Mix custard powder, sugar and a little cold milk to a smooth paste. Boil remainder of the milk, pour on to the ready-made paste, stirring the while. Reboil, if necessary, and serve.

327 Chocolate.

1 lb. Block cocoa.   2 lb. Cornflour.
2½ lb. Sugar.   2 gallons Water.

Method.—Shred or grate the block cocoa, place into a saucepan with a little water, add the sugar and stir over a gradual heat until dissolved. Add the remainder of the water and bring to boil, stirring occasionally. Dilute the cornflour with a little water and stir into the boiling chocolate, bring to boil and strain.

328 White (Sweet).

2 gallons Milk.   2 lb. Cornflour.
2 lb. Sugar.

Method.—Boil the milk and sugar, dilute the cornflour and stir into the boiling milk. Reboil and flavour with either vanilla or almond essence as desired.

329 Ginger.

2 lb. Sugar.   2 Lemons.
½ oz. Ginger.   2 gallons Water.
2 lb. Cornflour.

Method.—Boil water, add grated rind and juice of lemons, ginger and sugar. Dilute the cornflour and run into the boiling liquid. Correct colour with little browning and yellow colour and pass through a strainer.

330 Fruit or Jam Sauces.

3 lb. Jam.   2 lb. Sugar.
1 lb. Cornflour.   1 gallon Water.

Method.—Place 3 lb. jam into sufficient boiling water to make up to 1 gallon, add sugar and bring to boil, carefully stirring from time to time. Dilute the cornflour with a little cold water and pour into the boiling water and jam, stir until it boils again and colour, if necessary. Pass through a strainer.

331 Syrup.

2 sticks of Cinnamon.	4 lemons.
⅛ oz. Coriander seeds.	4 Bay leaves.
3 lb. Sugar.	4 qts. Water.

Method.—Boil up the water, sugar, cinnamon, coriander seeds, rind and juice of lemons, and bay leaves. Allow to cool.

CORRECT SAUCES TO SERVE WITH MEAT AND POULTRY.

Beef, roast	Horse-radish.
„ steak, fried	Tomato sauce.
Mutton, roast	Onion sauce or brown caper sauce.
„ boiled	Caper sauce or parsley sauce.
„ chops, fried	Tomato sauce.
Pork, roast	Apple sauce or piquante sauce.
„ chops, fried	Mustard sauce.
Ham, boiled	Parsley sauce.
Lamb, roast	Mint sauce.
Calf's head	Parsley sauce.
Chicken, roast	Bread sauce.
„ boiled	Egg sauce or parsley sauce.
Goose or duck, roast	Apple sauce.
Turkey, roast	Bread sauce.
Rabbit, roast	Bread sauce.
„ boiled	Onion sauce.

Eggs, Cheese and Pastry, etc

19 Curried Eggs and Rice.

    100 Eggs.
    5 lb. Rice.
    1 gallon Curry sauce.

Method.—Place eggs into a wire basket, plunge into boiling water for 8 minutes. Place into cold water, shell, reheat in boiling salt water. Place a little curry sauce in bottom of serving dish, cut eggs in two lengthways, sauce over and serve with border of plain boiled rice.

Rice.—Pick and wash, rain into boiling salt water; stir, bring to boil and allow to simmer approximately 15 minutes until grains are tender. Drain into a colander, refresh with cold water, then hot water, drain well and place on a baking tin in a cloth and dry off in warm oven or hot plate.

20 Egg Salad.

    100 Eggs.   2 lb. Beetroot.
    20 Lettuces. $\frac{1}{4}$ pt. Oil.
    2 lb. Watercress. $\frac{2}{3}$ pt. Vinegar.
    5 lb. Tomatoes.

Method.—Hard boil eggs for 10 minutes, then shell them. Wash lettuce, trim, wash and pick watercress, cut tomatoes in quarters, slice beetroot. Shred lettuce, (outside leaves), cut the hearts into six or eight pieces length-ways. Place the shredded lettuce in a dish, arrange the sliced eggs on top, arrange beetroot, tomatoes, watercress and lettuce around, and season with the salad dressing (*i.e.* 2 parts oil, 1 part vinegar, salt and pepper mixed well together).

21 Poached Egg, Macaroni or Spaghetti.

    100 Eggs. $\frac{1}{2}$ pt. Vinegar.
    7 lb. Macaroni or spag- Salt.
       hetti.   Pepper.
    3 lb. Grated cheese or
      2 qts. tomato sauce.

Method.—Place macaroni (broken in 2-inch lengths) in boiling salt water for 20 minutes. Well drain, add cheese or tomato sauce. Correctly season and place poached egg on top.

Poached Egg.—*See* recipe No. 16.

22 Poached Egg and Mashed Potatoes.

100 Eggs.	½ pt. Vinegar.
30 lb. Potatoes.	Salt.
3 pts. Milk.	Pepper.
8 oz. Margarine.	Nutmeg.

Method.—Poach eggs (*see* recipe No. 16).
Wash and peel potatoes, cook, pass through sieve, or mash, add boiling milk gradually, margarine, nutmeg, seasoning ; serve with poached egg on top.

23 Poached Egg and Minced Beef.

100 Eggs.	1 lb. Onions.
14 lb. Minced beef (cooked and prepared).	2 oz. Dripping.
1 qt. Thick brown sauce.	½ pt Vinegar.

Method.—Poach eggs (*see* recipe No. 16). Peel and chop onions finely, cook slowly in dripping. Add minced beef, sweat for 20 minutes until tender, season, add sauce, boil and cook together for 5 minutes.
Place in serving dishes and add a poached egg on top.

24 Poached (or Fried) Eggs on Fried Bread.

200 Eggs.	14 lb. Bread.
½ pt. Vinegar.	4 lb. Dripping.

Method.—Slice bread, cut in half and fry to golden brown in hot shallow fat. Drain, and place 2 eggs for each man on top. Serve hot.

Fried Eggs.—See recipe No. 2.

Poached Eggs.—See recipe No. 16.

25 Scotch Eggs with Sauce Mexicaine.

100 Eggs.	2 lb. Onions.
12 lb. Minced beef (raw).	4 oz. Dripping.
3 lb. Flour.	½ gallon Mexicaine sauce.
4 lb. Breadcrumbs.	

Method.—Hard boil the eggs. Peel and chop onions finely, sweat on in the dripping, allow to cool. Add to meat, season, and mould around each egg, 2 oz. mixture each. Make paste with flour and water, pass eggs through paste and breadcrumb. Fry in deep fat for 15–20 minutes ; drain and serve with mexicaine sauce, separate.

26 **Poached Eggs and Welsh Rarebit.**

100 Eggs.	1 oz. Mustard.
6 lb. Cheese.	Salt.
14 lb. Bread (sliced).	Pepper.
1 qt. Thick white sauce.	

Method.—Poach eggs. *See* recipe No. 16.

Chop cheese finely and melt down slowly with a little stock. Add white sauce, mustard and seasoning. Spread on either toasted or fried bread. Brown in very hot oven and place a poached egg on each.

27 **Scrambled Eggs and Ham.**

150 Eggs.	2 lb. Chopped lean ham
2 qts. Thick white bread	(cooked).
sauce.	8 oz. Margarine.
14 lb. Sliced bread.	

Method.—Fry bread (or toast).

See recipe No. 15 for scrambled eggs.

When scrambled eggs are prepared, add 2 lb. lean chopped ham and serve on slices of buttered toast or fried bread.

28 **Scrambled Eggs and Tomato.**

150 Eggs.	14 lb. Sliced bread.
2 qts. Thick white bread	12½ lb. Tomatoes.
sauce.	

See recipe No. 15 for scrambled eggs.

Method.—Blanche tomatoes, skin, squeeze out pips, cut in ¼-inch dice, lightly stew in margarine. Season with salt and pepper. Place the scrambled eggs on slices of buttered toast or fried bread and place a spoonful of tomato on each or mix the tomatoes lightly with the eggs.

SAVOURY CHEESE DISHES

29 **Cheese—Onion Savoury.**

12 lb. Cheese.	1 qt. Thick white sauce.
1 lb. Finely chopped	1 oz. Mustard.
onions.	12 lb. Sliced bread.
4 oz. Margarine.	

Method.—Stew onions in margarine until tender. Add chopped cheese, and melt slowly. Add white sauce, mustard, and spread on fried or toasted bread.

30 Cheese—Potato Pie.

25 lb. Potatoes.	3 lb. Dripping.
6 lb. Cheese.	4 oz. Baking powder.
2 lb. Onions.	Salt, pepper.
8 lb. Flour.	4 qts. Milk.

Boil and mash potatoes. Grate cheese. Make short paste. Chop onions finely. Stew without taking colour. Layer with mashed potatoes, cheese, onions, and cover with short paste. Bake in moderate oven for 1 hour.

Another method.—Slice potatoes and onions. Season with salt and pepper. Arrange in alternate layers with grated cheese. 3 parts fill the pie dish or baking dish with milk or stock, cover with a short crust and bake for approximately 1 hour.

31 Cheese—Scrambled Eggs.

150 Eggs.	Pepper.
2 lb. Grated cheese.	2 qts. White bread
Salt.	sauce.

Scrambled eggs. *See* recipe No. 15. Sprinkle with grated cheese.

Grated cheese may be added and mixed *with* the eggs.

32 Fried Cheese Pastie.

6 lb. Cheese.	3 Eggs.
8 lb. Flour.	4 lb. Breadcrumbs.
3 lb. margarine.	2 qts. Thick white sauce.
2 oz. Baking powder.	Salt, pepper, nutmeg.
Water for paste.	

Method.—Make short paste of flour, margarine, water and baking powder. Chop cheese, and melt slowly. Add thick white sauce and seasoning. Cut out paste in 4-inch circles, place 2 oz. Welsh rarebit in centre, egg wash sides, fold over, egg and breadcrumb, and fry in hot deep fat. Drain well and serve hot with tomato, piquante, lyonnaise, or curry sauce.

33 Macaroni and Cheese Fritters.

8 lb. Macaroni.	2 lb. Flour.
4 lb. Cheese.	6 Eggs.
3 qts. Thick white sauce.	8 lb. Breadcrumbs.
4 Eggs.	$\frac{3}{4}$-gallon Tomato sauce.

Vegetables

The uses of Potatoes .. Yeast in Pastry

25% to 50% potatoes may be used in lieu of Flour in Puddings, Cakes, Powder Goods, Yeast Goods.

Yeast Goods.	Short Pastry.	Puddings Suet
4½ lbs. flour.	9 lbs. flour.	8 lbs. flour.
1½ lbs. potatoes	3 lbs. potatoes.	4 lbs. breadcrumbs.
½ lb. margarine	1½ ozs. salt.	4 lbs. potatoes.
5 ozs. sugar.	4½ lbs. margarine	8 ozs. B. P.
2 pts. milk (approx	Water ad. lib.	4 lbs. suet.
Egg Colour.		7 pts. milk or water
2½ z. Yeast.		
		Fruits, Spices & Sugar to produce various types.

Baking Powder. All recipes are for the best quality B. P., ie 2 parts Cream of Tartar to 1 part Bi-Carbonate of Soda. ¾ ozs. to a lb. flour for powder goods. If using Greens B.P. use 1½ times as much as it contains a % of rice flour.
If using N. A. A. F. I. double the quantity as it contains a % of ground rice.

POTATOES

173 Baked Creamed.

65 lb. Potatoes (unpre-
pared).
1 lb. Brown breadcrumbs.
2 oz. Salt.

2 qts. Milk.
2 lb. Margarine.
Pepper and nutmeg to
taste.

Method.—Peel and wash potatoes. Place in container
and boil for 20 minutes. Strain off all water, replace
lid and dry off. Pass through a sieve, replace the
potatoes in container on a warm part of stove; add
salt, margarine, pepper, and grated nutmeg to taste;
add boiling milk. Mix well to a creamy consistency.
Place in a serving tin and sprinkle finely with brown
bread crumbs, a little melted margarine and brown off
in top of the oven.

174 Baked in Jackets.

65 lb. Potatoes (unprepared)—served whole.

Method.—Scrub suitably-sized potatoes until clean.
Place on the racks of a medium oven and bake until
cooked; approximately 1 hour. Serve whole, or cut
in half with the addition of a little margarine on each.

175 Boiled.

65 lb. Potatoes (unprepared).

Method.—Peel and wash potatoes. Cut to an even
size. Place in a container with salt, cover with water
and boil for approximately 20 minutes. Strain off
water and place potatoes on a warm part of the stove
for a few minutes. Allow them to dry before serving.
Shake the container gently so as to give the potatoes a
floury appearance.

176 Croquette.

65 lb. Potatoes (pre-
pared).
2 lb. Flour.
6 Eggs.

1 pt. Milk for batter.
6 lb. Breadcrumbs.
2 oz. Salt.
Pepper and nutmeg (to
taste).

Method.—Peel and wash potatoes and cook in a
steamer or boil for approximately 20 minutes. When
cooked, strain and pass through a sieve. Season with
salt, add pepper and grated nutmeg to taste, add yolks

of eggs and mix thoroughly. Allow to cool. Shape into croquettes, pass through batter, breadcrumbs and fry in deep fat until golden brown.

Care must be taken that the mixture is made as dry as possible, hence steaming is preferable to boiling.

The white of eggs should be used in the batter.

177 Fondante.

65 lb. Potatoes (unpre-pared).	4 qts. Stock.
	2 oz. Chopped parsley.
1 lb. Margarine or Dripping.	2 oz. Salt.

Method.—Peel and wash potatoes. Place in a baking tin three parts covered with seasoned stock and cook in hot oven. From time to time the potatoes should be brushed with melted margarine to impart a brown gloss when cooked. Before serving sprinkle with chopped parsley.

178 Fried.

65 lb. Potatoes (prepared).

Method.—Peel and wash potatoes. Cut into strips approximately ½ inch square and well wash. Drain potatoes thoroughly and place into frying basket. Blanch in hot fat until lightly coloured, then remove them from the fat and allow to drain.

When fat is reheated, refry until crisp on the outside. Sprinkle with salt and drain on a cloth before serving.

179 In Tomatoes.

65 lb. Potatoes (unpre-pared).	4 qts. Stock.
	2 lb. Flour.
1 tin Tomato purée.	2 lb. Bacon trimmings.
2 lb. Onions.	

Method.—Peel and cut the onions in dice. Dice the bacon trimmings, add the flour and stew together. Add tomato purée and stock, season to taste. Bring to boil, add the peeled and washed potatoes, cook in a medium oven, or slowly on the side of the stove. Serve carefully and sauce over.

180 Lyonnaise.

65 lb. Potatoes (unpre-pared).	2 oz. Chopped parsley.
	3 lb. Dripping.
7 lb. Onions.	

Method.—Scrub potatoes and cook in a steamer for approximately 18 minutes. Allow to cool, peel and cut into slices about ¼ inch thick. Fry in shallow fat until nicely brown and mix with fried sliced onions.

181 Macaire.

    65 lb. Potatoes (unprepared).
    1 lb. Margarine.
    3 lb. Dripping.

Method.—Scrub potatoes, place in a medium oven on the racks and bake. When cooked cut in half, remove potatoes from the skins and place in a container. Add salt, margarine and roughly mash. Shape into cakes and fry both sides in shallow fat until brown. This method is only suitable for small messes. For large numbers, cook in baking dishes and cut into portions after cooking.

N.B. Left over boiled potatoes may be used.

182 Parmentier.

65 lb. Potatoes (unprepared).	2 oz. Salt.
2 oz. Parsley.	Pepper and nutmeg to taste.
3 lb. Dripping.	

Method.—Wash, peel, and cut potatoes in approximately ½-inch cubes. Rewash and drain well. Heat dripping in frying pan or baking tins, sufficient to cover the bottom. When hot place in potatoes, season with salt, and sauté for approximately 5 minutes. Place in a moderate oven to finish cooking and colour a golden brown. Remove from pan and serve.

183 Parsley.

65 lb. Potatoes (unprepared).	4 oz. Chopped parsley.
1½ lb. Margarine.	1 pt. Stock.

Method.—Peel and wash potatoes. Cut to an even size. Place in a container and cover with water, add salt and cook for approximately 20 minutes. Drain off all water and place on a warm part of the stove for a few minutes to dry. Shake gently to give floury appearance. Melt margarine, add it to the stock, and with blanched chopped parsley sprinkle over potatoes before serving.

184 Roast.

    65 lb. Potatoes (unprepared).
    3 lb. Dripping.
    2 oz. Salt.

Method.—Peel and wash potatoes. Cut to an even size. Heat dripping, place in potatoes, and allow to colour lightly on top of the stove ; place in oven until cooked to a golden brown. During cooking baste frequently. Strain off fat, season and serve.

185 Sauté.

    65 lb. Potatoes (unpre-   3 lb. Dripping.
      pared).   Salt and pepper.
    2 oz. Chopped parsley.

Method.—Scrub potatoes, cook in a steamer for approximately 18 minutes ; when cooked allow to cool. Peel, cut into $\frac{1}{4}$-inch slices, lightly brown in hot shallow fat, drain off, season and sprinkle with chopped parsley when serving.

186 Savoury.

    65 lb. Potatoes (unpre-   2 lb. Dripping.
      pared).   2 qts. Stock.
    7 lb. Onions.   Salt, pepper and nut-
    2 oz. Chopped parsley.   meg to taste.
    2 lb. Grated cheese.

Method.—Peel and wash potatoes. Cut into slices $\frac{1}{8}$ inch thick. Peel and shred the onions, mix together with the potatoes and season with salt and pepper. Place potatoes and onions in a greased serving tin, three parts cover with stock, sprinkle with grated cheese, Cook in a hot oven. Sprinkle with chopped parsley before serving.

187 Steamed.

    65 lb. Potatoes (unprepared).

Method.—Peel and wash potatoes. Cut to an even size. Season with salt and cook in a steamer for approximately 20 minutes.

188 Stewed with Cheese.

    65 lb. Potatoes (unpre-   1 lb. Margarine.
      pared).   1 gallon stock or water.
    2 lb. Grated cheese.

Method.—Peel and wash potatoes. Melt the margarine. Grate the cheese. Slice the potatoes $\frac{1}{4}$ inch thick. Place in a serving tin, three parts cover with seasoned stock, sprinkle with margarine, grated cheese and cook in a moderate oven.

189 Mashed.

65 lb. Potatoes (unprepared).	2 oz. Salt.
2 qts. Milk.	Pepper.
1 lb. Margarine.	Nutmeg.

Method.—Peel and wash potatoes. Place in a container, cover with water, season with salt and boil for 20 minutes. When cooked drain off water and pass potatoes through a sieve. Place on a warm part of the stove ; add margarine, salt, pepper, grated nutmeg and boiling milk. Mix thoroughly and serve.

VEGETABLES

190 Braised Cabbage.

40 lb. Cabbage (unprepared).	2 qts. Stock.
	1 qt. Fat from stock pot.
1 lb. Carrots.	2 qts. Brown sauce.
1 lb. Onions.	Aromates in bag.
1 lb. Bacon trimmings.	1 oz. Salt.

Method.—Clean the cabbage, cut into quarters, cook in boiling salted water for 10 minutes. Drain in a colander. Peel and slice carrots and onions, place into saucepan, add bacon trimmings, fry on lightly. Add aromates. Place quartered cabbage on sliced carrots, onions, etc., half cover with stock and white stock-pot dripping, cover with greased paper and bring to the boil. Cover with lid, and braise in oven until tender. (Time approximately 1 hour.) Remove cabbage, strain stock, remove all fat, reduce stock and add to the brown sauce. Serve with the cabbage.

191 Braised Celery.

25 Large heads celery.	$\frac{1}{2}$ gallon Espagnole sauce.
2 qts. Stock.	
1 qt. Fat from stock pot.	1 Tablespoon vinegar.
	2 oz. Salt.

Method.—Trim celery, remove outside leaves, if necessary, scrub and remove outside fibres with a vegetable knife. Wash well. Put vinegar and salt into water and bring to the boil; place in the celery and boil for 20 minutes. Refresh under cold water and rewash. Allow water to run between leaves. Place into a saucepan and cover with stock and fat from stock pot. Add salt. Cover with a few crusts of bread and greased paper. Bring to boil. Cover with lid and cook in the oven. When cooked strain off liquor, remove fat, reduce stock and add to espagnole sauce. Split celery lengthwise in sections and fold evenly with the head of celery uppermost. Serve, masked round with espagnole sauce.

192 Braised Onions.

33 lb. Onions.
⅓ gallon Espagnole sauce.
1 qt. Brown stock.
4 oz. Sugar.
1 oz. Salt.
4 lb. Stockpot fat.

Method.—Select onions of an even size and carefully peel. Place a little fat in roasting tin, allow to get hot, add onions and fry to a light golden brown. Strain off all fat, and moisten with fat from stock pot and brown stock. Season, bring to boil and place in the oven. When cooked strain off stock, remove fat, reduce the stock and add to espagnole sauce. Serve onions masked with sauce.

193 Brussels Sprouts.

40 lb. Brussels sprouts (unprepared).
4 oz. Salt.

Method.—Trim off bottom of sprouts and remove all discoloured leaves. Steep in plenty of salt water. Wash, drain and place in plenty of boiling salted water. Boil steadily until tender. Strain and serve.

194 Boiled Cabbage.

50 lb. Cabbage (unprepared).
4 oz. Salt.

Method.—Remove outside coarse leaves, cut into quarters. Remove thick stalks and thoroughly wash in cold salted water. Bring plenty of water to the boil

and add salt.   When boiling, place in washed cabbage,
bring quickly to the boil again and allow to steadily
boil.   When cooked strain and press between two plates.
Cut into portions and serve.

N.B. The outside leaves can be used for soups.

195 Boiled Carrots.

40 lb. Carrots (unprepared).
2 oz. Salt.

Method.—Peel and cut into sections.   Cover with
cold water.   Add salt, bring to boil and allow to boil
steadily until tender.   Strain and serve.

196 Butter Beans.

10 lb. Butter beans.	1 lb. Margarine.
1 Ham knuckle.	1 oz. Salt.
10 oz. Carrots.	Faggot.
10 oz. Onions.	36 Peppercorns, in bag.

Method.—Soak beans overnight in plenty of cold
water.   Well wash, place into saucepan, cover with
cold water, bring to the boil and skim.   Add whole
carrots, onions, knuckle of ham, salt, a faggot and
peppercorns.   Allow to boil steadily until tender.
When cooked, remove garnish, reduce liquor to an
essence, add margarine to form an emulsion round the
beans and serve.

197 Butter Beans (Parsley style).

10 lb. Butter beans.	12 oz. Carrots.
4 oz. Chopped parsley.	1 oz. Salt.
1 lb. Margarine.	Faggot.
1 Ham bone.	36 Peppercorns, in bag
12 oz. Onions.	

Method.—*See* recipe No. 196.   Sprinkle with chopped
parsley and serve.

198 Buttered Cabbage.

50 lb. Cabbage (unprepared) (chopped after cooking).	2 lb. Margarine. 2 oz. Salt.

Method.—Plain boil cabbage, *see* recipe No. 194.
When cooked strain and chop.   Return to saucepan.
Add margarine, well mix, correct seasoning and serve.

INDIAN DISHES

Takara Purrie

caution Chillies are very pungeant use sparingly

Ingredients

Pastry Flour or Atta oil or Ghee Salt and Water

Vegetable Purrie

Potatoes, Marrow or Pumpkin or any other
suitable vegetable Chillies Indian Saffron.
onions and Salt

Method

Make a pastry of flour or Atta oil, salt and Water
prepare and Boil Potatoes or other suitable
vegetables and onions Mash up add chillies
saffron and salt   Press out pastry and cut
into Shapes (oblong or circle) Place a portion
of the mixture on half and fold over pastry
and seal the edges as in a normal turnover
Place Ghee or oil in a vessel and bring to the Boil
and Put in Pastries cook until a light Brown colour

TIME 10 MINUTES deep fat frying

INDIAN DISHES   CONTINUED

Sweet Pastries or Puffs
Ingredients
Flour or Atta, salt to flavour and water

1. Sugar, Sultanas Bread crumbs (mixed)
2. Sugar, Apricots, Bread. Fruit partly cooked and moist
3. Home made jam.

Prepare as for Takara Purrie and cooking

Marrows or Pumpkin Bhujie
Ingredients
Onions or suitable vegetable Chillie, saffron.
Salt and Ghee
Method
Prepare and cut vegetables into cubes Partly
Boil and then fry off in Oil

Chappatties
Ingredients
Flour or Atta. Water Ghee or cooking oil

Method
Make a pastry with flour or Atta add Ghee
or cooking oil and fry in Ghee.
Bake Indian method or on chappattie Plates

INDIAN DISHES   CONTINUED

Puraties
Ingredients
as for Chappatties and Dhall
Method
Make a paste of cooked Dhall or Vegetable Purrie Place the Dhall or Vegetable Purrie on Pastry and fold over.

Burtas
Macedoined vegetable are useful for using up remains of Potatoes. Burtas or cubed Potatoes mixed with fryed onions and well seasoned. Another variety Potatoes, Cabbage, Cauliflower Peas and Bringals Bringals roasted or Baked and skins removed. The pulp mashed fryed in oil and lime juice added.

Dhall Purrie
Boil the dhall until tender and add Indian spices make a flour or Atta Pastry take a small portion of this and press out place in a small Portion of prepared dhall and press outside edges inwards as for Potatoe cutlets and fry.

Plain Stew

Some simple dishes from one foundation

Ingredients

Meat	50 lbs	Vegetables	7 lbs
Onions	3 "	Flour	3 "
Salt	2 oz	Pepper	1 oz.

Stock or Cold Water as required

Sea Pie add Pastry and 50 lb Potatoes (Camp Kettle)	Curry and Rice 2 lb Curry Powder 8 lb Rice 3 lb Dressing
Stew and Dumplings add Dumpling. (Camp Kettle)	Turkish Pillau. omit Vege add Herbs, Rice and Kayenne Pepper
Meat Pie omit Vege. add Pastry (oven)	Irish Stew (Mutton.) omit Vege add 50 lb Potatoes Camp Kettle
Meat Pudding. omit Vege. add Pastry (Basin and Boil)	Potatoe Pie Cottage Pie. Hot Pot Shepherds Pie
Savoury Pie add Pastry (oven)	Hunters Pie omit Vege add 50 lb Potatoes oven
Brown Stew (in oven)	Mince - Roll. omit Vegetables add Herbs and Pastry
Plain Tomatoe Stew Add 15 lb Tomatoes camp Kettle or oven	Brown Tomatoe Stew add Tomatoes
Toact in the	Hole add Batter.

BACON DISHES, ETC.

1 Bacon and Bubble and Squeak.

12¼ lb. Bacon (prepared). Salt.
25 lb. Cabbage (cooked). Pepper.
25 lb. Potatoes (cooked).

Method.—Bone, trim and remove the rind of the bacon and cut into slices 1/16 inch thick (No. 5 gauge on Berkel slicer). Ration 2 oz. for each man.

Lay the slices on a tray with the lean part uppermost, grill or cook in a hot oven.

Chop the cabbage finely and mix with the mashed potatoes, season with salt and pepper. With the aid of a little flour, shape into medallions approximately 4 oz. each. Place in hot frying pan with a little fat, cook on both sides to a golden brown and serve with the bacon. A thick brown gravy can be served with this dish, if required.

2 Bacon and Egg and Chips.

12½ lb. Bacon (prepared).
100 Eggs.
30 lb. Potatoes.

Method.—Prepare the bacon as for recipe No. 1.

Wash and peel the potatoes, cut into fingers, wash again to remove excess of starch and dry in a cloth. Place in frying basket and fry in very hot clean fat. Cook until tender, but not coloured, remove, drain and place into a tray until required. To serve, replace in very hot fat, fry until golden brown, drain on a cloth and season with salt.

Frying pans must be used for frying eggs when available. Heat sufficient bacon fat to cover bottom of pan, when hot, break in the eggs, one by one, testing first for freshness ; apply a gradual heat to set the white and pass through the oven to set the yolk.

See Timetable for cooking, Sect. 11, para. 16.

3 Bacon and Potato Pie.

12½ lb. Bacon (prepared). 8 lb. Flour.
50 lb. Potatoes. 3 lb. Dripping.
4 lb. Onions. Water.
4 qts. Stock. Salt.

Method.—Utilize all trimmings of cooked bacon or ham not suitable for other purposes. The onions should be chopped, and stewed in bacon fat until tender to a light golden colour. Pass the trimmings of lean bacon and ham through a coarse mincer or cut into dice. Prepare a dry mashed potato and correctly season. Grease a pie dish or baking dish, arrange a layer of potato bacon and onions in the centre and cover with mashed potatoes. Mark the top, sprinkle with a few breadcrumbs and oily bacon fat and bake in a moderate oven for approximately 40 minutes. Cut into portions and serve with good ham liquor, piquante, or lyonnaise sauce.

For quantities as laid down, slice the bacon, slice the onions and potatoes in $\frac{1}{4}$-inch slices (2 oz. each) and season. Prepare a short crust. Arrange the potatoes in the bottom of a pie dish or baking tin. Lay rashers of bacon on this, cover with sliced onions and potatoes, three-parts fill with stock, cover with short paste. Brush over with little diluted milk and bake approximately 1 hour.

4 Fried Bacon.

> 30 lb. Bacon (unprepared).

Method.—It is essential that the utmost value is obtained from the bacon ration, and for that reason trim and bone as sparingly as possible. When cut, it should be placed on a baking tray. When cooking the tendency should be to warm through, instead of applying extreme heat, thereby losing as little of the fat as possible in the process of cooking. When served, the fat should still be soft and not crisp.

Preferably backs and streaky only should be used.
See Timetable for cooking, Sect. 11, para. 6.

5 Fried Bacon and Beans in Tomato Sauce.

> $12\frac{1}{2}$ lb. Bacon (prepared).
> 10 lb. Haricot beans.
> 4 qts. Tomato sauce.

Method.—Cook the beans as for haricot beans, heat tomato sauce and serve with the fried bacon.

6 Fried Bacon and Egg.

>12½ lb. Bacon (prepared).
>100 Eggs.
>*Method.—See* Recipe No. 2.

7 Fried Bacon and Sausage.

>12¼ lb. Bacon (prepared).
>12¼ lb. Sausages.
>*Method.—See* Timetable for cooking, Sect. 11, para. 41.

>*Recipe for sausages.*
>
>| | |
>|---|---|
>| 16 lb. Lean beef. | 6 lb. Soaked bread. |
>| 6 lb. Fat beef. | 8 oz. Seasoning. |

>*Method.*—Bread should be soaked and squeezed almost dry, mixed with passed meat and seasoning. Pass all through mincer again before fitting into sausage casings.

>*Seasoning :*
>
>| | |
>|---|---|
>| 10 oz. Salt. | 1 oz. Mustard. |
>| 3 oz. White pepper. | ½ oz. Cloves (ground). |
>| 1 oz. Grated nutmeg. | 1½ oz. Brown sugar. |
>| 1 oz. Thyme. | |

8 Fried Bacon and Tomatoes.

>12¼ lb. Bacon (prepared).
>25 lb. Tomatoes (8 to 1 lb. = 2 each).

>*Method.*—Cut the tomatoes in halves horizontally, season, and place into a baking tin with a little bacon fat. Cook in oven until tender. Serve in mess-tins with the fried bacon.

9 Bacon and Boston Beans.

>| | |
>|---|---|
>| 12¼ lb. Bacon (prepared). | 1 lb. Onions. |
>| 10 lb. Haricot beans. | 1 lb. Carrots. |
>| 1 Ham or pork bone. | 4 qts. Espagnole sauce. |

>*Method.—See* recipe No. 5. Replace tomato sauce with espagnole sauce.

10 Bacon and Mashed Potatoes.

>| | |
>|---|---|
>| 12½ lb. Bacon (prepared). | 2 oz. Salt. |
>| 30 lb. Potatoes. | Pepper. |
>| 1 qt. Milk. | Nutmeg. |
>| ½ lb. Margarine. | |

>Prepare the bacon as before. For mashed potatoes, *see* recipe No. 189.

3—(2060)

11 Bacon and Fried Bread.

> 15 lb. Bacon (prepared).
> 12 lb. Bread slices.

Method.—Cook the bacon as before. In the mean-time, cut the bread in ½-inch slices. Having removed the bacon, fry the slices of bread in the bacon fat and additional dripping to a light golden colour both sides, taking care not to dry up. Serve 1 slice of bread with 4 oz. of bacon a head.

12 Bacon and Liver (Thick Gravy).

> 12½ lb. Bacon (prepared).
> 12½ lb. Liver.
> ½ gallon Espagnole sauce.

Method.—Defrost, skin and cut the liver into 2-oz. slices. Season with salt, at the last minute. Pass through flour, fry slightly underdone in shallow fat until pearls of blood appear, turn over and complete cooking. Serve equal slices of liver and bacon in mess tins and sauce over with espagnole sauce.
See Timetable for cooking, Sect. 11, para, 27.

13 Boiled Gammon and Sauce.

> 30 lb. Gammon (unprepared).
> 2 pt. botts. of Sauce.

Method.—*See* Timetable for cooking, Sect. 11, para. 23.

14 Bacon and Sausage Cake.

> 12½ lb. Bacon (prepared).
> 12½ lb. Sausage cake.

Method.—Form sausage cake into 2-oz. medallions, dust with flour, sauté in shallow bacon fat until the blood percolates through. Turn over and sauté the other side a nice golden colour. Can be sautéed lightly either side and finished off in a slow oven until they are firm to the touch. Fry the bacon and serve.

15 Bacon and Scrambled Eggs.

> 12½ lb. Bacon (prepared).   ½ lb. Margarine.
> 100 Eggs.   Salt.
> 2 qts. White bread sauce.   Pepper.

Method.—Prepare a bread sauce :—

1 lb. Diced white bread or white breadcrumbs.
2 qts. Milk.

Soak the bread or crumbs in the milk, carefully bring to boil and stir with a wooden spoon until smooth.

Break the eggs into a basin, being very careful to ascertain their freshness, season with salt and pepper, and beat up with a whisk. Heat the margarine in a saucepan and place in the eggs. Apply a gradual heat, stirring with a wooden spoon until a creamy mass is formed. Add the bread sauce. Fry the bacon and serve.

16 Bacon and Poached Egg.

12½ lb. Bacon (prepared).
100 Eggs.
½ pt. Vinegar.

Method.—Boil water and vinegar together, place approximately 12 eggs in a wire basket and plunge into the boiling water for a second to release the white from the shell, gently break the eggs into the water. Bring to the boil, cover with a lid and allow to stand for three minutes without boiling, until set. Remove from the water carefully, with an iron spoon, and place into cold water. When required place eggs in hot salted water to heat through. Remove, and drain. Fry the bacon and serve.

17 Ham.

30 lb. Ham (unprepared).

Method.—Forehocks and gammons. *See* Timetable for cooking, Sect. 11, para. 23.

18 Sausage Cake.

1×4 oz. each or 2 × 2 oz. each. 2 lb. Flour.
25 lb. Sausage meat (prepared). 2 lb. Dripping.
¼ gallon Chutney sauce.

Method.—Mould the sausage meat into 4-oz. balls or 2×2-oz. cutter shapes. Wash with a light dusting of flour. Cook slowly in shallow dripping until well done as recipe No. 14, and serve in mess tins with chutney sauce or any other appropriate sauce, served separately.

Chutney Sauce.

¼ gallon good espagnole sauce. Add to this ¼ lb. chopped chutney.

VII.—SAVOURIES

94 Cheese and Potato Pie

25 lb. Potatoes	Salt
6 lb. Cheese	Pepper
2 lb. Onions	4 qt. Milk
8 lb. Flour ⎫ shortpaste	
3 lb. Dripping ⎭	
2 oz. Baking powder	

Method.—Boil and mash potatoes. Grate cheese. Make short paste (Recipe No. 97). Chop onions finely. Stew without taking colour. Layer in baking dish with mashed potatoes, cheese, onions, and cover with short paste. Bake in moderate oven for one hour.

Another method.—Slice potatoes and onions. Season with salt and pepper. Arrange in alternate layers with grated cheese. Three parts fill the baking dish, add milk or stock, cover with a short crust and bake for approximately one hour.

95 Fried Cheese Pastie

6 lb. Cheese	4 lb. Breadcrumbs
8 lb. Flour	2 qt. Thick white sauce
3 lb. Margarine or dripping	Salt, pepper, nutmeg
Water for paste	4 lb. Flour
2 oz. Baking powder	

Method.—Make short paste of flour, baking powder, salt, margarine, water (Recipe No. 87). Chop cheese, and melt slowly. Add thick white sauce and seasoning. Roll and cut out paste in four inch circles, place 2 oz. cheese mixture in centre, and damp the sides, pass through a thin batter, breadcrumbs and fry in hot deep fat. Drain well and serve hot with a brown sauce.

96 Welsh Rarebit

6 lb. Cheese	Salt
14 lb. Bread (sliced)	Pepper
1 qt. Thick white sauce (Recipe No. 90)	
1 oz. Mustard	

Method.—Chop cheese finely and melt down slowly with a little stock. Add white sauce and seasoning. Spread on either toasted or fried bread. Brown in very hot oven.

97 Cheese and Oatmeal Pudding

8 lb. Oatmeal	4 lb. Suet
4 lb. Breadcrumbs	Salt
2 lb. Flour	Pepper
4 lb. Grated cheese	Stock or water

Method.—Mix all the dry ingredients together. Mix to a stiff batter by adding cold stock or water. Place in greased pudding basins or jam tins, three parts full. Cover with pudding cloths or greaseproof paper. Boil or steam for 2½ hours. Serve with a white, creamy sauce.

98   Toasted Cheese

12 lb. Cheese
14 lb. Bread for toast

Method.—Slice cheese, place on bread or toast and brown quickly in very hot oven.

99   Cornish Pastie

9 lb. Potatoes or carrots
3 lb. Onions
9 lb. Preserved meat

12 lb. Flour
4 lb. Dripping or margarine
3 oz. Baking powder
Salt and pepper

Method.—Make pastry with flour, dripping or margarine, baking powder and salt (Recipe No. 97). Roll out the pastry until 1/8 inch thick. Cut out rounds with a large cutter. Wet the edges. Cut the preserved meat into cubes, add the onions, which have been previously diced and fried to a golden colour, and the potatoes or carrots, also cut into small cubes. Mix well together, season well with salt and pepper, moisten slightly. Place 3 oz. of this mixture in the centre of each round of pastry, fold over towards the centre, place edges together, wash with a little milk. Place on a tray, bake for 35 minutes in hot oven.

100   Oatmeal Steaks

25 lb. Minced Beef (raw) lean 70%; fat 30%
5 lb. Oatmeal
2 lb. Onions

Method.—Chop the onions finely and fry lightly in dripping. Cook the oatmeal as for porridge but using less water to keep it on the thick side. Add salt and allow it to cook slowly for three-quarters hour to one hour. Let it get cold and mix it with the meat and onion seasoning. Shape into round steaks. Flour lightly and fry in shallow fat. Serve with brown sauce.

101   Vegetable Pie

Pastry—
12 lb. Flour
4 lb. Dripping or Margarine

2 oz. Salt
4 oz. Baking powder

Method.—(See Recipe No. 87).

Filling—
12 lb. Carrots
7 lb. Turnips
4 lb. Marrow fat peas cooked
or
4 lb. Haricot beans cooked
4 lb. Onions or leeks

6 lb. Cauliflower
6 qt. Stock
1 lb. Dripping or margarine
Seasoning
Salt and pepper

Method.—Prepare the pastry as indicated in Recipe No. 87, soak the beans or peas overnight and cook, clean and prepare the vegetables, cut into cubes, heat the dripping or margarine in a sizeable pan, add the diced vegetables and cook very slowly without taking any colour, add the stock, season, salt and pepper, stew until tender: boil cauliflower separately, place the vegetables into dishes, equally divide the peas or beans in each pie dish, also the cauliflower, cover with pastry and bake until the pastry is cooked and brown.

N.B.—Tomatoes, when in season, make an excellent addition.

102 Vegetable Hot Pot

25 lb. Potatoes (peeled)
12 lb. Carrots
7 lb. Turnips
4 lb. Butter beans cooked
or
4 lb. Haricot beans cooked
4 lb. Onions or leeks

4 lb. Marrowfat peas cooked
4 lb. Lentils cooked
6 qt. Stock
1 lb. Dripping
Seasoning
Salt and pepper

Method.—Soak the beans and peas overnight and cook until tender. Slice the potatoes into ¼-inch slices, cut the vegetables into dice, heat the dripping, add the vegetables, fry without taking colour, place all the ingredients in layers in deep baking tins, section the layers, cover the top with a layer of potatoes, add stock to just cover the vegetables, brush over with a little melted dripping, cook in a moderate oven. *N.B.*—Tomatoes, when in season, make an excellent addition.

103 Preserved Meat Curry

30 lb. Preserved meat
1½ gal. Curry sauce

7 lb. Rice

Curry Sauce as follows:—

8 lb. Onions
1 lb. Sultanas
4 lb. Flour

1 lb. Apple rings
½ lb. Curry powder
Good stock

Method.—Chop the onions finely, fry until golden colour, add the curry powder, allow to cook for five minutes, add flour, allow this to cook until a sandy mixture. Add sultanas and apple rings (previously soaked). Pour in stock, bring to the boil, correct the seasoning, simmer 1½ hours.

Prepare the preserved meat by cutting into slices approximately three inches by one inch, arrange in serving dish down the centre, sauce over with curry sauce, heat to required temperature in slow oven and garnish with plain boiled rice.

104 Preserved Meat Roast

30 lb. Preserved meat
3 lb. Carrots
3 lb. Onions
3 lb. Turnips (if available)
4 lb. Bread

4 qt. Good brown sauce
1 lb. Dripping
2 oz. Salt
Pepper to season

Method.—Fry chopped onions to a golden colour, allow to get cold. Soak and press the bread. Pass the meat, bread, cooked carrots and turnips through a mincer, season, add the onions cold, mix well. Divide into sections each sufficient for 12 portions, roll out to the shape of a large roll, place in greased baking dishes and baste with a little dripping, bake in a medium oven for one hour, roll in breadcrumbs, colour off in oven. Slice and arrange neatly on dish, serve with good brown sauce.

105 Cheese Spread

6 lb. Cheese
6 lb. Dripping or margarine

Method.—Grate cheese, mix with dripping or margarine, season well, pass through mincer or mix to a smooth paste.

106 Oat Cakes

12½ lb. Oatmeal	1 lb. Sugar
3 lb. Dripping	Salt

Method.—Place oatmeal in a mixing bowl and add pinch of salt, dripping and sugar; mix well together with water and leave for 2½ hours. Shape into three-corner cakes of 2 oz. each and bake until brown. Serve two for a portion.

107 Oatmeal and Cheese Cakes

4 lb. Oatmeal	Pepper and salt to taste
4 lb. Cheese	
4 lb. Flour	
3 lb. Dripping	

Method.—Cut up cheese into small pieces and pass through mincer; add oatmeal, flour and dripping, and work into a stiff dough with water roll out into a paste, and cut into circular cakes, bake in hot oven for 15-20 minutes.

108 Scotch Cakes

6½ lb. Oatmeal	4 lb. Dripping or margarine
Milk for dough	2 lb. Sugar
5 lb. Flour	Salt

Method.—Mix the flour and the oatmeal, then thoroughly rub in the dripping or margarine. Add the remaining dry ingredients and mix well with milk to attain the correct consistency. Roll out and shape into rounds. Mark each round into four scones.

109 Baked Biscuit Suet Pudding

16 lb. Biscuits (crushed)
6 lb. Suet or dripping
2 oz. Salt.
8 oz. Baking powder
8 pts. Milk or water

Method.—Proceed as for plain suet pudding, and bake in baking dishes or frying pans (No. 1 cooker), immediately mixing is completed. *N.B.*—Is improved considerably by the addition of dried fruits or jam.

110 Biscuit Pastry Jam Tart

16 lb. Biscuits (crushed and powdered)
6 lb. Dripping or margarine
1 oz. Salt
4 oz. Baking powder
6 lb. Jam

Method.—Powder the biscuits, add salt, baking powder, and work in the dripping or margarine. Mix lightly into a medium paste with cold water. Roll out to a thickness of quarter inch and place in well-greased dixie lids or baking dishes. Partly bake immediately mixing is completed, then spread on sufficient jam and return to oven to finish baking. Time about 35 minutes. This pastry, without the jam, can be used for meat pies and puddings.

111 Biscuit Scones

16 lb. Biscuits	4 lb. Sugar
4 lb. Dripping or margarine	3 tins Milk
4 oz. Baking powder	

Method.—Powder the biscuits, add baking powder, the sugar, mix in the dripping or margarine and mix well. Add sufficient milk to make a pliable paste, and break into 1 lb. pieces. Roll out and divide into four pieces. Bake in a moderate oven for 20 minutes. Scones should be served hot. They are improved by adding a little dried fruit or jam.

112 Biscuit Porridge

12 lb. Biscuits	3 tins Milk
1½ lb. Sugar	30 pts. Water

Method.—Boil the water in the camp kettle. Crush the biscuits, and add to the boiling water, stirring until it becomes quite thick. Remove from the fire. Stir in the sugar and milk. Time required, 20 minutes.

113 Biscuit Dough-nuts

12 lb. Biscuits	1 oz. Salt
4 lb. Flour	Jam
6 lb. Dripping or margarine	
2 lb. Sugar	
1 tin Milk and water for dough	
8 oz. Baking powder	

Method.—Powder the biscuits, and add baking powder, salt, dripping, sugar and flour, and mix well together. Make a hollow in centre, and add milk and water. Mix into a stiff dough. Roll out and cut into round cakes. Fry in hot fat till brown. Jam should be served with them for tea meal.

114 Biscuit Yorkshire Pudding

14 lb. Biscuits crushed and powdered	2 oz. Baking Powder
Stock	2 lb. Dripping
Pepper	8 pts. Milk
	8 pts. Water (approximate)
	12 eggs
	1 oz. Salt

Method.—See Recipe No. 25.

* Flour may be used instead of biscuits.

RICE—VARIOUS METHODS OF PREPARATION

1. Rice has now been re-introduced to the Middle East Ration Scale. In the past substantial quantities of this valuable commodity have been wasted. The primary cause of this waste is undoubtedly due to unsatisfactory cooking and lack of variety in the dishes prepared.

2. It should be noted that supplies of potatoes in the Middle East are very inconsistent, and there is no guarantee of continuity even with the present reduced scale.

3. The most satisfactory bulk-producing substitute is rice, and, when properly treated, considerable variety can be added to the "Daily Bill of Fare."

4. Particular attention is directed to Recipe No. 1, which is the basic method of cooking as an adjunct to curries, meat stews, and as a vegetable.

5. Units should bear in mind that whilst rice is locally produced, thus saving shipping space, stocks are not unlimited and will not permit of waste in any form.

115 Plain Boiled Rice

7 lb. Rice
4 oz. Salt

7 gals. Water

Method.—Pick over, and thoroughly wash rice until the water is clear of all scum. The rice should then be rained into boiling salt water while stirring; simmer for approximately 15 minutes until the grains are tender. Wash under running cold water, preferably in a sieve or strainer, until cold, and the grains are free.

When required for service, plunge into hot salt water, strain off well, place on cloths or tray and keep in a warm place until required.

N.B.—Rice for Made-up Dishes

Method.—Use up to one-third of the total quantity of ingredients for all dishes such as fish cakes, meat patties, rissoles, etc. Cook the rice as above, and when cold add to other ingredients and pass through mincer.

SOUPS

116 Rice Soup

14 lb. White stock
8 qts. Milk
12 Yolks of egg (if available)

10 lb. Rice
Seasoning

Method.—Wash the rice well and add to the boiling stock, simmer gently until thoroughly cooked, rub through a fine sieve, re-boil, add the milk and bring to the boil and remove from the stove. Beat up the yolks with a little milk or stock and add to the soup; stir well, add seasoning and serve. Do not re-boil, as eggs will separate.

117 Carrots and Rice Soup

25 qts. Stock
14 lb. Carrots
4 lb. Rice (2 lb. to be cooked in soup and 2 lb. plain boiled for garnish)

4 lb. Onions
½ lb. Margarine
4 oz. Salt
Pepper to taste

Method.—Melt the margarine, add the sliced onions and thinly sliced blanched carrots. Cover with a lid and stew slowly until tender. Add the stock and bring to boiling point. Season with salt and pepper. Add the rice and simmer for one hour. Pass through strainer, re-boil. correct seasoning and consistency.

118 Potato, Carrot and Rice Soup

10 lb. Potatoes (prepared)
2 lb. Onions or 1 lb. leeks
25 qts. White stock
4 lb. Rice as garnish

½ lb. Dripping
7 lb. Carrots
4 oz. Salt
Pepper

Method.—Melt the dripping, add the diced onions and carrots. cover with a lid and stew slowly until tender, add stock and potatoes cut into cubes; bring to boiling point, season with salt, simmer for 1 hour, skim, correct seasoning and consistency, serve with garnish of boiled rice.

119 Rice and Green Pea Soup

5 lb. Rice	2 lb. Carrots
25 qts. Water or stock	Bacon trimmings
7 lb. Green peas	4 oz. Salt
2 lb. Onions or 2 lb. leeks	Pepper
1 lb. Celery	

If white stock is available, utilise instead of water.

Method.—Wash the green peas, soak overnight, drain and cover with the water or stock; add salt, bring to boiling point, skim thoroughly, add the vegetables cut into dice, rice and bacon trimmings, simmer until cooked, skim carefully; correct seasoning and consistency.

120 Mullagatawny Soup

25 qts. Stock	12 oz. Apple rings
2 lb. Dripping	2 lb. Rice as garnish
1 lb. Curry powder	1 tin Tomato purée or equal
7 lb. Onions	quantity of fresh tomatoes
3½lb. Flour	(7 lb.)
36 Peppercorns in bag	4 oz. Salt
3 Bay leaves	

Method.—Soak the apple rings. Melt the dripping, add the chopped onions and fry to a golden colour. Add the curry powder, mix well and fry on the side of the stove for a few moments. Add the flour and dry out. Moisten with stock, add the tomato purée and the remainder of stock, bringing to boiling point and skim. Add the soaked chopped apple rings and seasoning. Simmer for 1 hour, pass through a soup machine, strainer or sieve and re-boil. Remove the scum, correct the seasoning and consistency, add the plain boiled rice as a garnish.

121 Minestroni Soup

25 qts. Stock	1 lb. Marrowfat peas
1½lb. Carrots	1 lb. Cabbage
1 lb. Haricot beans	1 lb. Leeks
1 lb. Turnips	1 lb. Macaroni
2 lb. Rice	½ lb. Fat bacon
1½lb. Onions	2 oz. Chopped parsley
7 lb. Tomatoes	

Method.—Melt the fat bacon, add the root vegetables sliced, also shredded leeks and cabbage, and fry to a golden colour: sprinkle with flour, fry out, add stock, stirring gradually, add the half-cooked peas and beans, and simmer for 1 hour. Break the macaroni into inch lengths and add with rice to the soup. Continue to simmer until all ingredients are tender, correct the seasoning, add the chopped parsley and serve.

136 **Apple Rings and Rice (South African Recipe)**

8 lb. Rice (washed)	1 lb. Suet
½lb. Dripping	4 lb. Apple rings
3½lb. Sugar	1 oz. Ground cloves

Method.—Wash and rewash the rice, rinse the apple rings and soak with the rice in sufficient water to cover, for 6 to 8 hours. Place the apple rings, rice and water in which they were soaked into a cooking vessel and set to simmer for 1½ hours. Remove the skin from the suet, chop very finely and add with the sugar and cloves to the apples and rice. Place in greased baking dishes with a sprinkling of dripping on top and bake in a quick oven till cooked to a golden brown.

137 . **Baked Rice Pudding**

6 lb. Rice	4 lb. Sugar
1 oz. Nutmeg	16 pts. Milk
4 oz. Margarine	

Method.—Wash and pick over the rice, place in the dishes, add sugar and boiling milk, mix well, sprinkle with nutmeg and small pieces of margarine and bake in a moderate oven till tender.

138 **Rice and Raisin Pudding**

4 gals. Milk	3 lb. Sugar
4 oz. Margarine	1 oz. Nutmeg
2 lb. Raisins	4 lb. Rice

Method.—As 137.

139 **Baked Chocolate Rice Pudding**

5 gals. Milk	5 lb. Rice
3 lb. Sugar	1 lb. Cocoa

Method.—Make paste with cocoa and a little water, add milk and pour over rice and sugar, pour into baking dishes and bake until rice is tender.

140 **Baked Rice and Date Pudding**

4 gals. Milk	3 lb. Sugar
4 oz. Margarine	5 lb. Rice
3 lb. Stewed dates	

Method.—As 137.

141 **Rice and Fruit Slices**

8 lb. Flour	3 lb. Margarine
Water	4 oz. Baking powder
1 oz. Salt	

Method.—Sift flour, baking powder and salt together. Rub in fat lightly and mix quickly to a stiff dough with water. Keep in cool place till required.

Line baking trays with this paste and prick the bottom. Half bake. and then fill with creamed rice as shown in Recipe 133, and finish baking the pastry and allow to cool. Well drain any canned fruits and arrange on top of the cooked rice. Cut into suitable portions and brush over with boiling hot diluted jam.

Another method is to prepare strips of paste the length of trays 4 in. wide, wet the edges, and place a band of paste down each side. pinching the edges, prick the bottom, half bake and continue as above. Cut into slices.

Christmas Day Menus

This pamphlet contains suggestions for making the most of the rations being provided over the Christmas period in order that all troops shall have a really Merry Christmas.

S.T.Directorate
HQ ALFSEA
Nov '46.

WOT NO SNOW?

We may live without poetry,
      Music and art;
We may live without conscience and
      Live without heart;
We may live without friends, we may live
      without books;
But civilized man cannot live without
      cooks.
He may live without books - what is
      knowledge but grieving ?
He may live without hope - what is
      hope but deceiving ?
He may live without love - what is
      passion but pining ?
But where is the man that can live
      without dining ?

SUGGESTED - BILLS OF FARE FOR CHRISTMAS PERIOD.

24th DEC - 26th DEC '46.

CHRISTMAS EVE

B R E A K F A S T

Porridge or Cereal

Fried Bacon and Scrambled Egg (D)

Bread - Butter - Jam

Tea - Coffee.

*

D I N N E R

Vegetable Soup

Cornish Pastie - Brown Sauce

Croquette Potatoes

Creamed Cabbage - Carrots

Banana - Custard Flan

Coffee

*

T E A

Tea - Cakes - Sandwiches (Cheese and Cucumber)

*

S U P P E R

Cold Meats (Tinned).

Potatoe Salad - Green Salads

Mock - Mayonaisse - Sauce

Pickles

Open - Jam - Tart

Cheese - Biscuits

Tea - Coffee

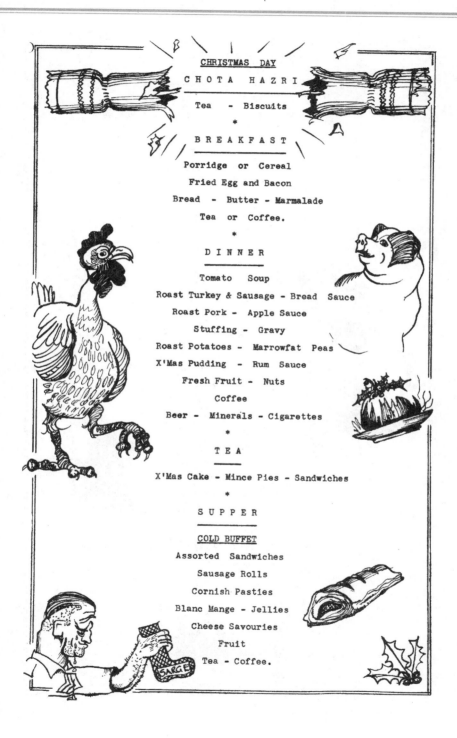

CHRISTMAS DAY

C H O T A   H A Z R I

Tea - Biscuits

*

B R E A K F A S T

Porridge or Cereal

Fried Egg and Bacon

Bread - Butter - Marmalade

Tea or Coffee.

*

D I N N E R

Tomato   Soup

Roast Turkey & Sausage - Bread Sauce

Roast Pork - Apple Sauce

Stuffing - Gravy

Roast Potatoes - Marrowfat Peas

X'Mas Pudding - Rum Sauce

Fresh Fruit - Nuts

Coffee

Beer - Minerals - Cigarettes

*

T E A

X'Mas Cake - Mince Pies - Sandwiches

*

S U P P E R

COLD BUFFET

Assorted Sandwiches

Sausage Rolls

Cornish Pasties

Blanc Mange - Jellies

Cheese Savouries

Fruit

Tea - Coffee.

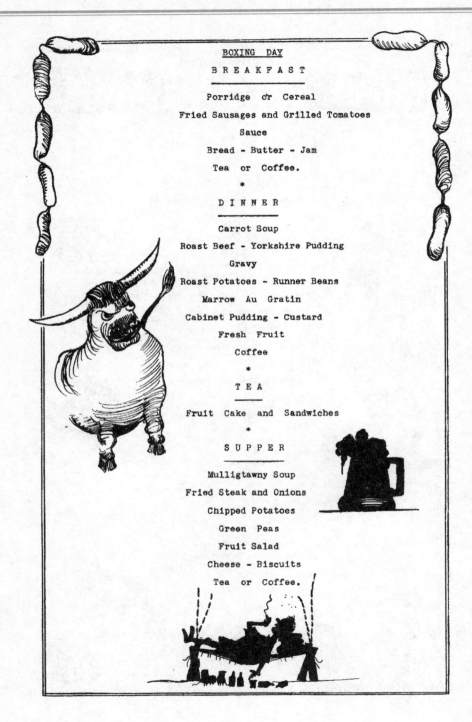

BOXING DAY

B R E A K F A S T

Porridge or Cereal

Fried Sausages and Grilled Tomatoes

Sauce

Bread - Butter - Jam

Tea or Coffee.

*

D I N N E R

Carrot Soup

Roast Beef - Yorkshire Pudding

Gravy

Roast Potatoes - Runner Beans

Marrow Au Gratin

Cabinet Pudding - Custard

Fresh Fruit

Coffee

*

T E A

Fruit Cake and Sandwiches

*

S U P P E R

Mulligtawny Soup

Fried Steak and Onions

Chipped Potatoes

Green Peas

Fruit Salad

Cheese - Biscuits

Tea or Coffee.

R E C I P E S

CALCULATED FOR 100 MEN.

SOUPS.

VEGETABLE SOUP.

Stock	50 pts.	Turnips	2 lb.
Carrots	4 lb.	Large cabbage 1	
Leeks	2 lb.	Margarine or	
Potatoes	7 lb.	dripping	8 oz.
Onions	3 lb.	Salt	4 oz.

Method:

Melt the dripping, add the diced carrot, leeks, onions, cabbage and turnips, cover with a lid and stew on the side of the stove until tender.
Moisten with stock, add the cubed potatoes, bring to the boil and skim.
Simmer until tender and pass through the soup machine or sieve, reboil, remove the scum, correct the seasoning and consistency.

TOMATO SOUP.

Stock	50 pts.	Ham Bones	2 lb.	Tomato Td.	10 lb.
Carrots	3 lb.	Cooking Fat	8 oz.	Flour	4 lb.
Onions	3 lb.	Salt	4 oz.	Sugar	8 oz.

Method:

Chop ham bones and fry in cooking fat. Add diced carrots and onions, fry to a golden colour. Mix in flour and cook on side of stove to golden colour. Add tomatoes, then stock, stir until boiling. Season with salt correct seasoning and consistency.

CARROT SOUP.

Stock	50 pts.	Bread	6 lb.
Carrots	14 lb.	Faggot	
Onions	4 lb.	Salt	4 oz.
Margarine	½ lb.	Black	
		peppercorns in	
		bag.	36

Method:

1. Melt the margarine.
2. Add the diced onion and thinly sliced blanched carrots.
3. Cover with a lid and stew slowly until tender.
4. Add the stock, bring to the boil, season and add faggot and peppercorns.
5. Cut bread into squares and bake in an oven to a light colour.
6. Add 5 lb. of bread to the soup, simmer for 1 hour; then remove faggot and peppercorns.
7. Pass through a soup machine or sieve.
8. Bring up to the boil, correct seasoning and consistency, and serve with remainder of the bread.

Note:- Care must be taken with the preparation of this soup not to allow it to boil after passing otherwise it will decompose.

MULLIGATAWNY

Stock	50 pts	Apple rings	11 oz.
Dripping	2 lb.	Tomato purée	1 tin
Curry Powder	1 lb.	Peppercorns in	
Onions	7 lb.	bag.	36
Flour	3½ lb.	Salt	4 oz.
Coconut	8 oz.	Bay leaves	3 oz.

Method:

1. Soak the coconut and apple ring.
2. Melt the dripping, add the chopped onions and fry to a golden colour.
3. Add the curry powder, mix well and fry on the side of the stove for a few minutes.
4. Add the flour and dry out.
5. Moisten with stock, add the tomato purée, bring to boiling point, and skim.
6. Add the soaked chopped apple rings and coconut, and the aromates.
7. Simmer for one hour, remove aromates, pass through a soup machine or sieve and reboil.
8. Remove any scum, correct the seasoning and consistency, and serve

CORNISH PASTIES.

Meat (cooked and prepared)	12 lb.	Flour	12 lb.
		Dripping	4 lb.
Onions	3 lb.	Baking Powder	4 oz.
Parsley	4 oz.	Pepper	
Potatoes	12 lb.		

Method:

1. Make a short pastry and roll out 1/8 in. thick.
2. Cut into 4 in. rounds, wet the edges, place 3 oz. of the mixture in the centre, fold over, press edges together and wash with a little milk.
3. Bake for 35 minutes in a hot oven.

ROAST PORK.

Pork (bone in)	37½ lb.	Gravy	8 pts.
Pork (boneless(	28½ lb.		

Method:

1. Cut into sizeable joints of 8 lb. in weight, season, chop through the chine bones, score the outside of the joints with a sharp knife, and place in baking dishes or camp kettle lids on a few thick slices of potatoes.
2. Baste with very little dripping and set off in a hot oven for 15 minutes.
3. Reduce temperature and cook slowly, basting from time to time.
4. When pork is cooked remove joints.
5. Run off excessive fat from the dishes, set the pan on the stove, swill out with stock, add to gravy, allowing approximately 2 tablespoons for each man.
6. Season and serve with pork.

STUFFING.

Shredded suet	1 lb.	Parsley	4 oz.
Dripping	½ lb.	Bread (soaked)	8 lb.
Onions	4 lb.	Salt and pepper	
Sage	3 oz.	Sprayed Egg	2 oz.

Method:

1. Finely chop the onions, parsley and sage.
2. Reconstitute the sprayed egg.
3. Stew the onions in the dripping to a golden colour and allow to cool.
4. Add the rest of the ingredients and mix well.

TURKEY. (1 lb tins)

Method:

1. Open tins carefully with tin opener.
2. Place meat in dishes.
3. Add a little good well seasoned stock.
4. Place on stove (not open fire) with cover, and thoroughly warm through. Do not allow stock to boil.
5. Serve small portions, as there is no waste.
6. Serve gravy piping hot.

BREAD SAUCE.

Milk	8 pts.	Margarine	½ lbs.
Onions	1 lb.	Pepper	
Cloves	¼ oz.	Salt	
Breadcrumbs	2 lb.		

Method:

1. Place the milk, onions and cloves in a saucepan, and bring slowly to the boil.
2. Simmer for 15 minutes.
3. Remove the onions and cloves and add the breadcrumbs.
4. Stand on a warm part of the stove for 15 minutes so that the breadcrumbs may absorb some of the milk.
5. Bring to the boil again and stir in the margarine, and add correct seasoning.

APPLE SAUCE.

Cooking apples	12 lb.	Cloves	3
or Apple rings	4 lb.	Water	4 pts.
Sugar	2 lb.		

Method:

1. Soak apple rings overnight (or peel, core and cut up the cooking apples).
2. Place in a stewpan, add sugar and cloves, cover with water, allow to boil for 30 minutes until cooked, pass through a sieve and serve hot.

BANANA CUSTARD FLAN.

Milk	12 pts.	Salt	2 oz.	Jam	2 lb.
Sugar	2½ lb.	Bananas	32		
Flour	8 lb.	Margarine	3 lb.		

Method:

Make flan paste as follows : Sieve flour and salt, make a
bay and mix sugar and margarine together in the centre, add
1 pt. water and work lightly to make a fairly stiff paste.
Care must be taken not to over work paste on account of
sugar. Line dishes with this paste, prick the bottoms and
bake in hot oven (400 Fahr) for approx. 40 minutes.
Prepare a stiff custard, pour into the baked pastry cases
and leave to set. Slice bananas on the slant and place on
the custard overlapping. Boil up the jam with a little
water and glaze over bananas.

CHRISTMAS PUDDING.

100 portions		12 portions	
4 lb.	grated apple	¼ lb.	
4 lb.	flour	¼ lb.	
4 lb.	breadcrumbs	¼ lb.	
4 lb.	suet	¼ lb.	
4 lb.	currant or raisins	¼ lb.	
2 lb.	chopped dates	4 oz.	
4 lb.	chopped prunes	8 oz.	
2 lb.	peel	4 oz.	
4 lb.	grated carrot	¼ lb.	
4 teaspoonful	mixed spice	¼ teaspoonful	
4 teaspoonful	ground ginger	¼ teaspoonful	
4 teaspoonful	grated nutmeg	¼ teaspoonful	
3 lb.	treacle (black for	2 tablespoonful	
3 lb.	brown preference)	4 oz.	
	sugar	pinch salt	
4 teaspoonful salt			
Milk to mix			

Method:

1. Prepare the breadcrumbs and mix them with the flour, suet,
   spices, salt, ginger and sugar.
2. Grate the apple and carrots, and add.
3. Chop the dates and prunes (previously) soaked and stoned),
   and add them with the currants (washed) and the chopped
   peel.
4. Add the treacle and mix to a moist consistency with fresh
   milk or tinned sweetened milk and water.
5. Put into greased pudding basins, cover with grease paper or
   pudding cloths and steam or boil for at least 4 hours - the
   longer the better.
6. Keep in a cool, dry place and re-boil for 2 hours when using.

Puddings should not be stored for longer than 14 days.

MINCEMEAT.

Sugar	3½ lb.	Sultanas	2 lb.
Fresh apples (peeled, chopped and cored)	9 lb.	or raisins	2 lb.
		Spice	¼ oz.
or dried apple rings (soaked and chopped)	3 lb.	Suet	12 oz.
		Vinegar	1 pt.
Prunes (stoned and chopped)	4 lb.		
or currants	4 lb.		

Method:

1. Chop the suet, add the dry ingredients and apples.
2. Moisten with the vinegar and allow to stand.

Note:- Production 21 lb.

MINCE PIES OR TARTS.

Mincemeat	6 lb.	Flour	8 lb.
		Salt	1 oz.
		Margarine	3 lb.
		Water for paste	

Method:

1. Prepare a short pastry, roll out thinly and cut into 3½ inch rounds, moisten half of them with water and place a little mincemeat on each.
2. Place another round on each and press well down all round.
3. Wash with milk, sprinkle with sugar and allow ½ hour's rest before baking.
4. Can also be made on making dishes or camp kettle lids and cut afterwards.

MOCK MINCE PIES OR TARTS.

Flour	8 lb.	Chopped apples	3 lb.
Margarine	3 lb.	Breadcrumbs	8 oz.
Salt	¼ oz.	Mixed spice	1 oz.
Mincemeat	3 lb.	Water for paste	

Method:

1. Prepare a short pastry, roll out thinly and cut into 3½ inch round, moisten half of them with water and place a little mincemeat on each.
2. Place another round on each and press well down all round.
3. Wash with milk, sprinkle with sugar and allow ½ hour's rest before baking.
4. Can also be made on baking or camp kettle lids and out afterwards.

RUM SAUCE.

Flour	1 lb.	Milk	9 pts.
Margarine	¼ lb.	Sugar	1 lb.
		Rum	1 bot.

Method:

1. Melt margarine in saucepan without frying.
2. Add the flour, stirring to a smooth paste, care being taken to keep the mixture from sticking to the sides of saucepan.
3. Allow the mixture to cook without taking colour until it attains a sandy texture then allow to cool slightly. (This is technically known as a white roux).
4. Boil the milk and add gradually to the roux, mixing well to prevent lumpiness.
5. When all milk is absorbed, allow to boil gently for ½ hour.
6. Add sugar.
7. Rum should be added just before serving.

MOCK MAYONNAISE.

White sauce	3 pts.	Mustard	1 oz.
Vinegar	1 pt.	Salt and pepper	
Yellow colour, a few drops.			

Method:

1. Prepare a white sauce.
2. Mix the mustard with the vinegar, pour into the boiling white sauce and add colouring matter.

WHITE SAUCE.

Flour	1 lb.	Milk	8 pts.
Margarine	3/4 lb.		

Method:

1. Melt margarine in saucepan without frying.
2. Add the flour, stirring to form a smooth paste, care being taken to keep the mixture from sticking to the sides of saucepan.
3. Allow the mixture to cook without taking colour until it attains, a sandy texture then allow to cool slightly. (This is technically known as a white roux).
4. Boil the milk and add gradually to the roux, mixing well to prevent lumpiness.
5. When all milk is absorbed, allow to boil gently for $\frac{1}{2}$ hour.
6. Season with salt if required for an unsweetened sauce.

Special Note:- It should not be necessary to pass this sauce if it is correctly mixed at the beginning. More milk or other flavouring must be added as required.

Another method (using milk powder).

Milk powder	2 lb.	Margarine	1¼ lb.
Flour	1¼ lb.	Water for reconstituting milk powder	16 pts.

Method:

1. Reconstitute milk powder.
2. Make a roux with the margarine and flour and cook in a slow oven or on top of the cooking range until sandy in texture, without taking colour and allow to cool.
3. Bring milk to the boil and gradually work into the roux, stirring with a wooden spoon.
4. Cover with a lid, simmer for 15 minutes.
5. Season with salt if required for an unsweetened sauce.

CABINET PUDDING.

Stale cake	7 lb.	Vanilla essence	¼ oz.
Stale bread	3 lb.	Milk	20 pts.
Mixed fruits	4 lb.	Sugar	2 lb.
Sprayed egg	5 oz.	Custard sauce or	16 pts.
		Jam sauce	8 pts.

Method:

1. Cut up the stale bread and cake into approximately ¼ inch squares.
2. Arrange in the greased and sugared dishes or basins in alternate layers with the fruit.
3. Prepare a custard with the sprayed egg, milk, sugar and essence; mix well together and strain over the dry ingredients.
4. Let stand for ½ hour to soak, then carefully bake in a slow oven (or cook in a bain-marie) until set.
5. Serve with a custard or jam sauce.

CUSTARD.

Sugar	1 lb.	Custard powder	1 lb.
Milk	16 pts.		

Method:

1. Mix custard powder, sugar and a little cold milk to a smooth paste.
2. Boil remainder of the milk, pour on to the ready made paste stirring the while.
3. Reboil, and serve.

Another Method:

Milk powder	1 lb.	Sugar	1 lb.
Milk tins	3 tins	Custard powder	1 lb.
Water for reconstituting milk powder			8 pts.
Water for reconstituting tinned milk			8 pts.

Method:

1. Reconstitute the milk powder and tinned milk and mix the two milks together.
2. Add the sugar and custard powder to 3 pts. of the reconstituted milk and work into a paste.
3. Bring the remainder of the milk to the boil and pour into the paste.
4. Reboil and stir frequently to avoid lumpiness.

JAM SAUCES.

Jam	3 lb.	Sugar	2 lb.
Custard powder	1 lb.	Water	8 pts.
Colouring (red or yellow) as required.			

Method:

1. Place 3 lb. jam into sufficient boiling water to make up to 8 pts., add sugar and bring to boil, carefully stirring from time to time.
2. Dilute the custard powder with a little cold water and pour into the boiling water and jam, stir until it boils again and colour as required.
3. Bring to the boil, correct consistency and pass through a strainer.

CHRISTMAS CAKES

RECIPE "A".

Flour	6 lb.	Milk	2 pts.
Lard or margarine	4 lb.	Bicarbonate of	3/4 oz.
Sugar	3¼ lb.	soda	
Mixed fruit	6 lb.	Ground ginger	1/8 oz.
Sprayed egg	¾ lb.	Spice	¼ oz.
Water for reconstitution.	1½ pts.		

Method:

1. Cream the sugar and fat.
2. Add the fruit, spice, ginger, flour and the reconstituted well beaten eggs.
3. Lastly add the milk with the soda dissolved in it.
4. Bake for 3 hours in a slow oven.
5. This mixture can be made into slab cake form or baked in a number of small moulds and will produce approximately 100 x 3 oz. portions.

RECIPE "B".

Margarine	1 lb.	Dried egg.	6 oz.
Sugar	1 lb.	Water for reconstitution	¾ pt.
Flour	1¼ lb.		
Salt		Baking powder	¼ oz.
Vanilla essence		Fruit (sultanas,	
Grated rind of 1		mixed peel,	
lemon and 1 orange		currants).	1¼ lb.

(This mixture is sufficient for one 6-lb. cake or three 2-lb. cakes).

Method:

1. Cream margarine and sugar.
2. Add reconstituted egg little by little.
3. Fold in the flour lightly (baking powder and salt incorporated).
4. Add the fruit and essence.
5. Place mixture into prepared tins.
6. Bake for approximately 2¼ hours in a moderate oven.

BUTTER CREAM.

Milk	2 tins.	Margarine	1 lb.
Sugar	2 oz.	Vanilla essence (a few drops)	

Method:

1. Cream the margarine and sugar.
2. Beat in the milk gradually until all is absorbed and add a few drops of essence.
3. Care should be taken that the margarine is smooth each time before milk is added.
4. If inclined to curdle, warm slightly.

Index

'Airborne Pannier' 80
'Aldershot Oven' 21, 22, 39, 49, 52–55
Anti-Aircraft Command 72
'Armoured Fighting Vehicle Pack' 80
Army Catering Corps (ACC) (all) 26,
    28–31, 33, 35, 59, 66, 68, 78, 86, 95–96,
    100, 112–113, 115, 117
Army Schools of Cookery
  Accra, Ghana 35
  Aldershot, England 20, 26–27, 33
  Arungabad, India 35
  Chilsteton, England 27
  Genifia, Egypt 26, 35, 112
  Mesopotamia 26
  Poona, India 96
  Russia 26
  Safarand, Palestine 26, 112
  Salonika 26
  Sidi Farouche, Algiers 113
  St Omer Barracks, France 33, 35
Auxiliary Territorial Service (ATS) 35
baking 13, 14, 16, 21, 98, 120
Beck, Major General E.A., 27
beer 12, 13
'Benghazi Burners' 106–108
biscuit 12, 13, 21, 22, 69, 71, 73, 95, 112,
   136–137

Bluff Range 39, 42
Board of Trade 64
boiling 13, 14, 22, 25, 41, 72, 98, 120
Bonaparte, Napoleon 11, 12
braising 25, 120
bread 12, 13, 14, 16, 21, 49, 61, 64, 73, 95, 134
British Expeditionary Force (BEF) 21, 29
'bully beef' 21, 23, 71
butter 13, 21, 64, 71
Byford CBE MVO, Colonel R.A.A., 117
Cabinet Food Policy Committee 64
cassava 91, 101
cheese 13, 21, 22, 26, 64, 71, 81, 180, 202
coffee 14, 16, 26, 95
Commissariat 13, 15
'Compo Ration' 62, 72–76, 78
Cooker Portable No.1 ('Hydro burner')
   39–41, 59, 106
Cooker Portable No.2 39, 106
Cooker Portable No.3 39, 106
Cooker Triplex No.4 39
'coppers' (cooking pots) 14
D-Day (6 June 1944) 61, 68
desert warfare 41, 62, 66, 91, 101, 112
'dixie' (kettle) 21, 22, 39, 41, 43
'Dog Fritter' 112
eggs 26, 66, 78, 95, 180

Eighth Army 35, 59, 101, 112
Elizabeth II, Queen 33, 35
Falklands conflict 16
First Army 113
First Gulf War 16
First World War (Great War) 16, 23, 26, 50, 64, 68–69
fish 80, 98, 100, 101, 166–167
Fourteenth Army 59, 95, 96, 101
Frederick the Great 11
fruit 49, 60, 71, 95, 98
frying 22, 25, 39, 43, 66, 120
George V, King 28, 30–31
'hayboxes' 22, 39, 50
Home Front 12, 63–64, 66
Hore-Belisha, Leslie 27, 28
India 95–97, 100
'Iron Ration' 22, 69
'Jungle Ration' 99
jungle warfare 62, 78, 80, 91, 95, 98–100
Keys, Dr Ancel 80
Kola nuts 101
'Koolgardie Meat Safe' 70–71
'K-Rations' 80, 84–85
'Landing or Assualt Ration' 72
'M and V' (meat and vegetable) stew 72
'Machonochie' ration 21, 23
Marlborough, Duke of 13
meat 12, 13, 14, 16, 20–22, 26, 49, 64, 69, 71, 80, 95, 100, 101, 117, 133, 156–165, 196–200
mess-tin 14, 22, 59, 68, 69, 72, 86, 89, 98
'Mess-Tin Ration' 69
milk 21, 49, 64, 71, 72
'Mountain (Arctic) Pack' 80–81
Navy, Army and Air Force Institute (NAAFI) 26, 66
Normandy 66, 68, 78, 81
Operation Dynamo (Dunkirk evacuation) 30
'Pacific 24-Hour Ration' 80, 82–83
'Pacific Compo Ration' 80
'pan-packs' 22
Pemmican 80
Peninsula War 11–15
pies 20, 26, 49
porridge 50, 72, 114, 135
potatoes 14, 16, 49, 64, 95, 185–189

pudding 20, 50, 135–150, 221–222
Rations Scale 37, 66, 114
rice 16, 21, 98, 101, 206–209
Richards, Private Frank 22
Richelieu, Cardinal de 11
roasting 14, 16, 20, 21, 25, 43, 49, 98, 120
Royal Air Force (RAF) 66
Royal Army Medical Corps (RAMC) 22, 35, 117
Royal Army Service Corps (RASC) 26, 30, 33, 59–60, 117
Royal Indian Army Service Corps 95
Royal Logistic Corps (RLC) 115
Royal Logistic Corps Museum 35
Royal Wagon Train 15
Royal West African Frontier Force 100
Salmon MP, Sir Isidore 27
Second World War 12, 16, 28–31, 33, 59, 63–64, 71–72, 91, 101, 113, 115
Siege of Sebastopol, 15–16
soup 14, 16, 26, 50, 89, 168–172
'Soya Link' sausage 95
Soyer, Alexis 15
'Soyer Stove' 15–19, 21, 22, 39, 41
'Spanish Ulcer' 12
steaming 16, 39, 60, 98, 120
stewing 16, 20, 21, 22–23, 26, 49, 50, 72, 120
sugar 21, 22, 64, 72, 95, 98
'Sutler' 12–13
tea 14, 16, 20, 22, 26, 50, 64, 72, 86, 91, 95, 98, 106, 120
The Beck Committee 27
The European Cookery School, Nigeria 100–101
'Tommy Cooker' 22, 86
'Trombone Oil Burner' 58–59
vegetables 12–14, 21, 39, 64, 78, 95, 120, 184–191
Venning, Quartermaster-General, General Sir Walter 30
water 11, 12, 15, 43, 50, 71, 72, 78, 89, 98, 106
Wellington, Duke of 12–13
wine 12, 13
Women's Voluntary Service (WVS) 30
Wyndham, Horace 20